in

Third Edition

P. J. North

Longman

To Judy

LONGMAN GROUP LIMITED
Longman House, Burnt Mill, Harlow, Essex CM20 2JE, UK
and Associated Companies throughout the World.

First published 1985
ISBN 0 582 33210 9

Set in Linotron Times 10/12
Printed in Great Britain by Mackays of Chatham, Ltd

Contents

Preface

People in Society is now in its third edition and continues to provide a valuable text for students coming to sociology and the social sciences for the first time. Within the new edition the opportunity has been taken to expand the range of topics covered and to revise the original sections where new material has become available. Two new sections have been introduced, covering Socialisation and Social Interaction, and The Mass Media. Changes in the political and economic face of Britain have made it necessary to revise extensively the chapters which deal with politics and employment. Throughout the text statistical sources have been brought up-to-date and the findings of recent research have been included.

As with previous editions the aim is to provide the new student with a broad overview of current British society drawing on the insights and perspectives of the sociologist with an increased emphasis on economic and political concepts. The methods of social science research are considered in detail and the student is introduced to sociological theories and concepts.

Since the appearance of the first edition of *People in Society* there has been considerable growth in the range of resource material available to the student at this level. The range of supporting texts is now quite extensive. The companion volume, *Understanding Evidence*, provides a variety of short extracts linked to the basic themes within *People in Society*. Together they provide a sound basis for students preparing for G.C.S.E. examinations, as well as for a number of other introductory courses.

A number of individuals have contributed to this text over the years and the list is becoming far too long to acknowledge in its entirety. I am particularly indebted to the pupils of Crown Woods School, Kidbrooke School and Thomas Tallis School who have, over the years, provided me with many insights into the problems of studying the social sciences for the first time, and to the many teachers on in-service courses at Avery Hill College who have provided a valuable focus for debate.

P. J. North
1985

Acknowledgements

We are grateful to the following for permission to reproduce copyright material:

Fabulous Music Ltd (part of The Essex Music Group) for first verse 'My Generation' by Pete Townshend (Lyrics only) © 1965 Fabulous Music Ltd; New Left Review for an adapted extract from *Work 2* by Jack Pomlet & Ronald Fraser; Penguin Books Ltd for an adapted extract from p 132 *Just Like a Girl* by Sue Sharpe, 1976; Routledge & Kegan Paul Ltd for extracts from pp 1, 8, 9, 93, 94 & 101 *Power, Persistance and Change* (A Second Study of Banbury) by Stacey, Batstone, Bell & Murcott, 1975; the author, Margaret Stacey for extracts from *Traditions and Change* published by Oxford University Press, 1960.

We are grateful to the following for permission to reproduce illustrations:

Blondel, *Voters, Parties and Leaders*, Penguin Books Ltd, figures 44, 45; British Library, figure 64; Coates and Silburn, *Poverty, the Forgotten Englishman*, W Murray, figure 56; Controller of Her Majesty's Stationery Office, figures 4, 11, 14, 17, 18, 19, 20, 21, 22, 23, 28, 30, 36, 37, 41, 54, 55 and tables 13, 16, 17, 19, 20, 22, 34, 37; Douglas, *The Home and School*, Hart Davis MacGibbon Ltd, figure 30 and table 23; Erving Goffman, *Gender Advertisements*, Macmillan, figure 80; *The Guardian*, figure 77; Hargreaves, *Social Relations in a Secondary School*, figure 31 and Young and Willmott, *The Symmetrical Family*, figure 74, Routledge and Kegan Paul; Hoineville and Jowell, *Survey Research Practice*, Heinemann Educational Books Ltd, figure 9; Independent Broadcasting Authority, figures 71, 73; Inner London Educational Authority, Research and Statistics Group, figure 34; R K Kelsall, *Report on an Inquiry into Applications for Admissions to Universities*, Association of Commonwealth Universities, 1957, figure 29; W Murray, *Boys and Girls*, Ladybird Keywords Reading Scheme, Ladybird Books, 1964, figure 35; National Union of Mineworkers, figure 46; Ann Oakley, *The Sociology of Housework*, Martin Robertson, 1974, tables 23, 28, 29; C Shaw and Henry McKay, *Juvenile Delinquency in Urban Areas*, The University of Chicago Press, 1969, figure 65.

Introduction
Doing Sociology

A good way to start doing sociology is to take a close look at the ordinary, everyday things that surround you. Perhaps the most exciting thing about sociology is the way it helps us to look at the things we normally take for granted. Someone once compared it to watching people playing a game the rules of which are unknown to you. As you watch you begin to get an idea of the rules and the different parts the players play. Sociology is rather like that but it is more as well. Above all we must remember that the sociologist is not only an observer watching the game. He, or she, is also a player who has played similar games with similar rules. None of us can escape from being in the world we try to understand.

As you work your way through this book and other books about the social world you will build up an idea of what sociologists do, the questions they ask, the methods they use and the subjects that interest them. In Chapter 1, we are going to look at one particular group of sociologists and the work they did. In Chapters 2, 3 and 4 we will consider some of the concepts and theories which help us to understand that particular piece of sociology. Chapter 5 is concerned with the methods which sociologists use. The remainder of the book considers some of the main features of life in modern Britain starting with the pattern of population. Later chapters consider the family, schooling, work, government, rich and poor, crime and deviance, mass media and religion.

1
Banbury – A Case Study

Banbury is in Oxfordshire, very close to the centre of England. There has been settlement on the site for nearly two thousand years. For the last eight hundred years, since a Norman baron built a castle there and the country people came for protection, Banbury has been an important centre for farmers in the area. For four hundred years it has been a market town and farmers would come on market day to buy and sell, and to gossip. The town is situated at the centre of a triangle of towns made by Stratford-upon-Avon to the north-west, Oxford to the south and Northampton to the north-east. The River Cherwell rising on the high ground away towards Northampton flows south through a long valley before it reaches Oxford to join the River Thames. At the centre of that valley is the town of Banbury. In the early 1950s when the town was studied by a team of sociologists many things could be seen to remind them of the town's past, and many things had changed.

In 1830 there were 6 400 people living within the borough of Banbury; most of them made their living by some form of trade, usually connected with the weekly market. The majority of the remainder were craftsmen – wheelwrights, blacksmiths, millers and harness-makers – closely linked to the needs of agriculture. In 1848 a new industry came to the town. A factory making farming implements was set up and soon afterwards the railway arrived. These new developments required a new kind of worker. They did not need the craftsmen employed in earlier times. They needed engineers, machine workers and factory hands. Many of these new workers came in to the town from outside. New cottages were built to house them. These were not the traditional stone cottages which may still be seen in the villages of Oxfordshire. They were built of red bricks, in long lines, by the side of the canal or the railway.

The new industries did well and expanded. The population of the town also expanded as more and more workers were needed. In 1841 the town's population stood at 7 200; by 1871 it had risen to

11 700. This growth was not continued. The foundry, which at its height employed 2000 people, fell on hard times and in 1920 the town's population scarcely reached 13 000. New inventions, changes in fashion, and declining markets meant that Banbury was in danger of becoming a depressed area. Jobs were scarce.

In 1929 a worldwide aluminium company showed an interest in a site for a new factory, just outside of the town. A group of leading citizens joined together to give support to the idea and four years later the factory opened. Two thousand jobs were created and the whole pattern of life in the town began to change. 'The Ally' had arrived, and with it came many people in search of work. The demand for labour was such that workers were attracted from all over the country. The ripples of population began to flow inwards towards Banbury.

The town began to grow and in the 1950s and 60s more industries moved in. Most important of these was a food manufacturing plant and a large car-parts factory. The 'ripples' were replaced by large movements of people encouraged by overspill agreements between the Banbury council and councils in London and Birmingham.

By the early 1950s the population of the town had reached 19 000. At the end of the 1960s it was over 40 000. The old market town had become a modern, bustling, industrial centre no different from many other towns in Britain.

THE SOCIOLOGISTS AND CHANGE

Banbury first attracted the interest of sociologists shortly after the end of the Second World War. A team of researchers led by Margaret Stacey went to live in the town for three years to attempt to build up a picture of life there and of the ways in which it was changing. Their report *Tradition and Change* (the first study) was the result of three years' field work and six years spent analysing and sifting the data. The purpose of the research was to study Banbury and the effect of the introduction of large-scale industry on the town.

While the research was being done the members of the team made their homes in or near Banbury. Participation in the life of the town was the main method of the work. Each research worker took part in a different sphere.

But participation and discussion with people met in everyday life are by themselves not enough to give you a full picture of a town the size of Banbury. The published records about Banbury were analysed. A questionnaire followed by a more detailed survey of over a thousand households was used to find out more about the people who lived there, their homes, families, and the religious and political groups to which people belonged. All the leading members of the community were interviewed. All the local organisations were studied by an analysis of their records. The aim of these investigations was to examine the composition of the leadership and membership of the various organisations, to show to what extent their leaderships overlapped and to what broader social group the organisations were connected. Margaret Stacey recorded the changes:

> The years around 1930 represent a divide. Life in Banbury before then would have been more easily recognisable to a man who had lived a hundred years earlier than to one living at the present day, only twenty years after (1950). Speak to any born Banburian of middle age or older and he will recall a town and a way of life which seem very remote. He will tell of the scores of carriers' carts which came rattling and rumbling in from the villages; of steaming cattle tethered in the streets; of the shouting drovers and the muck on the pavements. He will tell of the dark ill-lit streets of tiny family shops, of the drunkenness and brawling at night, and of the constable waiting in the shadow outside at closing time with his truncheon ready to help laggards on their way with a whack on the backside.
>
> The market place now has a tarmac surface on which ironmongers display their goods, patrons of the cinema park their cars and the St. John Ambulance stands ready. Where children used to play marbles at the Cross there are zebra crossings. Traffic streams past it along the north-south road between London and the south and the conurbations of the Midlands. A modern cinema looks on to the Horsefair car park. The shops in the brightly lighted High Street have plateglass windows and, though a few remain as family concerns, in this part of town most are branches of national chains, run by managers: Woolworths has taken the place of the 'Red Lion', farmers who used to do business at the bar have given place to young mothers with their prams. W. H. Smith stands in place of 'The Fox' where at fair times, and not only then, the fights were bloody and blasphemous. While, out of sight in the green fields beyond the town, surrounded by ten feet of barbed wire, immaculate flower beds, orderly bicycle ranks and lines of neatly parked cars, lies the aluminium factory. (Stacey 1960)

The coming of the aluminium factory in the 1930s changed more than just the market place and the High Street. There were far

5

deeper changes in the pattern of life in the town, in the fabric of the community and in people's social relationships.

BANBURY PEOPLE

Four people typical of Banbury as it was in the past are Sir William, Mr Shaw, Mr Grey, and George. Margaret Stacey describes them:

> Everyone looks up to Sir William, who comes of an old local family and who has lived in the same village, just outside Banbury, for the past thirty years. They acknowledge his public service and his work for charity. Sir William accepts his status. He is an active councillor because he regards 'public service as a duty which a man in (his) position owes'. He feels, too, that he should 'set an example' and is, therefore, punctilious in his dress and manners. He is a member of the church council in the village and reads the lesson at Matins. In the town itself, Mr Shaw, a prosperous tradesman who owns a business which has been in the family for three generations and in which his son also works, is an acknowledged leader. He, too, knows where he stands in the old-town society and accepts his position. Like Sir William, he considers that 'service to the community' is a duty. He has been Mayor of the town and gives freely to local charity. Mr Grey, another of the leading trades-people, is very like him in his social position and in many of his attitudes. But Grey is a 'pillar of the Methodist Church' and a Liberal in politics, while Shaw is a sidesman at the parish church and a member of the Conservative Association.
>
> George is an example of a traditional worker in Banbury. He has been employed at one of the old family businesses for twenty-five years. He accepts the leadership of Sir William and of the Shaws and Greys in the town. For he feels that 'the ordinary working man hasn't got the education' and that 'it's better to leave things like that to people who know about them'. So he does not belong to a trade union and avoids political discussion. He votes Conservative and is 'Church', but his neighbour, a native of Banbury like himself, with a similar job, is a staunch Baptist and a Liberal.
>
> Thus, Sir William rides with the Hunt. Shaw and Grey play bowls with the Chestnuts, while George and his neighbour belong to the Borough Bowls. Shaw drinks at the 'White Lion' in the town centre, but George goes to the pub at the end of the street. Grey, like George's neighbour, does not drink. George is a member of the British Legion (Sir William is its president). (Stacey 1960)

6

To men like these Banbury was the centre of their life. They could look back on Banbury as it was. Their ideas of politics, of religion and of life gave them security. Theirs was an established order in which each man 'knows his place'. To them the most important question to ask of a man was 'Who is he?'

But, since the pre-war expansion of Banbury, people who do not recognise such traditions have been drawn to the town. Men whose ideas and values are 'non-traditional'; whose roots are often far away. To them the key question is not 'Who is he?' but 'What does he do?'

Sir William is matched, for example, by Lord A. who was chairman of a group of engineering companies. Lord A. owns a hall in the district, but he is not often there because his work takes him to various parts of the country, to London, to the United States. He has no roots in the locality and belongs rather to an international society. He does not belong to the traditional status system, for he derives his status, not from his family as Sir William does, but from his position in industry.

Mr Shaw and Mr Grey are matched by Mr Brown. He is a technologist on the staff at the aluminium factory. He is a graduate from a provincial university. Like Lord A. he did not inherit his position but earned it on merit. He came to Banbury to work and if he does not get promotion in the factory, he will apply for a better post elsewhere.

George is matched today by people like Ted, who was brought up in an industrial city. He, like his father, has been a 'union man' ever since he started work. He is a Labour councillor. The class system for him is a matter of worker or not worker. He accepts his status as a worker and is proud of it, but, unlike George, he will not receive patronage from his 'betters'. 'The workers look after their own', he says. He does not accept that he has 'betters' like Sir William, Shaw and Grey. He supports the Labour Party. He wants to improve the lot and the chances of the workers as a class. (Stacey 1960)

THE SECOND STUDY

In 1966 Margaret Stacey returned to Banbury with a new team of sociologists.

The first field-work team left Banbury before the end of the age of austerity which followed the 1939–45 war: food was still rationed, hardly any post-war private houses had been built. In the period between the two studies the 'affluent society', the 'permissive society', the age of the pop group and youth culture all emerged. Communications were radically altered: television was in wide-spread use by the time of the restudy and the once-empty Oxfordshire lanes filled with cars faster than most that were on the road when the first study was made. These, of course, were technical and cultural changes that affected the whole nation. They have undoubtedly reduced the relative isolation of Banbury in a number of ways. Once distant neighbouring towns, already nearer by road in 1950 than they had been in 1900, were now nearer still. Furthermore, the improved communications, both TV and motor car, were shared by large sections of the population. They were not the privilege of the few. At the same time rail 'improvements' have reduced the connections of Banbury with the outside world.

The town itself now sprawls over a much wider area. Its cattle market, under cover and discreetly hidden, bears little resemblance to the old cattle market in the open streets about which people still talked in the late forties. Highly capitalised and organised, the market has progressed from being the 'largest in southern England' to the 'largest in England' and now, they claim, is the 'largest in Europe'. Despite this, and the twice-weekly street market, Banbury by 1966 had much more the air of an industrial town than of a market town. Along the road north out of Banbury there is a complex of factories where once the aluminium factory stood in splended isolation among the fields.

To a field-worker returning from the first study the most dramatic visual change is the many acres of erstwhile fields now covered in new housing estates. The land between the main roads has been progressively filled in: the Council Estate between the Broughton and Warwick roads, the superior private housing between the Broughton and Bloxham roads, and the less expensive housing between the Bloxham and Oxford roads. All the country walks, at one time so close to the town centre, seem to have disappeared and with their disappearance the character of the town seems to have changed. There are no longer tongues of open country penetrating wedge-shaped behind the ribbon development which fronted each main road in the thirties, forties and early fifties.

Some inhabitants express a mixture of awe, horror and pride as they point out to those returning on a visit to the town the 'acres' of new houses. One elderly Banburian, talking with nostalgia of the pre-war days, said, 'One thing I regret is the growth of Banbury; life in old Banbury made people terribly matey.' Another, having stated her disapproval of the rapid growth of the town which had already taken place, retorted with regard to the proposals for further expansion of the town, 'They might as well build a New Town, it won't be Banbury any more.' (Stacey and others 1975)

To the sociologist looking at Banbury in 1950 the most obvious feature of the town was the division between the traditional way of life of the old market town and the new developments which followed the growth of industry. By 1965 much of the old Banbury had disappeared. It was not only shops and buildings that had changed with housing estates covering what were once green fields. Attitudes changed. Men like Ted and Mr Brown became the majority. Whereas in 1950 they were newcomers, fifteen years later they were established members of the community. Margaret Stacey describes two streets in 1950.

> Tracey Avenue is known locally as 'Little Rochdale' because of the origin of its residents. Most of the men came from the depressed areas during the 1930s to look for work. When they found it they looked for houses for their families. Tracey Avenue was just being completed and naturally attracted them. This 'community within a community' was a much more comfortable setting for the immigrant than being surrounded by neighbours who were natives of the town.
> In Sonniton Street, a street mainly of Banburians, a middle-aged woman from the north found it impossible to get into the charmed circle of 'respectable' people, even though she attended the local church and joined the local Conservative Women's Association. In the same street a Scots family lived in complete isolation from other residents because they thought them 'unfriendly'. Their problem was undoubtedly increased because Sonniton Street is an established street with a defined structure. A substantial number of its residents have lived there for thirty or forty years. (Stacey 1960)

In the second study of Banbury the researchers looked closely at One End Street, a terrace of small Victorian houses, and Little Newton, a new housing estate on the edge of town.

> Although the personnel of the Little Newton estate was in many ways so different from that of One End Street, particularly in being younger, non-Banburian and better-off, the sociological determinants of neighbour relations appeared to be essentially the same. Thus it was seen in One End Street that those neighbours

9

who interacted with each other as neighbours were those who had other roles in common: kinship; common stage in the family circle; having children at home; place of origin, especially residence in the area. So it was in Little Newton, although there was some variation in the roles which were held in common.

In One End Street long residence together and especially having been born in the street, tended to lead residents to be friends as well as neighbours. In Little Newton everyone was a relative

Fig. 1. *Reasons for moving to Banbury*

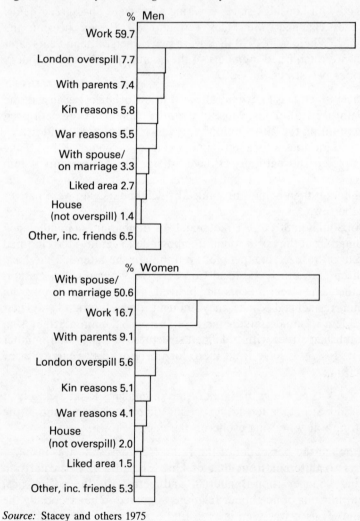

% Men

Work 59.7
London overspill 7.7
With parents 7.4
Kin reasons 5.8
War reasons 5.5
With spouse/ on marriage 3.3
Liked area 2.7
House (not overspill) 1.4
Other, inc. friends 6.5

% Women

With spouse/ on marriage 50.6
Work 16.7
With parents 9.1
London overspill 5.6
Kin reasons 5.1
War reasons 4.1
House (not overspill) 2.0
Liked area 1.5
Other, inc. friends 5.3

Source: Stacey and others 1975

newcomer. Common place of origin in a sense replaced long residence together as a basis for developing neighbour relations. Thus it was noticeable that Banburians were friendly with each other; some had been to the same school, others had been brought up in the same part of Banbury before they came to Little Newton.

In Little Newton, as in One End Street, availability to neighbour, i.e. being about in the locality, was important. Thus those who were around the house for long periods of time were in a position to develop neighbour relations. As in One End Street, among domestic groups where the wife went out to work there were few neighbour relations compared with those where she was at home. In Little Newton the men were younger and at work for the most part. Neighbouring for the men, as for the working wives, was thus largely confined to exchanges in the evening or at the weekends. The neighbour relations of working women and men were largely of the coincidental kind, superficial exchanges when working in the garden, hanging out the clothes, or cleaning the car. Without other over-lapping roles, such exchanges seemed

Table 1. *Employment in Banbury*

	1967%
Metal manufacture	10.0
Distribution	12.3
Transport	8.3
Clothing	2.4
Government	5.1
Building	10.7
Services except professional	8.7
Professional and commercial services	13.0
Food and drink	9.7
Woodworking	0.6
Electrical machinery, engineering	7.5
Printing	2.7
Agriculture	3.4
Gas, water, electricity	1.2
All other	4.4
Total	100.0

Source: Stacey and others 1975

rarely to develop into any other form of interaction. In contrast, those women who did not work and more particularly those who were the mothers of young children (and these categories overlapped very largely) were not only available in the locality for a great many hours, but also had the mother-role in common and children who played together and/or went to school together. For them the chances of establishing interaction with neighbours were higher because availability and overlapping roles coincided. (Stacey and others 1975)

As well as these small-scale studies of particular neighbourhoods (in which some of the researchers lived while working on the study), the team also collected evidence on the town as a whole.

They investigated the reasons people moved to Banbury in the first place.

From the census they discovered how many people lived in Banbury, their age and sex. They considered the industries in which people worked.

They collected evidence on religion in the town and the membership of the various churches.

Table 2. *Church members: 1950 and 1967*

Denomination	Denominational % of Church members	
	1950	1967
Church of England	36.5	27.7
Methodist	23.3	21.1
Baptist	4.6	7.2
Salvation Army	3.7	4.8
Congregational	3.7	2.8
Roman Catholic	28.2	36.4
Total	100.0	100.0
Total in sample	1 939	2 489

Source: Stacey and others 1975

They examined the links between people's jobs and their involvement in clubs and societies.

Table 3. *Occupation and voluntary associations*

Number of associations belonged to	Non-manual workers	Manual workers
	%	%
None	36	46
One	24	29
Two or more	40	25
Total	100	100

Source: Stacey and others 1975

They looked at the way people voted.

Table 4. *Voting of non-manual and manual workers, by date of arrival in Banbury*

Non-manual

Date of arrival	Since 1945	1930–45	Before 1930	Banbury born or brought up	Total
	%	%	%	%	%
Conservative	55.0	49.2	75.0	55.7	55.4
Labour	18.1	37.3	12.5	13.5	18.2
Liberal	8.4	4.5	8.3	6.5	7.2
Did not vote	12.0	1.5	4.2	16.5	12.3
Rest	6.4	7.5	0.0	7.8	6.8
Total	99.9	100.0	100.0	100.0	99.9

(Table 4, continues overleaf)

Manual

Date of arrival	Since 1945 %	1930–45 %	Before 1930 %	Banbury born or brought up %	Total %
Conservative	25.7	25.8	34.7	28.1	27.5
Labour	44.0	46.4	38.8	40.3	42.0
Liberal	5.2	5.1	4.1	6.5	5.8
Did not vote	19.4	13.4	12.2	18.4	17.8
Rest	5.6	9.3	10.2	6.7	6.8
Total	99.9	100.0	100.0	100.0	99.9

Source: Stacey and others 1975

All of this evidence made it possible for the team of sociologists to build up a picture of life in a fairly ordinary English town. They were able to show how life had changed and the things that had caused it to change.

Reading about Banbury may have raised some questions in your mind. What is the point of studying a place like Banbury? What use might be made of the findings? Why do we call studies like this 'sociology'? By the end of this book you should have a clearer idea how to answer these questions and others like them.

2
What is Sociology?

The two studies of Banbury provide a unique picture of life in an English town over a period of twenty years. They also provide an indication of the sort of things sociologists are interested in and how they study them.

Having read about Banbury and the research that was done there you may be wondering why it is called sociology. A great deal of what you have read could have been history or geography. Sociology, history and geography are similar subjects and they overlap. They are all social sciences. Sociologists often used historical or geographical material in their work. The content of their studies is often similar. They are all concerned with aspects of man's life on earth. The differences appear when you consider how the content, the raw material, is used by the different subjects. Any subject that you study at school, college or university is more than a list of topics. It also includes methods – the ways in which evidence is collected and used, and concepts – ideas which are used to put the evidence into some kind of order. Sociologists also use theories which guide and influence the way they work. We shall be considering methods in much more detail in Chapter 4.

A concept: community

A sociological concept which is central to the Banbury studies is 'community'. It is fairly typical of many ideas used in sociology. Firstly it is a word which has an everyday meaning outside of sociology. Sociologists use it in a similar way but try to be more precise. Secondly, in everyday use 'community' has a number of meanings and they overlap. Think about the differences of meaning in these uses of the word 'community':
— local community
— community spirit

— Community Centre
— the school community

'Local community' refers to a geographical area; a town, or village, or even a collection of streets like those around Tracey Avenue or One End Street in Banbury. 'Community spirit' is what you might expect to find in 'a community'. It is made up of attitudes of people towards each other and their relationships. It need not be tied down to a geographical area. 'Community Centre' is a place, in a local community, where community spirit is expected to develop. You do not need a Community Centre to develop 'community spirit' and even if you do have one there is no guarantee that it will. In reality a Community Centre may be little more than the place where they hold whist drives and playgroups. 'The school community' also involves the idea of 'place' except that it is the place you go to, rather than the place where you live. School community is usually used to refer to the relationships which exist within the school.

Thirdly, because 'community' can be understood in a number of ways both in everyday use and by sociologists there are often debates and arguments about exactly what it does mean and how it is being used. These debates are an important part of sociology.

Fourthly, as long as we are clear about the ways in which we use the word 'community' it can help us to organise our knowledge. In sociology similar events and actions from real life are grouped together as examples of particular ideas, or concepts. For example, in Banbury we can find evidence for the existence of some kind of community relationship within both One End Street and Little Newton. People know each other, they help each other out, they share experiences. This helps us to build up some kind of pattern. We can link particular behaviour or particular ways of life to particular situations. By observing such patterns in everyday life we are able to predict what could happen in the future. Human social life is so complicated that we could never hope to be one hundred per cent accurate in our predictions but we can get some idea of what *might* happen.

Fifthly, the concept of community helps us to make comparisons. We can compare Tracey Avenue in 1950 and Little Newton in 1965. One is a street of people with a common background who have shared many common experiences over nearly twenty years, the other is a new estate made up of people who had very little in common before they moved there. You could go on to compare them with other districts including your own. Comparison such as this is useful to the sociologist because it enables him or her to get a more precise picture of how social life fits together.

Community and association

A sociologist who was particularly interested in the way communities changed was Ferdinand Tonnies. He was German and lived from 1855 to 1936. His most important work was a book entitled *Gemeinschaft und Gesellschaft*. In this book Tonnies describes two patterns of social life which he called Gemeinschaft and Gesellschaft. These two German words are translated into English as 'community' and 'association' but many sociologists still prefer to use the original words.

An important feature of change in society is the movement from societies which are *gemeinschaft* or communities, to those which are mainly *gesellschaft* or associations. This is not just a change in the size or scale of the society, it is a change in the way people behave towards each other.

GEMEINSCHAFT

A *gemeinschaft* type of society, or community, would be fairly small. It would not contain many people. The people within such a community would recognise each other when they met 'face-to-face'. They may not have a very close relationship but they would know a little about each other and, as in Banbury in the old days, 'everyone would know their place'. This often amounted to knowing the positions and duties each individual held within the community.

GESELLSCHAFT

Gesellschaft is only a partial society. It does not attempt to provide for all of the needs of its members. It usually has very precise and limited aims which only concern part of people's lives. Its membership may be larger than the membership of a *gemeinschaft* type of society but its members do not stay for ever. People come and go. Membership is temporary, not permanent. The relationships which exist under *gesellschaft* are sometimes called 'associational relationships'. People only come into contact with each other for specific purposes and relationships tend to be formal. There are often rules about how people should communicate with each other; these are sometimes referred to as 'the proper channels'. A large business concern, or a government department provides examples of *gesells-*

chaft or association. Modern city life is made up of a network of such associational relationships which interlock through the members of the society.

A village in the country

We can see some of the features of *gemeinschaft* if we look at life in a country village. In 1940 Alwyn Rees lived for a time in the parish of Llanfihangel-yng-Ngwynfa in mid-Wales. His description of this little community can be found in his book *Life in a Welsh Countryside*.

It would not be quite accurate to call Llanfihangel a village. It is a parish of three small hamlets and scattered farms spread over an area of 15½ square miles of Montgomeryshire. When Rees was there the population of the parish was about five hundred people and all but fifty of these lived in farms and cottages spread across the countryside. The largest of the three hamlets, Llanfihangel itself (known locally as the Llan), contained less than a dozen buildings. As well as the church and a rectory, the school and the school-house, there were two shops, a post-office, a village hall and two cottages.

Within eleven miles of the cluster of dwellings that made up Llanfihangel were the boundaries of eight other parishes, making a total of 177 square miles of countryside. Within these nine parishes 75 per cent of the householders of Llanfihangel were born, and 85 per cent of their wives. It was within these 177 square miles that the majority of the inhabitants lived out their entire lives.

There was a time when the farms were self-sufficient, growing their own food and only trading outside when they had a surplus. This had changed by the time of Rees's study. The isolation of the parish had been broken. The farmers now reared stock for the market away in Oswestry and shops-on-wheels were regular callers at even the most isolated farms. Over the years the parish had become more closely linked with the life of mid-Wales and the Borders.

In the Llan household the father combines many roles. He is father, employer, manager and workman, as well as husband. In years past he was also expected to lead the family in prayer and organise family entertainment. In most of the farmhouses 'the family' would include hired labourers who lived under the same roof and ate at the same table. These were often young men, sons of neighbouring farmers, who would one day have farms of their own. Local families were often closely linked together. Two-thirds of the households studied had members whose close kin (parents, brothers, sisters, sons or daughters) lived elsewhere in the parish. One-third of the households were linked with two other households in this way. At sheep-shearing time these kin, and others from farther afield, would be expected to come and lend a hand. Thus, whereas in Banbury the question might be asked of a man, 'who is he?' or 'what does he do?' in Llanfihangel the question would be, 'who are his family?'.

Within the family each member would have a special task. The men would work in the fields under the direction of the father. The women would work around the house and concern themselves with the poultry and the dairy.

Within this community each individual has many roles.

A shopkeeper interests himself in cures and his advice is sought in case of illness. He also takes a lead in the organisation of sports and coaches the local teams, while his wife plays the piano and has now succeeded her father as church organist. The latter, a retired blacksmith and part-time postmaster, was very well read, and good use was made of his literacy not only by his immediate neighbours but also by the inhabitants of the surrounding district. The postman makes walking sticks in return for which farmers give him presents of tobacco, and he is also the church bellringer and organ blower. (Rees 1950)

Llanfihangel provides a good example of *gemeinschaft*. It is a small community in which the inhabitants meet face-to-face. Each individual participates in the community in many ways, acting out many different roles, over a whole lifetime. It is not a 'pure' example of *gemeinschaft*. Some elements of *gesellschaft* come into it. The farmers trade with buyers from far away; their sheep end up on the dinner tables of Birmingham and London; the post office exists to maintain contact between the hamlet and the world outside; the school is part of a wider county education service, as is the mobile library. Few communities today are completely isolated and self-contained.

Ted

A single community does not give us a clear picture of the nature of *gesellschaft*. We can see it better if we follow one man around on a fairly normal day of his life. One of the people we met in Banbury was Ted. Ted was not born in Banbury. His parents lived in Birmingham and after school Ted got an apprenticeship as a sheet metal worker. After a few years he married and when his apprenticeship was finished he applied for a job with one of the newer firms in Banbury. He and his wife, Irene, moved out to Banbury and, after a year or so, managed to get a council house in the southern part of the town. When Ted is at work he wears a boiler-suit to protect his clothes. His foreman wears a white overall. Ted has a lot of contact with the foreman and with the works manager because he is the shop steward for his part of the factory. Ted's relationship with both these men is determined by the rules drawn up over many years by the firm and the unions together. Their relationships are also affected by the accepted manner of behaviour in the works. Ted, the foreman, and the works manager, all have expectations of how each should behave in the work situation. These rules and expectations do not apply to Ted when he is in the canteen with his mates, or at a union meeting. In Llanfihangel most of the farmers were there because that was where their families had always farmed. It seemed the natural thing for them to do. Ted works at the factory, and is a shop steward in the union, by choice. He does not have to join in these particular 'associations'. He could work elsewhere and he could belong to another union.

When Ted leaves the factory at five-thirty he leaves his 'factory life' behind him. On the way home he enters into other relationships of a partial kind. He gets on the bus and buys a ticket, making a short-term contract with the bus company through their appointed agent, the bus conductor. If Ted wanted to he could determine the precise nature of his 'contract' by reading the bus company's by-laws. He stops to buy an evening newspaper, and then some cigarettes. Each time he enters into an associational relationship with another individual. Each time the aim of the relationship is very specific – to travel home, to exchange money for newspaper or cigarettes, and the relationship is limited. Ted never meets the bus conductor anywhere else. He knows nothing about the tobacconist except that he stocks his brand.

When Ted gets home he enters into the nearest thing in his life to *gemeinschaft*. His family is close, and membership is natural rather than voluntary. It is a situation of face-to-face relationships. In the evening he goes out to the pub where he meets yet another group of people in yet another situation. Some evenings he has to attend council meetings, for he was elected to the local council a couple of years back. In the council chamber Ted's relationships with the Mayor and the other councillors are very formal. He is always addressed as 'Councillor Smith', and in turn he has to address all his remarks through the Mayor. As a councillor Ted often has to sort things out for ratepayers in his ward. This may involve contacting council officials, again 'working through the proper channels' in a particular role.

Ted is a fictional example of someone who could well exist. Most people in a modern city live lives not unlike Ted's. Moving from one limited relationship to another, seldom allowing relationships in different situations to overlap. In advanced industrial societies people live their lives at the centre of a large number of *gesellschaft* or 'associational' relationships.

Social roles

While considering the idea of community we have been using another important sociological concept, that of social roles. The word 'role' is borrowed from the theatre and describes the behaviour which is expected from people in particular social positions. We have already seen that in Llanfihangel individuals play a number of different roles in village life. Ted also has a number of different roles to play but he plays them to different audiences. Sociologists would say that in Llanfihangel each individual plays a number of roles to the same role-set while Ted plays different roles to different role-sets. In everyday life some roles are more clearly defined than others.

When you get on a bus you expect the conductor to sell you a ticket, possibly to tell you when you get to your destination and, if you are an old lady, to help you off the bus. You do not expect him to come round selling ice-cream, or to sing a selection of hit songs from *The Sound of Music*. A bus conductor's role is clearly defined. People know what sort of behaviour to expect from him. We can say that his role is 'specific'. But not all social roles are like this. If you tried to write down a list of the 'role content' of the role of 'mother' you would get a very long list. Our expectations of the behaviour involved in performing roles like 'mother', 'father', 'son', 'daughter', are not at all specific. We would say that they are more diffuse.

Richard Hoggart describes some of the things expected of mothers when he was young.

> Partly because the husband is at work but also because women are simply expected to look after such things, it will be the mother who has the long wait in public places, at the doctor's for 'a bottle', at the clinic with a child who has eye trouble, at the municipal offices to see about the instalment on the electricity bill. (Hoggart 1957)

In some situations roles are clearly defined. We can understand that bus conductors don't sell ice-cream because we accept a basic definition of the role of bus conductor. This is close to the way 'role' is used in the theatre to describe a part someone plays from a script.

In many situations roles are not defined at all and we have to decide for ourselves what roles are being played. Usually we can rely on clues about the roles people play. A bus conductor has a uniform which symbolises the role and a setting – his bus – in which to perform it. Take these away and you are left with very few clues. Should you meet a total stranger you would search for clues which might indicate who they are and what they are doing there. Often we are able to use our experience of similar situations in the past to help us.

William and Charlotte Wiser describe the problems faced by the people in an Indian village when they arrived in the village intending to carry out a sociological study.

> Our assistant brought in the news that after observing our camp, and considering the various rumours that had arrived in advance, the leaders of the village had concluded that the Sahib must be the settlement officer come to check the landholding and revise rents. They knew that he was not the district magistrate nor a deputy; neither was he a public official. There had been missionaries here before, and he might be classified as such. But he had secured maps of the area and had access to records of landholdings. Who would want these but someone interested in taxes? (Wiser and Wiser 1969)

As the villagers got to know the 'Sahib' and 'Memsahib' better they changed their ideas about who they were and what their role was. The original idea about their roles was redefined.

> Each year has bound us closer to the life of the community. Some of our neighbours have grasped the idea of our survey and are willing to cooperate in its preparation. Others have accepted us simply as friends. (Wiser and Wiser 1969)

We approach any new situation with a basic stock of knowledge about the behaviour that would be appropriate. As we gain more knowledge of the situation we are able to change our ideas and remodel our understanding of roles. It is important to remember that in real life, social roles are not fixed like the roles in a play. They are frequently 'negotiated' by the people concerned.

Social roles therefore concern the behaviour that is expected of people in certain situations. The behaviour that fits the role needs

22

to be learned and we learn what to expect in the performance of certain roles. But roles may also change and can be 'renegotiated' in the way individuals interact in real life.

The Banbury studies can also show us the different levels at which sociologists work. When Margaret Stacey describes life in Tracey Avenue or Little Newton she is describing the face-to-face relationships of people in their everyday lives. We would call this 'interaction'. It is the basic level of social life. However, when Stacey describes things like voting patterns, or church membership she is moving away from the individuals towards the larger social group. It is rather like a zoom lens at a football match. One moment you are focused right in on a handful of supporters and then you are zooming out to view stands packed with thousands of people. Some sociologists prefer the 'close-up' view while others study the large mass. Of course, they are not really very different. The great mass of fans in the long shot is made up of many small groups of supporters which may require different methods of study and may lead to different kinds of theories.

Trying it out

Margaret Stacey spent thirteen years working on her two studies of Banbury. She was helped by a team of researchers, typists and others. You do not need that much time and all of those resources to do sociology. You can start from where you are at the moment. For example, why are you bothering to read this book? Is it because you want to or because you have been made to? Are you reading it because you are interested in sociology and hope to learn more about it or because you want to pass an exam? If you are reading it out of interest, why pick on sociology? Why not Greek drama or nuclear physics? Why do an exam in sociology, and what is the exam for anyway?

The answers to questions such as these are likely to be connected in some way with the social world in which you live. The decision to read this book was unlikely to have been taken on the spur of the moment. The fact that you are reading it may reflect the power situation in which you find yourself, the need to pass examinations, relationships with particular people and so on. Sociologists often theorise in this way, suggesting possible reasons for behaviour on the basis of what they know about the social world.

You could go on asking questions about your reasons for reading this book. You could relate this one activity to a whole range of other ideas – career, qualification, interests, learning, and so on.

Another way of doing sociology would be to go back to the statistics and to look more carefully at Margaret Stacey's evidence. What concepts or ideas can we gain from the tables of voting behaviour, or from the link between social class and membership of voluntary associations? What kind of a town was Banbury and how has it changed?

You could move on from Banbury and look at some other research from the area of community studies.

Finally you could even go out and do some research of your own. Decide on an area you are going to study. See how much evidence you can collect from information in the local library – local histories, census figures, election results, etc., or from the local newspaper. Go out and talk to people either as part of a properly planned survey or by meeting people with special knowledge – local councillors, policemen, or old people who have lived there all of their lives. Look at the way the streets and houses vary by asking estate agents about house prices in different areas and by direct observation. A camera can be a useful tool in such studies.

When you have completed your study find some way of presenting it – either as a written report or on exhibition or even as a tape-slide presentation or a talk on local radio.

Throughout your study keep asking yourself 'why is life here organised the way it is?'. You may not discover the whole answer but trying to find out will be a valuable exercise.

In Chapter 5 we look in more detail at the methods you might use.

3

Socialisation and Social Interaction

At birth we know nothing of society. The world into which we are born is wholly new to us. Our first experience of the world is through our senses. We experience the world as sensations of warmth, hunger, closeness, pain, comfort and discomfort. Out of these sensations we begin to build a view of the world. As we grow older our attention is focused more and more upon other objects which also inhabit this world. The people around us are especially important to us for they give us the warmth and comfort we enjoy and they help us to overcome hunger and pain. We can also communicate with them. Our actions cause them to act. We smile and they smile back. We make noises and they reply. Slowly we begin to gain some control over the world in which we find ourselves and it begins to make sense to us.

We can see this in Leila Berg's description of how a baby begins to learn to speak:

Babies are international. Lying in his cot, babbling as he grows, a baby speaks the consonants and vowels of every race in the world. Energy galvanizes the whole of him, setting his body wriggling, his hands clutching, his legs waving and his tongue, lips and jaws babbling. He doesn't have to be taught to do this, any more than a bulb has to be taught to send up a shoot. His speech is part of his vitality. With every movement of every part of him he is sending something of himself into space, he is launching himself into the world. *Mmmmm* and *nnnn* he says, like a sexy woman, snuggling, desiring. And *p p p* and *d d d* he says, delighting in play. All over the world, mamans, mums, nanas and nannies, dads, pappas, pas and babushkas, we cry 'That's me!' and turn his expressive sounds into the role we choose to play, answering him. The baby is amazed and delighted. HE makes his magic sounds again and again, and again we exclaim with joy and admiration, identifying ourselves as his family, and he crows in shared delight.

Still international, he continues to explore all the other sounds he can make, joyously feeling out his abilities. But now he begins to notice that he has scored a bullseye. So he concentrates on the sounds these important adults like best, the ones they have chosen for their language, the ones they respond to; and he practises them. He has plenty of time to practise. None of this – neither the rich exploration, nor the mutual response nor the selection, nor the concentration – has been taught him. He listens to tones of speech, and long before he can speak an English sentence speaks an English tune – or more accurately, the tune of an English people who are important to him and who respond with delight. (Leila Berg 1972)

Making sense of the world

Growing-up means more than becoming physically bigger, or learning to walk and talk. Growing-up means becoming part of a social world, learning what it is to be a member of a particular community. It means becoming fully human and takes place within social groups. This is a process we call *socialisation*. We do not acquire our knowledge and understanding of the world on our own. We rely on those who are around us for our ways of seeing the world. In other words we depend upon others for our socialisation.

The world that we grow up into is already there before we are born into it. We do not have to make it for ourselves. We receive it from others who in their turn received it from previous generations. Imagine a time when there was no society. Individuals made lives for themselves and discovered their own ways of surviving. Then, one day, two human beings met. Their first need was to communicate. Signs and gestures developed into words and language was created. Without some form of communication there could be no society. Other humans joined them and social life began to take shape. The earliest inhabitants of this society had no need to describe what they were doing. Eventually, however, they would have had children needing to be taught about the ways of the group and what it means to live in society. The children would come into a society which was fully established. It would appear to them as the only way in which to live. Instead of being something which has to be 'made' it would be something which is 'there'. Although this is an oversimplified view of how social life began it does tell us three things. Firstly, the social world is made by people. Secondly, it needs to be passed on to each new generation, and thirdly, it appears to us as something which has always existed. It seems to be natural.

This process of 'world-making', or *social construction* still continues. Every day new forms of social organisation arise out of the social interaction between individuals and this is passed on to others. For example, when two people marry they bring together different ways of life. The differences may be great, as when a couple from very different backgrounds marry, or small, as when they share similar experiences. But, they will be different. In setting up a new home they will have to work out their own ways of doing things. They will need to build their own society. To the children who are born into the family this will appear as the natural way for families to live. Each family constructs its own social world and hands it on to its children. This does not, of course, mean that you will always want to live in that way. You will experience other families and will have your own ideas about family life. Your beliefs about family life will help you to carry out the task of building your own family, which in turn will appear natural to your children.

We acquire, therefore, a world that is presented to us. A baby cannot say 'I don't really want to grow up as the child of a bank clerk in Manchester, would you mind if I became an Eskimo instead?' Our worlds are made for us and having acquired them they seem to be so natural that we find it difficult to imagine how they might be different. We must not forget, however, that social worlds can be very different and that however great those differences are, and however strange they appear to us, they are seen as natural to those who have grown up within them. Our ways of life would appear equally strange to people brought up in other social worlds. Sociologists use the term *culture* to describe the beliefs, attitudes, ways of behaving, social roles and all of the other things we have to learn in order to become part of the society.

Culture

When we acquire an understanding of a particular pattern of social life we are acquiring a *culture*. Social scientists have defined culture as:

> the patterns of ideas, beliefs, values and knowledge that the members of a social group have about themselves and their social and physical environments.

We can think of culture as the whole way of life of a community or social group. This may be seen in those things which make living in Britain different from living in France or Germany or Sierra Leone.

It can be seen in the differences between patterns of everyday life in remote hill villages in Wales and in the centre of a big city like London or Liverpool. We may also use the concept of *sub-culture* to describe particular ways of life which can be found within a wider culture. Young people, for example, may have attitudes, forms of dress, and ways of behaving which are part of the wider British culture but which are distinctive enough to be recognised as a separate 'sub-culture'.

When we look at patterns of social life in different parts of the world we soon realise that there are many different cultures. Even within a single nation we can recognise different cultures. Britain has always been a multi-cultural society. The invasions of Saxons, Romans, Vikings and Normans each introduced new cultures. The later arrival of Jews, Irish, Huguenots, Poles, peoples from the Caribbean and from Africa and Asia have continued this tradition. At one time it was thought that newly arrived cultures should be *assimilated* or absorbed into the existing dominant culture. As the awareness of the strength and value of different cultures has grown so there has been a recognition of the need for *cultural pluralism* with different cultures existing side-by-side.

An important feature of culture is that it is learned. Acquiring a culture is an important part of the process of becoming a member of a particular community or social group. Many of the important features of a culture are expressed through symbols. Particular forms of dress, facial decoration, or hairstyle symbolise particular cultures. The Rastafarian wears his hair in long 'dreadlocks' as a symbol of his rejection of the wider society. A bride's white gown symbolises purity. The Jewish boy's Bar Mitzvah symbolises his coming of age. Although culture is learned it need not be seen as something which is fixed and unchanging. Cultures adapt when the circumstances of the community change. When cultures come together, when there is large scale migration, for example, the immigrants often adopt those features of life in the host community which they value while maintaining the important features of their own traditional culture. The children of the original migrants grow up with two cultures, becoming more like the host community but often still holding to the traditional ways.

Within sociology the concept of culture is important. It points us towards those things which hold social groups together. In considering socialisation we are concerned with the ways in which new members of the society come to acquire those attitudes, values and beliefs which are part of their culture.

Socialisation

The approach we have taken so far has considered socialisation as the process of learning a culture. This is known as *enculturation*. We can also think of socialisation as learning to gain control of our feelings, desires and impulses, as acquiring the behaviour which is needed in particular social roles or as the development of self. Socialisation can therefore have four meanings:

Enculturation
Impulse control
Role learning
Development of Self

IMPULSE CONTROL

Theories of socialisation which emphasise control of impulses and desires are usually derived from the work of Freud. Although most of Freud's work was done at the end of the nineteenth century his theories are still being debated. Freud believed that the human mind has two parts. Our normal everyday thinking involved the conscious mind. There is also an unconscious mind containing hidden memories and thoughts which have been repressed or hidden away by the conscious mind. Within the unconscious mind of the young child are certain basic drives, called the 'id'. If left uncontrolled these will lead to anti-social, animal-like, behaviour. The child needs to be socialised so that a conscience, or super-ego, can develop. The ego keeps the balance between the impulses and desires of the id and the moral conscience of the super-ego. In Freudian terms socialisation places social and moral controls over man's natural animal instincts.

ROLE LEARNING

We saw in Chapter 2 how each individual within society performs one or more roles. Linked to each role are expected ways of behaving, governed by social norms. Socialisation can be seen as the process of learning particular social roles and the behaviour which makes it possible for each individual to fit in to society. Socialisation is effective when each individual is properly fitted into an appropriate role. If the socialisation is not effective the individual will not function properly in society. Poor socialisation is blamed for deviant or 'anti-social' behaviour. This approach to socialisation, which is associated with a type of sociology known as *functionalism*, has been heavily criticised. It is a very static view. It is society which is in some way thought to determine how people grow up and live their lives. For this reason the functionalists have been accused of taking 'an over-socialised view of man'. It is an approach which does not explain how individuals take a hand in changing their roles or how society itself changes.

The fourth approach to socialisation accepts that individuals have an influence on how they grow up. There is an *interaction* between the child and its social environment. In discovering that the world contains other people the infant begins to get an understanding of himself or herself. Part of being human is being able to think about yourself in the same way as you can think about others. American sociologist, G. H. Mead, thought of this as 'I' and 'Me'. 'I' is my private self inside my own thoughts. 'Me' is the self that I show to the world. Language makes it possible for us to rebuild the world in words inside our heads. We can think about things that have happened and things that we would like to happen. Socialisation involves the development of the self. Mead thought that this happened in three stages.

At a very early age the child begins to think about itself. It has the ability to reflect. This is important for social learning for it means that the individual can not only observe the behaviour of others but can also think about it and compare it to his or her own behaviour. There comes a point in our lives when we can say to ourselves 'did I get it right?', 'did I do it properly?'. The second stage begins when the child starts to play and it is in play that children are able to construct their environment, trying out different roles. In the third stage the child's individual play is extended through social play with other children. This is the 'game' stage when roles may be tried out on a wider stage. Instead of roles that society has prepared for them children are taking a hand in constructing their own roles. Mead's 'interactionist' approach is very different from the functionalist view of socialisation.

Childhood

Childhood is a fairly recent invention. It appears during the eighteenth century. Before that time children were seen as little adults. Early portraits of children show them wearing the same sort of clothes as their parents. Children worked alongside the adults and in the cramped conditions of many houses shared in the same living and sleeping space. Many children died soon after birth. It was a common belief that children were naturally sinful and that play was the work of the devil. Children, therefore, needed strict discipline if they were to reach salvation. At the end of the eighteenth century a different view of childhood began to appear. Children were seen as being closer to nature than adults who are tainted by the ways of the world. Childhood innocence replaces ideas of sinfulness. Instead of strict discipline the child was thought to need to be allowed to develop free of the harmful effects of the world.

These different views of the nature of childhood are reflected in different views of the way children should be brought up. One view sees the child as a lump of clay waiting to be moulded into any shape that society might wish. We can call this a *tabula rasa* view of socialisation, meaning that the child is literally a 'blank slate' waiting to be written upon. The opposite view sees the child as a young plant pushing up through the soil only needing warmth and light and food to enable it to grow and blossom. Instead of being moulded and shaped the child should be tended and nurtured. This *child-centred* view focussed on the potential that existed within the child. Whereas the 'tabula rasa' approach focusses on the way in which the environment shapes the child the 'child-centred' view of socialisation looks at the ways in which the child gains control of the environment.

These different views influence the ways in which children are brought up. At one time it was thought wrong to give in to children. A firm discipline was needed. Later views changed and it was believed that children should be given freedom to grow in their own way. Popular writers of books about child-care communicated these different views to parents. American writer Truby King was an important influence on child-rearing in the 1930s.

> The leading authorities of the day – English, foreign and American – all agree that the first thing to establish in life is regularity of habits. The mother who 'can't be so cruel' as to wake her sleeping baby if he happens to be asleep at the appointed feeding time, fails to realize that a few such wakings would be all she would have to resort to . . . The establishment of perfect regularity of habits, initiated by 'feeding and sleeping by the clock' is the ultimate foundation of all-round obedience. (Truby King 1937)

Forty years later another baby-care expert, Dr Spock, was telling parents:

> Doctors who used to warn young parents against spoiling are now encouraging them to meet their baby's needs, not only for food,

31

but also for comfort and loving. These changes in attitudes and methods have benefited most children and parents. There are fewer tense ones and more happy ones (Benjamin Spock 1973)

In many of these theories of child development the growing child, and in the end the adult, are seen as the product of the way that they have been brought up. If parents, and others who care for children do the right things then the child will turn out properly. Both Truby King and Benjamin Spock based their advice on 'doing the right thing'. These views of child-rearing which see the child as a product of certain kinds of upbringing often ignore the fact that socialisation is a two-way process. Parents are as much influenced by their children as the children are by their parents. Psychologist Rudolph Schaffer has described this as a *transactional* approach to child-rearing.

The child, it was thought, came into the world as a formless, inert blob of clay which was then moulded by parents, teachers, society, or whatever other forces he happened to come into contact with, and the shape that he eventually assumed was therefore entirely due to the characteristics others had decided to implant in him. This view, we now know, is misleading. As detailed examinations of mother-infant interactions show, from the beginning the baby is active, not passive; his behaviour is organised, not 'absent'; and even to the earliest social interactions he brings certain characteristics which will affect the behaviour of other people towards him. A mother's task is not to create something out of nothing but rather to dovetail her behaviour to that of the infant's. (Schaffer 1977)

Patterns of child-rearing

There is no one right way in which to bring up children. There are not only different styles of child-rearing recommended by different experts but also different patterns of child-rearing in different communities. In Britain children are brought up by their parents within families. In other societies it may be done differently. In her study of adolescent girls on the Pacific Island of Samoa, Margaret Mead observed how the task of bringing up the youngest children fell upon the older girls.

The weight of the punishment usually falls upon the next oldest child, who learns to shout 'come out of the sun' before she has fully appreciated the necessity of doing so herself. By the time

Samoan girls and boys have reached sixteen or seventeen years of age these perpetual admonitions to the younger ones have become an inseparable part of their conversation, a monotonous, irritated undercurrent to all their comments. I have known them intersperse their remarks every two or three minutes with 'Keep still', 'Sit still', 'Keep your mouths shut', 'Stop that noise', uttered quite mechanically although all of the little ones present may have been behaving as quietly as intimidated mice . . . No mother will exert herself to discipline a younger child if an older one can be made responsible. (Mead 1928)

In some societies child-rearing is seen as a great burden and is carried out in a way which would shock many in Britain. Amongst the Ik of Northern Uganda children are seen as a liability.

We should not be surprised when the mother throws her child out at three years old. She has breast-fed it, with some ill humour, and cared for it in some manner for three whole years, and now it is ready to make its own way. I imagine the child must be rather relieved to be thrown out, for in the process of being cared for he or she is carried about in a hide sling wherever the mother goes, and since the mother is not strong herself this is done grudgingly. Whenever the mother finds a spot in which to gather, or if she is at the water hole or in her fields, she loosens the sling and lets the baby to the ground none too slowly, and of course laughs if it is hurt . . . Then she goes about her business, leaving the child there, almost hoping that some predator will come along and carry it off. (Turnbull 1973)

These two examples show quite different approaches to child rearing in two small-scale tribal societies. There are also many different patterns of child-rearing in Britain. John and Elizabeth Newson have carried out a long-term study of families in Nottingham. In following through a group of 700 children from birth to the age of seven the Newsons were able to see how different families responded to similar problems. They found that differences in how children were brought up were often closely linked to the social class of their parents.

The Newsons' first study looked at the patterns of infant care in the 700 families. They found that there were clear differences between the families of workers in office jobs (white-collar workers), and those of manual, or blue-collar, workers. The middle-class, white-collar, groups tended to start their families later as can be seen in Table 5.

Table 5. *Percentage of wives aged less than 21 at birth of first child*

Social Class:	
Professional and Managerial	24
Clerical and supervisory	25
Skilled Manual	40
Semi-skilled Manual	46
Unskilled Manual	53

Source: Adapted from Newson, J., and Newson, E., *Patterns of Infant Care*, 1963

Many of the differences found by the Newsons were linked to the situations in which the families lived. Over half of the middle-class infants slept in their own bedroom. Only one-fifth of the children of skilled manual workers slept alone and for the children of unskilled workers having a room of their own was very unusual with 97 per cent having to share. There were similar differences in the children's diets, with only 5 per cent of the children of professional workers having an inadequate diet compared to 13 per cent of skilled manual workers and 32 per cent of unskilled workers.

There were other differences in the ways in which children were brought up which were not related to the kind of houses in which the families lived, nor to how much money they could afford to spend on food. The children of manual workers were more likely to be given a bottle or a dummy to help them to get to sleep. They were more likely to be smacked and to go to bed later. These are differences in the ways families in different social classes behave towards their children.

When they looked at the families of the seven-year-olds they found that the differences between different social classes had continued. There were clear differences in approaches to discipline and in the freedom allowed to the children. By the time children get to seven years old they are getting far more independent. They are likely to be out on their own more and away from the direct supervision of their parents. When the children were seven the Newsons asked the parents, 'How would you describe him/her to someone who didn't know him/her at all? Would you call him/her an indoor child or an outdoor child?'

The replies fitted a clear pattern. The children from working-class families were more likely to be described as 'outdoor children'. In all social classes girls were less likely to be described as 'outdoor children' than were the boys. The middle-class children were more likely to be fetched from school, expected to say where they were going when they went out, have friends back to their homes to play and were less likely to 'wander off' on their own or play in the street. In the same way that girls in either social class were less likely be described as 'outdoor types' so all girls were more likely to be supervised and kept close to homes than the boys.

Middle-class and working-class parents used a variety of methods of disciplining their children. Like all parents they would use rewards, such as praise and 'hugs and kisses', as well as punishments, such as smacking. Each parent's approach to discipline, however, needed to be viewed as a whole.

> Smacking happens, not in a vacuum, but as part of a continuing dialogue of words and behaviour in which the mother's intent is conveyed in various ways. Hugs and kisses are one kind of message; smacks carry another; words are the vehicles for others again.

'Smacking' and 'talking to the child' happened within both social classes. The important difference the Newsons discovered was the context within which the punishment took place. Middle-class parents were more likely to have a *democratic* view of child-rearing which aimed at making a naughty child realise what he or she had done wrong and to learn self-control in not doing it again. In this way self-discipline becomes *internalised* within the child's personality. One of the middle-class mothers who was interviewed commented

> Often I feel that punishing him for something and not saying any more about it perhaps doesn't quite do the trick and I perhaps come back on the subject. Perhaps a day after I'll say 'You know yesterday you did this or that, and I gave you a smack', and explain to him why it's not very nice; then he usually feels sorry, and says so; or perhaps doesn't say anything, but just thinks about it.

At the other extreme are parents who are more likely to use words to threaten or 'bamboozle' the child into obedience or will use physical punishments without getting the child to understand the reasons. Smacking is often seen as a way of showing a child who is boss.

> If I didn't stop them, they'd be the gaffers of me all the while; so I've got to put my foot down one way, and shouting I don't always do it. So you might as well give them a good hiding and be done with it . . . Well, I think if they never have a good hiding

they think they can get away with a lot, now they do, when they get older. We had a lot of good hidings, yet we never did them things what's going on today, did we?

Threats may be used to make a child behave.

If he's naughty, I say 'We'll have to buy a new baby now'; and he says 'No, Mam, no, Mam, you've got to love me, love me'. I say 'All right, you'll be a good boy?' He says 'Yes'.

For these children discipline becomes something that is imposed from outside. The Newsons conclude by suggesting that the way in which a child comes to understand discipline is likely to influence how society itself is understood. The middle-class children, they argue, gain a knowledge of the inner workings of the system and are better able to find reasons for events. The working-class children, especially the least privileged, learn to view society as something that is imposed upon them.

Secondary socialisation

Socialisation does not come to an end with childhood. As people move through their lives they meet new situations, they learn new ways to behave, they acquire new ideas and develop an understanding of new cultures. Going to school, starting a job, joining a football club or moving to another community each means that we must change in some way. Even on our death bed we need to learn the behaviour appropriate to a dying person. This learning of new roles and new codes of behaviour which continues throughout our lives is called 'secondary socialisation'. Just as primary socialisation laid the basis for an individual's identity as a person, so secondary socialisation leads to changes in that identity.

We can think of our lives as a continuous 'career' made up of a large number of different situations, or 'settings', through which we move as we move through our lives. Within each setting there are different things to learn, different ways to behave, different attitudes and beliefs and different expectations. As we move from one situation to another we become socialised into the attitudes and patterns of behaviour which are appropriate to that setting. Secondary socialisation also involves coming to see ourselves in a new way.

CAREER

If you sat down and wrote your autobiography you would be able to describe how you had moved from one stage in your life to another. If your memory is good you might be able to remember life in your infants school, or when you were in the juniors. Life at secondary school is possibly easier to remember. You might even be able to remember how you moved up through the school from first year to second year and so on. If you left school a long time ago you might write your autobiography in terms of your married life or different jobs that you have had. When describing marriage you might describe courtship, engagement, marriage and parenthood. Each of these represents a different status within your overall career. To the sociologist a 'career' is a series of different statuses which make up the pattern of our lives. We can think of a 'career' as the pattern of a whole life or as part of it. We can, therefore, also talk of different 'careers', a school career, or a 'career' as a drug-addict, for example. As we move from one status to another we need to learn the behaviour which fits our new roles and positions. The change from one status to another may be marked by some kind of formal transition. There may be a ceremony or special event which indicates to all concerned that a new status has been gained. An eighteenth birthday party marks the beginning of adulthood. The beginning of married life is marked by a wedding. For a Jewish boy the Bar Mitzvah is an important event marking the time when he is able to join the older men in the synagogue. This movement from one status to another is often described as 'status passage'. The events which surround the status passage are the 'rites of passage'. Once within the new status we are likely to mix with others who share that position and from them we will learn the roles and behaviour that go with the status. This is all part of the process of secondary socialisation.

Peter Marsh has used this concept of career to describe the development of the role of football hooligan. The career of the football supporter can be seen as three or four separate statuses. The youngest recruits to the terraces are the 'little kids' of nine or ten who are only just beginning to learn how to behave. They are a source of embarrassment to the older fans.

'They'll go up and do all the signs and they'll chant 'Come on' and 'Up the aggro' and everything like that, and then as soon as anything happens they'll run everywhere and put everything into panic and you don't know where you are.' (Marsh 1978)

In time the 'little kids' move up to become part of the older group of 'rowdies' and may even move into the prized roles of 'aggro leader' or 'hard-case'. Within the career each status has its own behaviour and expectations. The 'hard-case' in the football crowd

37

is expected to lead the charge into the opposing fans. The 'nutter' is expected to do crazy things which no other fans would risk.

An important part of the change in status is the change in identity. It is through our interaction with others that we come to see ourselves in different ways. Erving Goffman has examined how a confidence trickster socialises his victim into rethinking how he sees himself. The 'con' is a way of obtaining money under false pretences from a 'sucker' or 'mark'. The confidence trickster is a talented actor who builds up a relationship with the 'mark' with the aim of taking away some, of his money. If at the end of the 'con' the 'mark' feels that he has been swindled he will go to the police and make life difficult for the trickster. Before he departs with the 'mark's' money it is important for the trickster to provide an explanation which enables the 'mark' to accept the loss without causing trouble.

The typical play has typical phases. The potential sucker is first spotted, and one member of the working team (called the 'outside man', 'steerer' or 'roper') arranges to make social contact with him. The confidence of the mark is won, and he is given the opportunity to invest his money in a gambling venture which he understands to have been fixed in his favour. The venture, of course, is fixed, but not in his favour. The mark is permitted to win some money and then persuaded to invest more. There is an 'accident' or 'mistake' and the mark loses his total investment. The operators then depart in a ceremony that is called the 'blowoff' or 'sting'. They leave the mark but take his money. The mark is expected to go on his way a little wiser and a little poorer.

Sometimes, however, a mark is not quite prepared to accept his loss as a gain in experience and to say and do nothing about his venture. He may feel moved to complain to the police or to chase after the operators . . . He may 'squawk', 'beef' or 'come through'. In order to avoid this adverse publicity an additional phase is added at the end of the play. It is called 'cooling the mark out'. (E. Goffman 1952)

After the 'sting' one of the team may stay with the 'mark' to 'cool' him. The 'mark' needs to be socialised into believing that although he has lost out on the deal it does not reflect on him as a person, that it could happen to anyone, and that there is nothing to be gained from going to the police.

In considering the problem of 'cooling the mark' Goffman presents one example of a situation in which an individual's view of himself has been challenged by events. He suggests that 'cooling out' is used in many other situations where individuals need to be helped to come to terms with events. Breaking off a close relationship, failing an important exam you had told everyone you would pass easily, being turned down for promotion that everyone thought you would get, are all examples of everyday situations to which individuals need to adjust. If the 'cooling out' is effective the individual will adjust to the event without seriously damaging his or her identity.

Society

Although this chapter has been considering ideas like culture, social roles, socialisation and career it has really been about society itself. It is impossible to separate a thing called 'society' from the ways in which people interact in everyday life; from the ways in which they make their social worlds and from the ways in which they pass those social worlds on to others. This approach has seen society as something which is continually being remade through the actions of individuals, but which also has an influence on how individuals become. Society has been seen as a process of becoming. Society is continually being made and remade through the actions of people.

It is important to remember this as we discover more about the ways in which social life is organised. We often treat society as a 'thing' which somehow exists on its own, yet we know that cannot be true. The word 'society' is often used as a shorthand way of describing this process of becoming at a particular point of time. Because 'society' appears to be like that at this moment of time does not mean that it has always been like that, nor that it will continue to be like that in the future.

4

Class, Status and Power

If you stand a short way away from the bottom of a cliff you can often see lines running along the cliff-face indicating the various geological layers, or strata. Sociologists have borrowed this term 'strata' from the geologists and use it to describe levels which exist in society. Social stratification refers to the division of society into a number of levels placed above and below each other. You are probably familiar with the idea of 'social classes' but before we go on to examine the idea of class we must consider certain other forms of social stratification.

Social stratification

FEUDAL ESTATES

In medieval England society was divided into feudal estates. These were divisions based on land-holding and the obligation to fight for your lord.

> At the top stands a royal family and a landholding, hereditary military aristocracy, closely followed by an allied priesthood, ranking on a par with the secular nobility. Below them are merchants and craftsmen while free peasants and unfree serfs form the broad bottom strata. (Mayer 1955)

They were essentially man-made divisions for both king and nobles had the power to promote someone of low estate to a higher position. Each estate had its part to play in the life of the nation. 'The nobility were ordained to defend all, the clergy to pray for all and the commons to provide food for all.' It was a part of the system of a feudal society and when that form of society went into decline the system of estates went with it. In Sweden the four estates of nobles, clergy, citizens and peasants survived until 1866, but it had died out in most other parts of Europe well before then.

Estates divided up the power in society and restricted each individual's ability to change his status. Because position, power and status were given at birth we would say that they were 'ascribed' (see page 46). Very few people were able to improve themselves by their own efforts. Only the most exceptional achieved the distinction of ennoblement by the king. People had to be satisfied with their position in the society. In the words of the Victorian hymn:

> The rich man in his castle,
> The poor man at his gate,
> God made them high and lowly,
> And ordered their estate.

Another reminder of the days of estates can be seen in the division of Parliament into Lords and Commons.

CASTE

In India a very different form of social stratification operates. This is a system of 'caste'. Each Hindu belongs to one of the four main castes or is casteless, an untouchable. As in the system of estates position, status and power are ascribed at birth. Caste is inherited and advancement in this life at least is limited. You cannot work your way up in a caste system. It is also difficult to marry into another caste. Indian society is endogamous and you may only marry someone of your caste. Caste is supported by the religions of India. Hindu religious culture has evolved rules, or *dharma*, which restrict contact between those of different caste. These religious rules affect ordinary social contact as well as marriage. A strict Brahmin, a member of the highest caste, would take care not to come into contact with a lower caste such as the Sudras, or with an untouchable. He would take care not to sit in the same seat or drink from the same cup, or even be touched by his shadow. Should he come into contact with someone of lower caste he would ritually wash himself as an act of purification.

In recent years the Indian Government has tried very hard to remove the worst injustices of the caste system. Mahatma Gandhi, the great Indian reformer, called the untouchables 'Harijans' or 'God's people' and they have now been given many social and political rights which were once denied them. Despite this the system still exists. In any part of India there might still be as many as 2 500 *jatis*, or subcastes, each centred on a particular occupation, restricted by the rules of endogamy, maintaining ritual distance from other *jatis* and obeying the *dharma*. By such obedience the Hindu believes that he will attain a good *kharma* and ensure rebirth into a higher caste in his next life.

THE IDEAS OF MARX

Much of our thinking about class originates in the writings of Karl Marx who lived from 1818 to 1883. Marx held that class was based on the organisation of production. The economic system of capitalism gave power to those who owned wealth and property. Marx pointed out that every aspect of life depended ultimately on how men provided themselves with 'material' things like food, clothing and shelter. In capitalist societies men and women provided for their material needs by selling their labour power to others who owned or controlled the forces of production. These forces of production included raw materials, factories, machines and the skills needed to use them. Various forms of production created particular relationships between the people involved. In a factory we find managers, foremen, charge hands, shop stewards, clerks, and many other types of worker. The social relationships between these different groups arose out of the way things are produced and Marx called these relationships the social relations of production.

For Marx the most important division of society created by the social relations of production was that between those who owned or controlled the forces of production – the capitalists – and those who sold their labour power – the workers or the proletariat. The differences of interest between these two groups inevitably led to conflict. In *The Communist Manifesto*, which Marx published with his friend Friedrich Engels in 1847, he wrote:

> The history of all hitherto existing society is the history of class struggles.
>
> Freeman and slave, patrician and plebeian, lord and serf, gildmaster and journeyman, in a word oppressor and oppressed, stood in constant opposition to one another, carried on an uninterrupted, now hidden, now open, fight, a fight that each time ended either in a revolutionary reconstitution of society at large or in the common ruin of the contending classes.

In this approach to social class Marx introduced a further important idea. It is not enough for a class to exist simply because people share a similar position in society. People should also be conscious of their shared position. Marx distinguishes between the *objective* view of 'a class in itself' in which groups and individuals can be seen to have things in common and the *subjective* 'class for itself' in which people have an awareness of themselves as a class.

Class and status

Marx's view of social class focussed on the relationship to the means of production and provides a valuable way of understanding the basic divisions of society. The Marxist approach is particularly useful when considering problems of the distribution of power and wealth in a society.

In our everyday use of the idea of class, however, we link these basic ideas of social and economic relationships to ideas of status and prestige. How do ordinary people see social class and how do they place others in a social class pattern? How, for example, would you 'class' the following occupations: tractor driver, carpenter, railway porter, barman and dock labourer? Are they all working-class, or proletariat, and therefore all at the same level, or would you say that a carpenter has a higher position than a barman, or vice versa? How would you decide? Obviously a system based only on an individual's job is not adequate. It does not fully explain how people really see social differences. We must clearly take other factors into account.

We must, in fact, consider the individual's status in society. If social class is derived from how you earn your money then social status depends on how you spend it. One refers to the individual as a producer, the other to the individual as a consumer. Society is made up of a series of levels or status groups.

Each individual's status depends on a number of things. Occupation is obviously important. A doctor has higher status than a road sweeper largely because of his job. But status also takes into account education, level of income, style of life, patterns of consumption and so on. If two men sit opposite each other in the morning rush hour they will have a fair idea of each other's status without a word being spoken. If one is wearing a pin-stripe suit, regimental tie, and a bowler hat, and is carrying a rolled umbrella and a copy of *The Times* he would be given a different status from his companion who might be wearing working boots, overalls, a donkey jacket and cloth cap and have *The Sun* newspaper sticking out of his pocket. These visual symbols are very important in enabling us to 'place' people correctly on a scale of status. This is not meant to imply that either individual is any better or worse than the other. Sociology aims to be a value-free science. No doubt if they got talking and found that they had a common interest in cricket, or gardening, or youth work, they would get on very well together. It may be that communication at that level never gets a chance because of the way each man 'reads' the symbols of dress and accent.

We can get an even clearer picture of class and status if we take a closer look at Margaret Stacey's work on Banbury described in Chapter 1.

Class and status in Banbury

Each of the individuals described in the first Banbury study recognised the existence of class and status in some form or another. They did not always agree, but they felt themselves to be part of a stratified system. If we consider their ideas closely we will find that they are more aware of status difference than they are of social class. We would also find that they had two different ways of thinking of class and status, something which arose out of the situation in Banbury at the time of the study.

Sir William, Shaw and Grey, George and his neighbour would have accepted a view of class and status which is based on tradition. Lord A., Mr Brown and Ted held a non-traditional view. The traditional view is shown in Table 6.

A TRADITIONAL VIEW

Table 6. *The traditional pattern of class and status*

Class	Status group
Upper	1. County
	2. Gentry
Middle	3. Upper middle
	4. Middle
	5. Lower middle
Working	6. Respectable working
	7. Ordinary working
	8. Rough working

Source: Stacey 1960

All those in the 'working-class' group were wage earners. They earned their living with their hands. George, for example, is likely to have been employed as a craftsman in a traditional industry – cabinet making, a cooper or a wheelwright – or as an unskilled labourer – on a building site or in a flour mill. The job he does determines his social class. Manual work puts a man into the

44

working-class group. Sociologists often speak of 'manual working-class' when referring to this group.

Within the working class there are subgroups whose membership is based more on 'how you live' than on 'what you do'.

> Within the working class in Banbury there are three status groups: the 'rough', the 'ordinary', and the 'respectable'. The 'roughs', often the poorest families, would like to lean heavily on their neighbours but they are discouraged. Their personal appearance and the state of their houses add to their unattractiveness as companions. The 'respectables' on the other hand are not expelled: they are 'stand-offish'. They are bent on improving their own social positions and close contact with neighbours is a part of the life of the social class they wish to leave behind. (Stacey 1960)

These groups have different levels of status within the working-class community.

The middle classes

Mr Grey and Mr Shaw are middle-class. Sociologists would say this because they earn their living in non-manual jobs. They have a certain status in the community. They behave in ways which are typical of middle-class people. For example, they live in larger houses than people like George and his neighbour. Shaw and Grey live in an area where many other middle-class people live.

> Their houses, sometimes with three bedrooms and sometimes four, are found on the hilly land to the south and west, where there is a prospect of fields and woods. It is here that the more 'well-to-do' live, the larger tradesmen and senior officials. Their houses, owner occupied, are set well back from the road. Some are semi-detached but a noticeable number stand on their own; in either case most have garages. (Stacey 1960)

Such houses are an indication of status. But so also are their other activities. Messrs Shaw and Grey are actively involved in church activities, in politics, and organisations like the Rotary Club and the tennis club.

An examination of class and status in Banbury also reveals a third group – an upper class, which includes men like Sir William. Some people feel that there is no 'upper class' any more. Certainly it is diminishing in the country as a whole. The sort of upper-class groups found in Banbury by Margaret Stacey, owning land and having inherited status, is fast dying out.

A NON-TRADITIONAL VIEW

Alongside this 'traditional' class system there is the non-traditional. Lord A., Mr Brown and Ted are typical examples of people who think of themselves in non-traditional class and status terms. The non-traditional view is shown in Table 7.

It is difficult to link this non-traditional class and status system to the traditional system. There are some similarities – in the working class, for example – but in the middle-class groups there is considerable overlap. And many people would say that there is no 'upper class' in a modern industrial society. Although Lord A. and his equals have many of the marks of an 'upper class' – large country houses, wealth, and power in politics as well as industry – they are often men who have 'made their own way in the world', often from quite humble origins. Their wealth, power, status and titles are seldom inherited from their ancestors, as it was for Sir William. In many ways this group merges with the 'upper-middle-class' group in a way which was not possible with the 'traditional' aristocracy.

Table 7. *The non-traditional pattern of class and status*

Class	Status group
Upper	1. Industrial upper
Middle	2. Senior managers and directors
	3. Newer professions
	4. Industrial technicians
Working	5. Respectable
	6. Ordinary
	7. Rough

Source: Stacey 1960

Status – achieved and ascribed

In a 'traditional' system position in society is established at birth; it is handed on from father to son. This process is termed 'ascription' and the status which is passed on in this way is 'ascribed status'. In more advanced industrial societies status goes to those who have done the most to earn it. It is 'achieved status'. Mr Brown gives us a good example of achieved status. His father was a coal miner in Durham. When 'young Brown' won a scholarship to the grammar school the family scrimped and saved to make ends meet. He did well in his 'A' levels and got to university where he studied metallurgy. He now works in Banbury in the research department of the aluminium factory. His roots are working class but his achievements have put him into the middle class. He is a good example of upward social mobility.

An important feature of advanced industrial society is this ability to move from one class in society to another. It is not something which can happen overnight. It can only be seen clearly when a son's job is compared to his father's. Because status in modern industrial societies is achieved, and depends on 'merit', such societies have been described as 'meritocracies'. This is in contrast to the traditional society which included an 'aristocracy'.

Power

The words 'meritocracy' and 'aristocracy' also refer to the way in which power is distributed in a society. In traditional societies 'power' was 'ascribed' and lay in the hands of an inherited 'ruling class'. In Britain today the amount of power a man has depends far more on what he has achieved – on merit. We can see this clearly when we compare Sir William and Lord A. in Banbury. Sir William possesses ascribed status and power. His family have been important in that area for generations and in the past have exercised considerable power. Once the entire country was ruled by men like Sir William and by the 'aristocracy'. Today his neighbour Lord A. has far more power. Lord A.'s power is not local; it is national. He is chairman of his own company and on the board of directors of many others. His advice is called for on many matters of national importance and he deals with governments and companies all over the world. Thousands of men's jobs come under his chairmanship, and though his power is not 'absolute' – his shareholders could give him the sack – it is still very considerable. Unlike Sir William, Lord A. did not inherit his position. He 'made his own way' in the world, starting from fairly ordinary beginnings. His title came somewhat late in life as a symbol of the recognition of his achievements. His son, who will not continue the title, is expected to make his 'own way in the world', too. His position in life will also depend on his achievements even though he had a far better start than his father.

In reality the division of power in Banbury is more complex. In the second study of the town Margaret Stacey concluded that there was no one group or individual holding complete power. She suggests that a number of elite groups are able to exert influence in different areas of life. Many important decisions for the town were made by politicians in London. Within the town decisions were influenced by a number of different groups: the trades council, the Chamber of Commerce, ratepayers' associations and a range of smaller 'pressure' groups (see Chapter 10).

It is clear, however, that power is not shared equally in Banbury, nor in any other community. Certain individuals and groups have more power to influence events, make decisions or affect the lives of others than do other individuals or groups.

MAX WEBER

These three main ideas – class, status and power – are brought together in the writings of Max Weber, a German sociologist who lived in the early part of this century. Weber's view of 'class' is similar to that of Marx. To Weber, however, 'class' is not simply a matter of owning or not owning capital but also includes the opportunities and advantages a person receives from his or her position in the economic system. A shop-floor worker in a factory is not only a seller of 'labour-power' to a capitalist. He is also a 'worker' as distinct from a 'manager', with different hours, different privileges and different opportunities.

Whereas class concerns the individual's position in a system of production, status is linked to 'consumption'. An individual's status depends on the way other people see them. In Weber's view status is a 'subjective' matter. We can see this in the division of the Banbury working-class groups into 'respectable', 'ordinary', and 'rough'.

Weber's third aspect of social stratification is 'power' which again while linked to class and status is not always so. The Queen is undoubtedly very rich and has very high status but is she more powerful than Parliament or the Prime Minister? Trade union leaders are not the highest paid people in the country, nor do they have great status but in certain situations they have considerable power. Class, power and status may be linked but they may also be quite separate. The barrow-boy who 'makes good' ends up with a chain of supermarkets, may have a large house, a chauffeur-driven Rolls Royce and a yacht at Monte Carlo but need not be accepted by his neighbours as a 'person of class'. Nor might he have power outside of his own business interests.

This chapter began with a view of stratification which compared it to strata on a rock face. We can now see that such a picture is too simple and that social differences depend on a number of different factors. This becomes clearer when we examine how class, status and power change.

Measuring social class

It should be clear by now that social class is not easy to define. Sociologists use a variety of different meanings which are very often different from those used in everyday conversation. This becomes a particular problem when social class is a feature of social research. The researcher needs to be able to put individuals into social class categories consistently and reliably. The categories used must also be as close as possible to real life, everyday categories.

THE REGISTRAR GENERAL

One social classification which is very widely used is produced by the Registrar General. It was first used in the 1911 Census and has been revised a number of times since then. It is still used in the ten-yearly Census of Population and in most government reports and surveys. It has a five-point scale with each group based on a

Table 8. *The Registrar General's social classification*

Non-manual occupations		
Class I Professional	Doctor, dentist, engineer, scientist, university lecturer, etc.	A
Class II Managerial and technical	Manager, librarian, teacher, nurse, other technical occupations: pharmacist, laboratory technician, owner of small business, etc.	B
Class III (non-manual) Clerical and minor supervisory	Clerk, commercial traveller, typist, draughtsman, policeman, secretary, shop assistant, etc.	C1
Skilled manual work		
Class III (manual) Skilled trades	Carpenter, cook, driver, electrician, fitter, hairdresser, instrument maker, painter, printer, tailor, toolmaker, etc.	C2
Semi-skilled and unskilled manual work		
Class IV Semi-skilled work	Assembler, bus conductor, farm worker, machine operator, postman, roundsman, stoker, store-keeper, waiter, etc.	D
Class V Unskilled work	Kitchen hand, labourer, messenger, office cleaner, porter, window cleaner, etc.	E

particular range of jobs. Group III is often divided into manual and non-manual sections.

Not all Government surveys use the Registrar General's social classification. A number make use of the classification of socio-economic groups. A variation of the classification of socio-economic groups is used by the General Household Survey.

While the social classification tries to arrange people's jobs into some kind of order based on status and skill, the socio-economic groups are merely groups of people whose 'social, cultural and recreational standards are similar'. They are not arranged in any particular order.

Table 9. *The socio-economic grouping*

1. Employers and managers in central and local government, industry, commerce, etc. – large establishments.
2. Employers and managers in industry and commerce, etc. – small establishments.
3. Professional workers – self-employed.
4. Professional workers – employees.
5. Intermediate non-manual workers.
6. Junior non-manual workers.
7. Personal service workers.
8. Foremen and supervisors – manual.
9. Skilled manual workers.
10. Semi-skilled manual workers.
11. Unskilled manual workers.
12. Own account workers (other than professional).
13. Farmers – employers and managers.
14. Farmers – own account.
15. Agricultural workers.
16. Members of Armed Forces.
17. Occupations which are inadequately described.

OTHER CLASSIFICATIONS

The Registrar General's scales are often criticised for being too vague and for being too much concerned with occupations. They do not reflect divisions of status clearly enough. A librarian in Class II may have the same status as a university lecturer in Class I, possibly higher. An alternative scale was developed by J. Hall and D. Caradog Jones by asking people how they rated various occupations. The resulting Hall-Jones Scale is a seven-point scale and takes status into account as well as just occupation.

A major use for social classifications is in the market research industry. Market researchers attempt, among other things, to discover the likely demand for new products about to be put on the market and the pattern of demand for existing products. Their customers include everyone from soap powder manufacturers to political parties. As class and status play an important part in determining a person's shopping habits it is important that the researchers have a clear classification to use. The usual market research classification is shown in the right-hand column of Table 8. The link with the Registrar General's scale is only very rough. Market research organisations take many more factors into account. They would be concerned with income, house ownership, education and subjective factors like speech, and attitudes. Similar scales are used by the opinion polls which test public opinion before elections.

Social classifications such as these are used to give general indications of links between social class and education, consumption, political attitudes and so on. They do not make it possible for sociologists to make predictions about the behaviour of individuals. Their main use is to indicate general trends over an average group of people.

How do people see themselves?

We now have a fairly clear idea of how sociologists see social class. But there is one final question we must ask: does it really work out like this? If sociology is a search for reality we must consider how far the sociologists' view actually fits real life. Would the ordinary man-in-the-street decide which class he belongs to in the same way as the sociologist does? Would he reach the same answer?

In considering this we need to understand the idea of reference group, or frame of reference.

Each one of us lives in a social world. Even the hermit living in his cave cannot escape from the knowledge and ideas gained through growing up in a society. Our membership of societies shapes our attitudes and beliefs about ourselves and about the way the world is. Those individual beliefs are not unique. We share them with those around us. They are part of our social world. Our frame of reference is that community of people who are most important in shaping our ideas and beliefs. Family, friends and neighbourhood are all important. Those we work with may also have an influence and the media – television and the newspapers – may introduce us to other groups to whom we may refer.

How each individual places himself in a social scale depends on his frame of reference. Whilst to a sociologist one individual may appear to be working-class he may claim to be middle-class. Perhaps

Fig. 2. *The frame of reference*

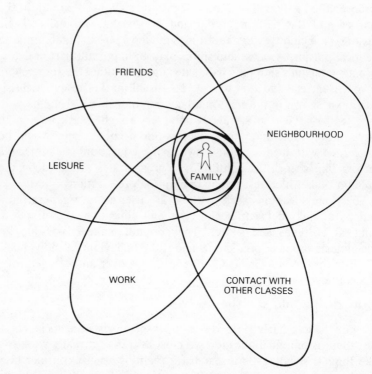

he wishes to keep himself at a distance from those he regards as beneath him. Perhaps he thinks he is on the way up, or his family background is middle-class. A large number of things are likely to influence the individual's self-image of class and status. Butler and Stokes (Macmillan 1969, Penguin 1971) found that this 'self-assigned' class was generally related to occupational status. But there were some major exceptions. Nine per cent of the unskilled manual workers interviewed regarded themselves as middle-class and one-fifth of the higher managerial group felt themselves to be working-class.

Obviously most people assign themselves to a social class which is close to their real position. Only 4 per cent of the Butler and Stokes sample did not see themselves in social class or status terms (including a jovial publican who said he was a member of the sporting class). In general, people are aware of inequalities in the distribution of wealth, prestige and power and through their frame of reference are able to place themselves within the class system. But not everyone sees the class system in the same terms.

Table 10. *Occupational status and social class*

	MANAGERIAL		NON-MANUAL		MANUAL	
	Higher	Lower	Supervisory	Lower	Skilled	Unskilled
	I	II	III	IV	V	VI
Claiming to be:	%	%	%	%	%	%
(*a*) *Middle-class*	78	65	60	32	17	9
(*b*) *Working-class*	22	35	40	68	83	91
	100	100	100	100	100	100

Source: Butler and Stokes 1969

(Butler and Stokes used an amended market research classification with group C1 divided into supervisory and lower non-manual.)

Ted – us and them

In the last chapter we read about Ted, a shop steward from Banbury.

> Ted, like his father, has been a 'union man' ever since he started work. He is a Labour councillor. The class system for him is a matter of worker or not worker. He accepts his status as a worker and is proud of it, but, unlike George, he will not accept patronage from his 'betters'. 'The workers look after their own', he says. He does not accept that he has 'betters' and rejects the leadership of people like Sir William, Shaw and Grey. He supports the Labour Party. He wants to improve the lot of the workers as a class. (Stacey 1960)

Ted sees social class as a division between bosses and workers, a conflict not unlike the Marxist view we studied earlier. In Ted's mind what really matters is the way power is exercised. The workers must stand together in order to have power. Society divides into 'us' and 'them', boss and worker. A worker who crosses the line between one and the other is a traitor to his class.

CLASS AS A LADDER

The alternative view sees social class as a ladder with many rungs. If you work hard you will climb the ladder and your status will increase. What matters most is to make your own way in the world using your abilities to the full. These two views are extremes. In reality most people's ideas come somewhere between the two. But the extremes can provide models of certain types of attitude which will help us to understand the reality which lies between.

53

MODELS OF CLASS

We can use the terms 'Status model' and 'Power model' to describe them.

	Status model	Power model
Social class	Mainly middle class	Mainly working class
Class perspective	Individualism	Collectivism
Image of society	'Status ladder'	'Us' and 'them'
Values	Stand on your own feet, don't sponge off others	Stick with your mates, make the best of things
Attitudes of education	Work hard at school to get a good start in life	Get a good job with a bit of money. Learn a trade
Attitudes to work	A chance to get on in life. Earn the respect of your colleagues	It brings in money to spend when you are not working. Work is not something you enjoy
Attitudes to poverty	Hard work is the best cure for poverty. Why should we support the idle?	It can happen to anyone. We may be next. A matter of 'luck of the draw'
Attitudes to trade unions	They have too much power. They prevent individuals from using their initiative and restrict the right to work	The workers must stand together. 'United we stand, divided we fall'
Politics	The Conservatives give a man the chance to better himself	The Labour Party stands for the working man. It is out to help the underdog.

These two models represent two separate systems of thought. They are extremes but they show how the different ideas of 'power' and 'status' can fit into a system of belief and attitudes which are total, covering all aspects of an individual's view of society.

54

Changes in social class

In 1876 the Secretary of the London and Westminster Bank told a Civil Service inquiry that 'the general social status of clerks' was 'upper middle' and that 'as a rule we would not introduce the sons of shopkeepers' but 'only sons of clergy, military and medical men'. However, a series of surveys in the 1950s showed that between one-third and one-half of clerical workers thought that they were working-class and that over 40 per cent were sons of manual workers. The status of clerical workers as a class had declined when compared to the status of skilled manual workers. This does not mean that clerks have become 'working-class' or that skilled manual workers have become middle-class but that the two groups cannot be separated as clearly as they could in 1876. The clerk's status position has become uncertain. He does not know quite where he stands on the status ladder. His style of life and working situation seem middle-class but his pay is often less than that of a factory worker. Sociologists term this 'status ambiguity'. The clerical worker's status is uncertain or ambiguous. He doesn't quite 'know where he stands' (see Chapter 9).

At the same time that the clerk's position has declined, other groups have imposed their status. The 'new professions' and 'industrial technicians' in Banbury's non-traditional status system are examples of this. Neither of these groups appears in the traditional pattern of class and status. They are new groups. Such occupations hardly existed at the turn of the century. These groups include research scientists, like Mr Brown, computer programmers, management staff and junior executives, teachers and lecturers, as well as laboratory technicians, supervisors, and junior administrative staff. The status of all of these groups is rising. Modern industry needs their skills. Membership of these groups depends on education and achievement, not on inheritance and ascription. They might be called a 'new middle-class' in contrast to the 'old middle-class' of men like Mr Shaw and Mr Grey. Mr Brown, with his univeristy education and his 'white-collar' job, is a good example of such a new middle class, and while he individually is making progress in his career he is a member of a profession which is also climbing.

The process by which some sections of the working-class seem to merge into the middle-class is known as 'embourgeoisement'.

THE AFFLUENT WORKER

This idea of 'embourgeoisement' (which means 'becoming bourgeoise', or middle-class) has been argued about for many years. It

55

begins with the attempt to explain why the revolution that Marx predicted did not happen in Britain. It has been suggested that modern capitalism, with the help of the Welfare State, has improved everyone's standard of living to such an extent that classes have almost ceased to exist. This is summed up in the phrase 'we are all middle-class now'. The old working-class life-styles are supposed to have disappeared with increases in real income, improved living conditions, greater home-ownership, urban re-development and so on. The worker has become affluent.

John Goldthorpe and David Lockwood (1969) did not accept this view. They thought it was too simple and ignored many of the real facts. From 1962 to 1968 they carried out a study of workers in Luton which aimed, among other things, at discovering if embourgeoisement had taken place. They chose Luton because it was an expanding prosperous town where you would expect to find lots of 'affluent workers'. If embourgeoisement was taking place anywhere it would, they argued, be taking place in Luton.

They focussed on three aspects of the lives of their sample of 300 industrial workers. Firstly – the work the men did; secondly – the social lives of the men and their families; and thirdly – their hopes for the future and views on life generally.

Not surprisingly they discovered that the work situations of the men had not changed greatly. They were still in the position of selling their skills to the employer and to achieve a 'middle-class' income required considerable amounts of overtime. Social life on the smart new Luton housing estates was seen to be different from traditional working-class life-styles. The differences were not seen as a movement to middle-class ways but as an adaptation of the old working-class patterns. The social networks were more likely to be based on the family and not on friends. Husbands and wives shared fewer friends and they belonged to fewer clubs or associations. Similarly, the affluent workers studied did not seem to have adopted middle-class attitudes.

'Therefore', they concluded, 'we held to the view that the thesis of the progressive embourgeoisement of the British working class was, to say the least, not proven; and that as usually presented, it involved a variety of confused and dubious assertions.'

Social mobility

As well as changes in the way the class system fits together there can also be changes in the positions of individuals within the system. As people move through their lives their social class may change. This movement of individuals within the class system is called *social mobility*. How much social mobility there is in any society depends upon the extent to which people gain their positions within that society by achievement rather than by ascription. In those societies in which status is based on birth, as in a strict caste system, there can be no social mobility. It is only when positions can be gained through an individual's achievements that social mobility can take place.

There clearly is social mobility in Britain. In the case study of Banbury Mr Brown was able to achieve changes in his class position. His *avenue of social mobility* was through education and success at work. The church, local politics and sport are other avenues whereby individuals can achieve a higher status. Not everyone moves into a higher class. Some people may also move down the class ladder. Within Britain there is, therefore, both upward and downward social mobility.

Studies of social mobility have focussed on three main problems. Firstly, how much movement is there between social classes? How many people are likely to change their position during their lifetime, and how far are they able to move? Secondly, what is it that makes it possible for people to move up the social class ladder, and why do some people move down rather than up? Thirdly, how far does improved mobility also allow individuals to rise to the top-most, or elite, positions within society. The early studies of social mobility in Britain carried out by class and others attempted to describe the extent of social mobility. The more recent studies by Blau and Duncan in the United States and by the Oxford Mobility Study in Britain have been more concerned with explaining why individuals in certain social groups appear to be more socially mobile.

The Oxford Mobility Study divided the male population into seven social classes. Classes I–IV are made up of people in non-

Table 11. *Origins and destinations. The percentage of men who were in the same social class as their fathers (1972)*

Social class of men at time of interview							
I	II	III	IV	V	VI	VII	All
%	%	%	%	%	%	%	%
48·4	22·6	10·8	24·9	16·6	29·6	34·8	28·0

Source: Oxford Mobility Study

Fig. 3. *Social mobility*

The percentages of men born into each social class by
the social classes they were in at the time of the survey.

Men born into Class I:

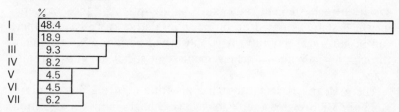

	%
I	48.4
II	18.9
III	9.3
IV	8.2
V	4.5
VI	4.5
VII	6.2

Men born into Class II:

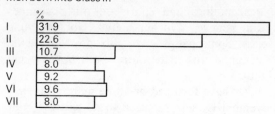

	%
I	31.9
II	22.6
III	10.7
IV	8.0
V	9.2
VI	9.6
VII	8.0

Men born into Class III:

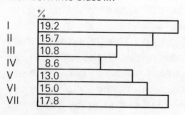

	%
I	19.2
II	15.7
III	10.8
IV	8.6
V	13.0
VI	15.0
VII	17.8

Men born into Class IV:

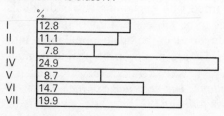

	%
I	12.8
II	11.1
III	7.8
IV	24.9
V	8.7
VI	14.7
VII	19.9

Men born into Class V:

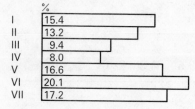

	%
I	15.4
II	13.2
III	9.4
IV	8.0
V	16.6
VI	20.1
VII	17.2

Men born into Class VI:

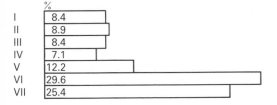

Men born into Class VII:

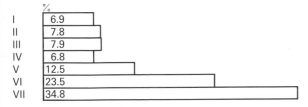

Source: Oxford Mobility Study 1972

manual, or white-collar jobs, while those in classes V, VI and VII are in manual, or blue-collar jobs. A sample of men aged 25–64 in 1972 were asked about their own occupation and that held by their fathers at a similar stage in their lives. Only 28 per cent of the sample had not moved into a different social class. Over two-thirds of them had been socially mobile. Most of the movement was 'short-range' movement across one or two boundaries.

Table 11 shows the proportion of men whose social class has not changed. It is clear that social mobility is greater for some classes than for others. Nearly half of the men whose fathers were in social class I remained within it. In Figure 3 it is possible to see where men born into different social classes were at the time of the survey. In general it supports the view that most mobility is fairly short-range. Much depends, however, on the categories that are used. If instead of seven different classes we only used two a slightly different picture emerges. Grouped on the basis of manual and non-manual occupations, (combining groups I–IV and V–VII), we find that one-third of those born into the manual working class have moved across into the non-manual middle class. If the dividing line is placed between the professional class, (Class I), and all of the other classes we find that only 14 per cent of those born below the line managed to cross it into the higher class. This means that mobility between the middle and working classes is far easier than movement into the social elite. The evidence also suggests that there is more movement upwards than downwards. This has been made possible by the increases in the numbers in the professions and in management. If instead of looking at where men who were born into particular social positions ended up we considered where the people in those positions came from a different pattern emerges. Although nearly half of those born into Class I remained there only a quarter of those found in Class I were born into it. This can only be explained by an increase in the size of the higher classes.

This still leaves us with the question 'how do people change their social class?' For those who do move between social classes there are two periods in which change can take place. Firstly there is the possibility of social mobility through education. For many people doing well at school and university provides a route into a higher class. Similarly failure at school can lead people into jobs which place them in a lower class. How well you do at school is not, however, the only influence. The second avenue of mobility is through the career that follows after a period of education. 'Working your way up' through the job is very important in determining which class you end up in. There are, however, differences in the routes taken by people in different careers. In a study by Goldthorpe less than 20 per cent of the industrial managers in Class I came from Class I backgrounds. Over half of them came from working-class homes (Classes V–VII). The senior administrators, particularly in the public services, were much more likely to come from middle-class homes in Classes II–IV although two-fifths of this group also had working-class backgrounds. Salaried professionals (university lecturers and senior scientists), were more likely to come from upper-middle-class homes, whereas self-employed professionals (doctors, lawyers and accountants), were more likely to have Class I backgrounds. This evidence suggests that while those in the professions were more likely to move up the social ladder through their educational achievements, a large proportion of the industrial managers and administrators were likely to come from the shop floor or from lower administrative and clerical positions.

So far we have considered social mobility as if it were only something that happens to men. This is a reflection of the way studies of social class and social mobility have been carried out. There are reasons for this, though they may not be very good reasons. Firstly, social class has been used as a 'family concept'. It has been the occupation of the father (who has traditionally been defined as the 'breadwinner)', which defines the social class of the whole family. On marriage women were assumed to take on the social class of their husband. The work that women did was not seen as a reliable indicator of social class. On this basis social mobility for women was a matter of 'marrying up' or 'marrying down'. This has been described as *marital mobility* and has the effect of making women more socially mobile than men. In very general terms it is more likely that a daughter will move into a different social class than will her brother. Leaving 'marital mobility' aside comparisons based on women's employment, rather than their husbands' employment, are more difficult. Many married women are in part-time jobs, often at lower pay than their husbands, and in many cases as a second, rather than main income. In these cases occupation is not a good measure of social class. On the basis of employment alone women, as a group, are more likely to be downwardly mobile.

Another comparison with male social mobility can be gained from studies of single men and single women. Here a different picture emerges. Single women as a group generally have better chances of upward social mobility than single men. This does mean that single women have equal opportunities. Far fewer women are able to move into the top jobs. It simply means that for a few women who remain single there is the possibility of moving up the social ladder. For the majority of women employment is not a good avenue of social mobility.

The picture that emerges is of a class system which is continually changing and within which there is movement in many directions. The changes do not affect everyone equally and the movements are not always easy to follow. Viewed as a whole the class system is far from rigid. In the chapters which follow we shall consider many other aspects of social class and the ways in which it is reflected in the lives that people lead.

5

Sociologists at Work

In Chapters 1 and 2 you read about the work of some sociologists. In this chapter, we will consider the methods used by sociologists in more detail. There are three things to remember before we do this. Firstly, sociologists do not always carry out their studies in the way textbooks say that they do. In real life the researcher must adapt the rule to fit particular situations. You would not expect a great artist to 'paint by numbers', nor would you expect a good sociologist to do everything as it is laid down in textbooks.

Secondly, sociologists are human. They have their own preferences and prejudices. They also make mistakes. They are on the whole honest and act in good faith when making judgements or carrying out research, but their work needs to be looked at critically. There is an old saying 'No one is ever perfect'. It is as true for sociologists as it is for all other scientists. When you read sociological studies you must watch out for any weaknesses or any statements with which you do not agree. Remember that we all have our own view of the world which influences the way we see events. If you feel that a piece of sociology is wrong, or biased, then say so. The ability to make sensible criticism is an important part of the work of the sociologist.

Thirdly, we should always remember that investigating the social world is very different from investigating the natural world. Unlike the chemist, who works in his laboratory studying substances in testtubes, or the physicist who probes the structure of a particular molecule, the social scientist studies something of which he is himself a member. The sociologist must never lose sight of the fact that he or she is part of that social world which is being studied. We have all grown up in it, have feelings about it and are affected by it. When we attempt to study it we cannot escape from being part of it. In a study using interviews, for example, the information we receive may be affected by whom we are, why we are doing it, how we speak or dress, or behave, to the person interviewed. A chemical in a test-tube is not going to bother about the chemist's accent, or how he dresses. A person being interviewed in a social survey may be influenced by such things, and it could affect the findings.

The sociologist as researcher

As we saw in Chapter 1 sociologists have a number of different ways of gathering information. We can sort these different research methods into four groups.

1. Research which relies on other people's evidence. We will call this a *documentary* method.
2. Research which seeks answers to particular questions from fairly large groups of people with fairly short, often very short, periods of contact. This we will call *survey* method.
3. Research which involves the sociologists working very closely among those he or she studies, often for quite long periods of time. This is an *observation* method. Sometimes the sociologists participate in the lives of those studied. This then becomes *participant observation*.
4. Research which involves carefully chosen groups of people who are placed in different situations to see what happens. This is an *experimental method*.

Very often these methods are combined to give different views of the same subject. As we saw in Chapter 1, documentary evidence on Banbury was combined with survey data and participant observation.

Whichever method, or combination of methods, is chosen the researcher must go through certain stages and apply certain basic rules. Any piece of research begins with a *creative* stage. The sociologist is faced by a problem and begins to look for explanations. He may begin with a 'why?' problem: 'Why do certain groups of people go to church?', 'Why do people cause trouble at football matches?'.

It may be a 'What if?' problem: 'What would happen to children if they were sent to different schools?', 'What would be the results of a general election next week?'. It may be a 'how' problem: 'How do the lives of people in Newcastle differ from those of people in London?'.

From the problem, and what is known about the world – including what has been learned from other sociologists – the researcher develops an hypothesis. This is a 'hunch' about what might be the answer. The hypothesis, or hunch, needs to be tested. This leads to a *technical* stage where the researcher must design an investigation,

63

choosing the methods which are likely to lead to the best evidence. The investigation must then be carried out. Finally there is a *theoretical* stage at which all of the information must be analysed and compared to the hypothesis before any final conclusions are reached. These three stages – creative, technical and theoretical, may take anything from a few weeks to many years. Often they run into one another with each new piece of evidence producing new hypotheses, requiring new or changed methods and leading to new conclusions.

IS IT GOOD RESEARCH?

In all of this the researcher must keep certain basic questions in his mind.

1 He must decide whether he is looking for evidence which will prove his hunch to be right or evidence that could prove it to be wrong. Both methods are used. Decide for yourself which gives the better result:
   (a) the study which produces evidence in favour of the hypothesis.
   (b) the study which is unable to find any evidence against the hypothesis (assuming that both studies were carried out with equal care and thoroughness).

2 He must make sure that the methods used, and the results gained are *valid*. Has the research, in fact, measured what it was supposed to measure. A survey on crime, for example, might use police statistics as a measure of how much crime occurs. Experience has shown this not to be a *valid* measure. Much crime is not reported to the police and therefore does not get counted in their statistics.

3 The methods used must also be *reliable*. Would the same methods used by different people in different places, even at different times, give the same results? You could test this for yourself by carrying out a simple survey in a shopping street or at a bus stop, in the morning, mid-day and evening. It is unlikely that you would get the same results each time.

4 When you analyse the results of any research you must look to see how close your results are to what you might predict from your hypothesis. They will never match exactly. You must decide how close is 'close enough'. Researchers use 'tests of significance' to measure the closeness of their original hunches to what the collected evidence shows. If the prediction and the evidence do not match you must decide whether your hypothesis is wrong, the methods are at fault, or it is a chance result. Sociologists must decide how close they must be for the result to be *significant*.

5 In sociology it is often difficult to *control* the various things which

might affect the result. A biologist studying the effect of light on plants can put a plant in a darkened cupboard, and leave an identical plant, treated the same in every other way, in sunlight. This second plant is the 'control'. The only difference between the two plants is the amount of light they receive. Sociologists cannot control the various influences on their research in quite the same way. Instead they try to build in statistical controls.

6 Many sociological studies are concerned with particular groups of people – housewives, office workers, people living in Grimsby, Methodists, etc. These are quite large groups and it would be very expensive and often inconvenient to interview them all, or to send them all a questionnaire. Therefore, researchers take a *sample* from the group and base their findings on them. Sampling is considered in more detail later in this chapter. The important question which concerns us now is 'how *representative* is the sample?' Are the answers the sample gives us the answers we would get from the whole group?

We often want to apply evidence from the study of one group of people to a larger group or to other groups. It is important to know if the groups studied are typical or if they differ in important ways. Is your school or college typical of all schools or colleges? Is your class typical? How far should evidence from your class, or school, or college be used to support hypotheses about classes, schools or colleges in general?

7 Finally, the sociologist must be prepared to put his research – its hypothesis and results – to the test of review by other sociologists. It must be compared to existing theories and to previous research. The research may just fill in a gap in our existing knowledge, or it may be so revolutionary as to make us rethink all that has gone before. If that does happen, other sociologists will want to test the results, even repeat the research before deciding whether to accept it or not. Sociologists call this *replicability*.

Whenever you read a piece of sociological research ask yourself these questions:

1 Did the research actually measure what it set out to measure and would someone else have got similar results using similar methods?

2 Are the results what you would have expected on the basis of your commonsense knowledge, and from other things you have studied?

3 Could any other factors have influenced the results in ways which the researcher might not have noticed?

4 How do the results affect the way I now understand things?

Using documentary evidence

Documentary evidence is often used in sociology. When working from documents the sociologist is using evidence which has probably been collected for some other purpose – either by official agencies or by other social scientists. This will often influence how such evidence is used. The researcher must decide how *reliable* the evidence is and how *valid*. It is not enough to accept documentary evidence at face value. You must always ask yourself three questions: Why was this evidence collected? Who collected it? How was it collected?

An American sociologist, Harold Garfinkel, attempted a study of patients in a hospital out-patient clinic. His main source of information on the way patients were dealt with by the clinic came from the patients' official records which had been kept by the nurses and doctors. These documents were supposed to contain basic information about the patient – such as age, sex, occupation – and details of diagnosis and treatment. Garfinkel soon found that these 'official records' were of very little help in his research. They were in fact 'bad' records. Other researchers working with similar official files had noticed the same thing. This led Garfinkel to ask the questions: 'Why are record files like these always so bad?' and 'Why are 'bad files' normal?'. The answers, he suggests, are to be found in the way the files are written up and in the people who write them up.

When people become doctors or nurses it is not because they want to spend their time filling-in official forms. They want to get on with the job of caring for people and making them well. If the information in an official file helps them to do that job they are more likely to give it time and care. Information for which they see no value is usually less well recorded. This is often the case with information that is required for 'official' records. More effort is needed to gain certain types of information. You can tell someone's 'race' or 'sex' usually at a glance. Guesses about 'age' are fairly accurate. Most people will tell you about their religion, if they are married or where they live. Information about their health, education or occupation takes a little more effort on the part of the form-filler. As the form-fillers are usually busy people with many other things to do they must decide if the effort needed in getting the information accurately is justified by its value to them in their work. Often it isn't and the 'official document' will be a 'bad' source of information.

Garfinkel realised that collecting information for official forms in the clinic was not a matter of putting the right answers in the right places on the forms. The form-filling, and the keeping of records

Fig. 4. *The census districts*
(a) Enumeration District (ED)

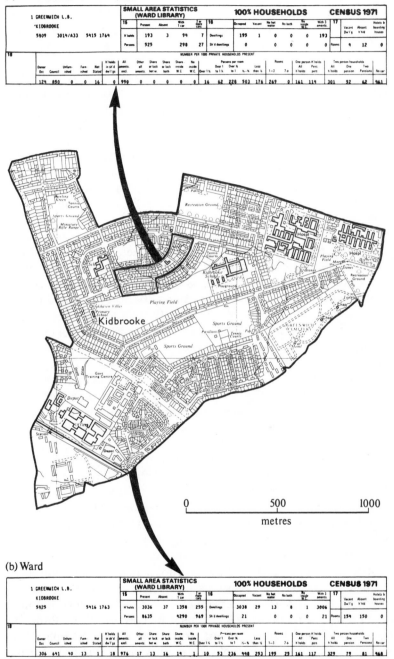

(b) Ward

about patients, was part of the relationship between a doctor and the patient. They were intended to be read by particular groups of people who knew the situation and understood the work of the clinic. To the doctors who used them they were probably quite good records. To the sociologist researching the organisation of the clinic they were very bad records.

The example shows some of the problems we must face when using any documentary evidence. Never accept anything at its face value. Try to imagine how a number or a heading came to be on a table of figures or on a graph. Think back to the point of time when that number was an actual person doing everyday things. How did the actions of that person, and of many others come to be a statistic?

THE CENSUS

An important source of documentary evidence is The Census of Population which is carried out every ten years, and has been since 1801 (with the exception of 1941 in the middle of the Second World War). It is a unique kind of survey which aims to count every man, woman and child in the United Kingdom on one Sunday night in April. Information is also collected on their families, the dwelling in which they live, education, work and a number of other topics.

The census is planned and co-ordinated by a Government department, the Office of Population Censuses and Surveys (OPCS). The information is collected by enumerators who distribute census forms and often help people to fill them in. Each enumerator works in an enumeration district (ED) which covers an area of roughly 150 households. The information from all the households is put together into overall figures for the enumeration district which are then added to the information from other EDs to produce the figures for the ward. The ward figures are then added to the figures from other wards to produce County or Borough tables which, in turn, go towards regional and national figures. Fig. 4 shows the Kidbrooke Ward for the London Borough of Greenwich. The enumeration districts can be seen and part of the ED data for one enumeration district is shown at the top of the page. At the bottom of the page you can see the same information for the whole ward.

It is some years before the census information is finally published, though Preliminary Statistics are available within a matter of months. Apart from the sheer size of the task of co-ordinating information from 102 000 census enumerators covering over 10 million households and residential institutions the Office of Population Censuses and Surveys must also carry out checks to ensure that the information gained is as accurate as it can possibly be. Post-enumeration surveys involving 40 000 households are carried out a few weeks after the main census date and the census figures are checked against the registers of births, marriages and deaths. These checks on the census show that as a whole the census is remarkably accurate. The total population recorded in the 1981 census was within 0·4% of the actual population based on the post enumeration survey. In a total population of 52 000 000 that is a possible error in the region of 0.1 per cent.

Inaccuracies may arise within the census for a number of reasons. There is always a danger that someone may be left off the census form when it is returned to the enumerator. This is most likely to happen where there are large numbers of people living in one place, particularly in multi-occupied houses. There may be a misunder-

Fig. 5. *The census form*

1971 CENSUS — ENGLAND

H Form For Private Households

To the Head (or Acting Head) of the Household.

Please complete this form and have it ready for collection on Monday 26th April. If you need help, do not hesitate to ask the enumerator.

The enumerator may ask you any questions necessary to help him to complete or correct the form.

The information you give on the form will be treated as CONFIDENTIAL and used only for compiling statistics. No information about named individuals will be passed by the Census Office to any other Government Department or any other authority or person. If anyone in the census organisation improperly discloses information you provide, he will be liable to prosecution. Similarly you must not disclose information which anyone else (for example, a visitor or boarder) gives you to enable you to complete the form.

The legal obligation to fill in the whole form rests on YOU, but each person who has to be included is required to give you the information you need. However, anyone who wishes can ask the enumerator or local Census Officer for a personal form which can be returned direct to the enumerator or local Census Officer and then you need answer only questions B1 and B5 for that person.

PLEASE TAKE NOTE

There are penalties of up to £50 for failing to comply with the requirements described above, or for giving false information.

When you have completed the form, please sign the declaration at the foot of the last page.

MICHAEL REED
Office of Population Censuses and Surveys,   Director and
Titchfield,   Registrar General
Fareham, Hants.

*A household comprises **either** one person living alone **or** a group of persons (who may or may not be related) living at the same address with common housekeeping. Persons staying temporarily with the household are included.*

To be completed by enumerator			
C.D. No.	E.D. No.	Form No.	Ref.

If sharing with another household :—

Hall, staircase, passage, etc., shared only/not only* for entry to accommodation.   *delete whichever is inapplicable.

Number of rooms shared.

Name and full postal address :

PART A   Answer questions A1—A5 about your household's accommodation and then answer questions B1—B24 overleaf and if appropriate answer questions C1—C7.

SPECIMEN

Where boxes are provided answer by putting a tick in the box against the answer which applies. For example, if the answer is 'YES': ☑ YES ☐ NO

PLEASE WRITE IN INK OR BALLPOINT PEN

A1
How do you and your household occupy your accommodation?

1 ☐ As an owner occupier (including purchase by mortgage)

2 ☐ By renting it from a Council or New Town

3 ☐ As an unfurnished letting from a private landlord or company or Housing Association

4 ☐ As a furnished letting

5 ☐ In some other way
(Please give details, including whether furnished or unfurnished)

Note: If the accommodation is occupied by lease originally granted for, or since extended to, more than 21 years, tick 'owner occupier'.

A2
Does your household share with anyone else the use of any room, or hall, passage, landing, or staircase?

☐ YES   ☐ NO

A3
How many rooms are there in your household's accommodation?

Do not count
Small kitchens less than 6ft. wide, bathrooms and toilets, sculleries not used for cooking, closets, pantries and storerooms, landings, halls, lobbies or recesses, offices or shops used solely for business purposes.

Note
A large room divided by a sliding or fixed partition should be counted as two rooms. A room divided by curtains or portable screens should be counted as one room.

A4
How many cars and vans are normally available for use by you or members of your household (other than visitors)?

Include any provided by employers if normally available for you or members of your household, but exclude vans used solely for the carriage of goods.

If None, write 'NONE'.

A5
Has your household the use of the following amenities on these premises?

a A cooker or cooking stove with an oven
1 ☐ YES — for use only by this household
2 ☐ YES — for use also by another household
3 ☐ NO

b A kitchen sink permanently connected to a water supply and a waste pipe
1 ☐ YES — for use only by this household
2 ☐ YES — for use also by another household
3 ☐ NO

c A fixed bath or shower permanently connected to a water supply and a waste pipe
1 ☐ YES — for use only by this household
2 ☐ YES — for use also by another household
3 ☐ NO

d A hot water supply (to a washbasin, or kitchen sink, or bath, or shower) from a heating appliance or boiler which is connected to a piped water supply
1 ☐ YES — for use only by this household
2 ☐ YES — for use also by another household
3 ☐ NO

e A flush toilet (W.C.) with entrance inside the building
1 ☐ YES — for use only by this household
2 ☐ YES — for use also by another household
3 ☐ NO

f A flush toilet (W.C.) with entrance outside the building
1 ☐ YES — for use only by this household
2 ☐ YES — for use also by another household
3 ☐ NO

1

PLEASE TURN OVER TO PART B➤

standing of the purpose of the census which leads to under-registration. In 1971 many people objected to census questions concerning the places of birth of their parents. Immigrants feared that the answers to such questions might one day be used to return them to countries which were no longer theirs. In addition there may be people who have entered the country illegally and would not want to be identified on a census return.

Another type of problem arises when people are not sure what parts of the census form mean. In 1951, for example, the number of rooms in some houses was not properly recorded. The definition asked for 'rooms used for living, eating and sleeping'. For many people this did not include unused 'spare rooms' and they were not counted. These ambiguities in the census return are usually corrected in the following census when definitions are brought up to date and new questions are included. Changes in definitions between censuses often make comparison difficult. In 1951 the census asked for 'the usual employment' of all wage-earners. Some who were unemployed put down their usual occupation and made no mention of unemployment; some who were trained in one job but were at that time doing something else wrote down what they were trained for. In 1961 this was tightened up by asking about their employment in the week before census day and in 1971 the question was for the 'main employment in the week before census day'.

Other problems may arise because of administrative changes, such as changes in local government boundaries or the school-leaving age; problems in sampling when a sample census is taken; and problems of misinformation as when someone enters the wrong age. The effect of these difficulties on the whole census is usually slight. They may be more significant in particular areas or among particular groups of people. These problems are not restricted to the census: they are also found in many other types of social survey.

OTHER SOURCES OF DOCUMENTARY EVIDENCE

Social scientists use many other pieces of documentary evidence in addition to the census. Nearly every organisation in the country publishes some kind of report and many of these contain information which is useful to the sociologist. These reports, which come from government departments, private and nationalised industries, trade unions and employer organisations, research associations, local councils and many other bodies contain three types of data. Firstly there are statistics which are collected in the normal work of the organisation. Your school or college will make regular returns of the number of pupils, their age, and sex; the police keep records of the number of crimes reported; the immigration officials record the numbers entering or leaving the country; employers keep records of the number of workers, hours lost through absenteeism, and so on. These data are collected and published at regular intervals.

The second type of information is also collected regularly but it involves a special survey: usually a sample of those concerned. The General Household Survey is a good example of this kind of fact-gathering. Information on housing, health, migration, education and a number of other topics is obtained from a sample of 15 000 households every year. In a similar way the Family Expenditure Survey collects information on the way families spend their money. The findings are published each year.

The third type of information is collected once only for a particular purpose. Many organisations conduct investigations to help them plan for the future or discover present needs. Government inquiries or Royal Commissions often collect large amounts of information. Some, like the Robbins Report on Higher Education, produce volumes of evidence which are longer than the report itself. Many reports of this type are published every day of the week. Often they can be found in local reference libraries or can be obtained directly from the organisations which produced them.

The most important and widely-used information from many of these sources is collected together into yearbooks, or abstracts. The *Annual Abstract of Statistics* published by the Central Statistical Office is the most important collection of easily available statistics on the United Kingdom. Monthly figures are published in the *Monthly Digest of Statistics* and local data in the annual *Abstract of Regional Statistics*. *Social Trends* and *Economic Trends* are regular publications which present the information in a simpler, and more readable form. In addition many organisations publish yearbooks covering national and international events though different methods of compiling statistics in different countries can make comparison difficult.

HISTORICAL EVIDENCE

One important area of documentary evidence is historical documents. These are frequently used by social scientists. Historians take great care when using historical evidence. They ask many of the questions social scientists ask and often work in similar ways. Sometimes their evidence is very full and accurate though frequently it is incomplete and has only a limited use. Historical evidence can be of great use to the social scientist but it needs to satisfy the same tests of reliability and validity that would be applied to other social science data.

Social surveys

Surveys are carried out for many reasons and by many different groups of people. If you are stopped by someone in the High Street and asked for your views on toothpaste, insurance or the government it is likely that you are being involved in a survey being carried out by a commercial social research agency. Such agencies carry out research for their clients. One week they may be doing market research on 'soft centres' for a chocolate manufacturer and in the following week an opinion poll on attitudes towards trade unions for a national newspaper. Surveys are also carried out by academic researchers based in universities and polytechnics and by public research bodies like the Government Social Survey. Many organisations have their own research departments. Research is big business with millions of pounds being spent each year on finding out what people want, like, enjoy, do, have, and believe. Whatever the reason for the research, whoever the client may be, whatever the topic, the basic problems faced and the methods used are much the same. The basic rules for conducting a survey are similar for a classroom-based study of pocket money, as they are for a national survey of political attitudes.

PLANNING A SURVEY

Planning a survey involves both the creative and technical aspects of social research. Remember what was said at the beginning of this chapter: sociologists do not always stick to the rule-book. Every piece of research, every survey, every investigation creates new problems. A good survey is the one which adapts the rules to fit the situation. The stages in conducting a survey are shown in Fig. 6. The researcher must find a way of investigating the problem as effectively as possible within the resources of time and money at his disposal. Some surveys are able to use teams of trained interviewers, using detailed questionnaires backed up by an army of statisticians and the very latest in computer technology. Other researchers produce equally useful findings working on their own with only a pocket calculator to help them.

We shall compare two pieces of research in this chapter. Ann Oakley's study, *The Sociology of Housework* (1974) is a good example of small-scale investigation using very limited resources.

Fig. 6. *A flow chart of a survey*

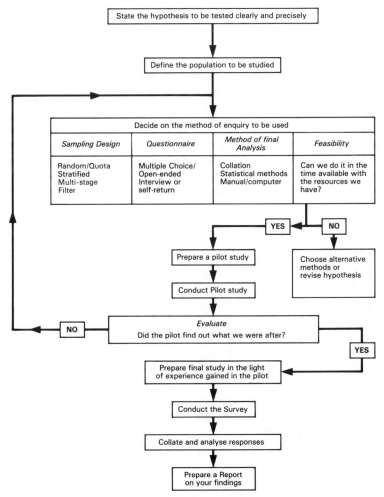

The Symmetrical Family (1973) by Michael Young and Peter Willmott lists 60 interviewers, 14 coders and 8 typists as well as statisticians, computer programmers, supervisors and a host of advisers. Both studies have their good and bad points and provide valuable insight into the topic of family life. Neither the size of a survey nor the amount of money it can spend are guarantees that it will produce useful research. Whatever the resources available the researchers must be able to solve certain basic problems. The main technical problems are those of sampling, questionnaire design, interviewing and analysis.

SAMPLING

It is only very seldom that social researchers want to know about everyone. The census is one example of a survey which does include everyone. More often the researcher is concerned with a particular group of people. Ann Oakley was interested in housewives. Young and Willmott wanted information on people who lived in or near London. This group of people studied is called a *population* or a *universe*. If you carried out a survey on people in your school or college the *population* studied would be all of the people who attended the school or college. If you did a survey on the sixth form or part-time students then sixth-formers and part-timers would be your populations. The population is made up of all the people who make up the group that is being studied. Survey populations are usually stated very precisely, for example: 'men over 35 years old working in Luton', 'families with 2 or 3 children in South Yorkshire', and so on.

Researchers have discovered that they can get an accurate picture of the population studied without having to survey everyone. Instead they only interview a sample and, if the sample is large enough and chosen carefully enough, they will get results which are as accurate as they would have been if they had interviewed everyone – and they can do it at much less cost in time and money.

The best method of sampling uses a *random* sample. In such a sample every individual has an equal chance of being sampled.

The first stage in preparing any sample is to decide on your *sampling frame*. This is a list of all of the people, families, groups or organisations found from which the sample will be drawn. This list must cover the whole of the population to be surveyed and it must be complete. A survey on attitudes to work in a factory might use the pay-roll of employees as a sampling frame. If the pay-roll only covers weekly-paid workers and not casual or temporary workers then it does not cover the whole population. If the pay-roll is not up to date and does not include new employees then it is also incomplete.

Ann Oakley (1974) used the lists of patients of two London doctors for her sampling frame. From the doctors' lists she collected the names and addresses of all married women between 20 and 30 years old with at least one child under 5. An alternative to doctors' lists is the Register of Electors for each area. Young and Willmott (1973) used these lists as a sampling frame in their research into the symmetrical family. For the area of their study concerned with

Fig. 7. *A random sample*

Sample

Population

75

managing directors, Young and Willmott used a published *Directory of Directors* as the basis for their sampling frame.

The sample is taken from the sampling frame in various ways. A simple *random sample* uses special lists of 'random numbers'.

Table 12.

```
72 59 93 76 24

74 35 08 90 61

43 62 23 50 05

17 58 53 78 80

53 08 70 94 25     Source: Kendall and Smith 1939
```

If you wished to sample 25 people from a list of 100 names using this section of a random number table you would use the 72nd name, 59th name, 93rd name and so on.

Random numbers give a more reliable sample than you would get if you took every fourth name on the list, a method known as *systematic sampling*. Both random sampling and systematic sampling can sometimes give unsatisfactory results. Small samples, for example, are less reliable than large ones. Often a researcher can only afford to use a small sample. To prevent any errors creeping in he could use a different type of sample.

Table 13. *Ages of men and women in the London region*

	Men		Women	
	Survey 1970	Census 1966	Survey 1970	Census 1966
17–19	4%	7%	3%	6%
20–24	10	10	6	9
25–29	9	9	10	8
30–39	18	18	15	16
40–49	20	18	20	16
50–59	18	19	18	18
60–64	7	7	9	8
65–69	6	5	7	6
70 or over	8	7	12	13

Source: Young and Willmott 1973

Stratified samples are used where it is possible to divide the population into a number of relevant groups. Young and Willmott found, for example, that their sampling methods gave them fewer men and women between 17 and 19 than they would have expected on the information they had from the census.

It would have been possible to have stratified their sample on the basis of the percentages in the census. They would then have sampled 7 per cent of men and 9 per cent of women aged 17–19, 10 per cent of men aged 20–24 and so on. This would have given them a more reliable sample than they actually achieved using a random method.

Young and Willmott did in fact use a *multi-stage* method of sampling.

> We needed something as near as we could get to a cross-section of the adult population of the London metropolitan region. If we had simply picked a sample of individual people scattered all over the region, it would have taken far too long (and have been far too expensive) to go and interview them. We had to follow the familiar method and proceed in two stages, first selecting a sample of places in which the interviewing would be concentrated and then picking samples of people in each place. (Young and Willmott 1973)

They used a two-stage sample (sampling the places and the people) but three- or even four-stage samples are not unusual. To get a sample of school children to interview you might first make a sample of Local Education Authorities (LEAs). From these you would sample a number of schools from which you would sample a number of children. That would be a three-stage sample (Fig. 8).

This could be combined with a *cluster sample*. Instead of sampling individual pupils from each school you might sample a number of classes. The research would then be based on *clusters* of children in particular classes. In this way class 4B would be 'a cluster'.

Another commonly used method is a *quota sample*. A market research interviewer may be given a quota of people to interview. This may include 10 upper-middle-class families, 20 lower-middle-class families and 15 working-class families. This method, however, relies on the judgement of the interviewer and not on a strict sampling process.

Very often it is not possible to locate the people you want to interview on the basis of the information which you have. Often the researcher has to filter out particular groups of people for particular aspects of a study. This involves *multi-phase* or filter sampling.

Fig. 8. *A multi-stage sample*

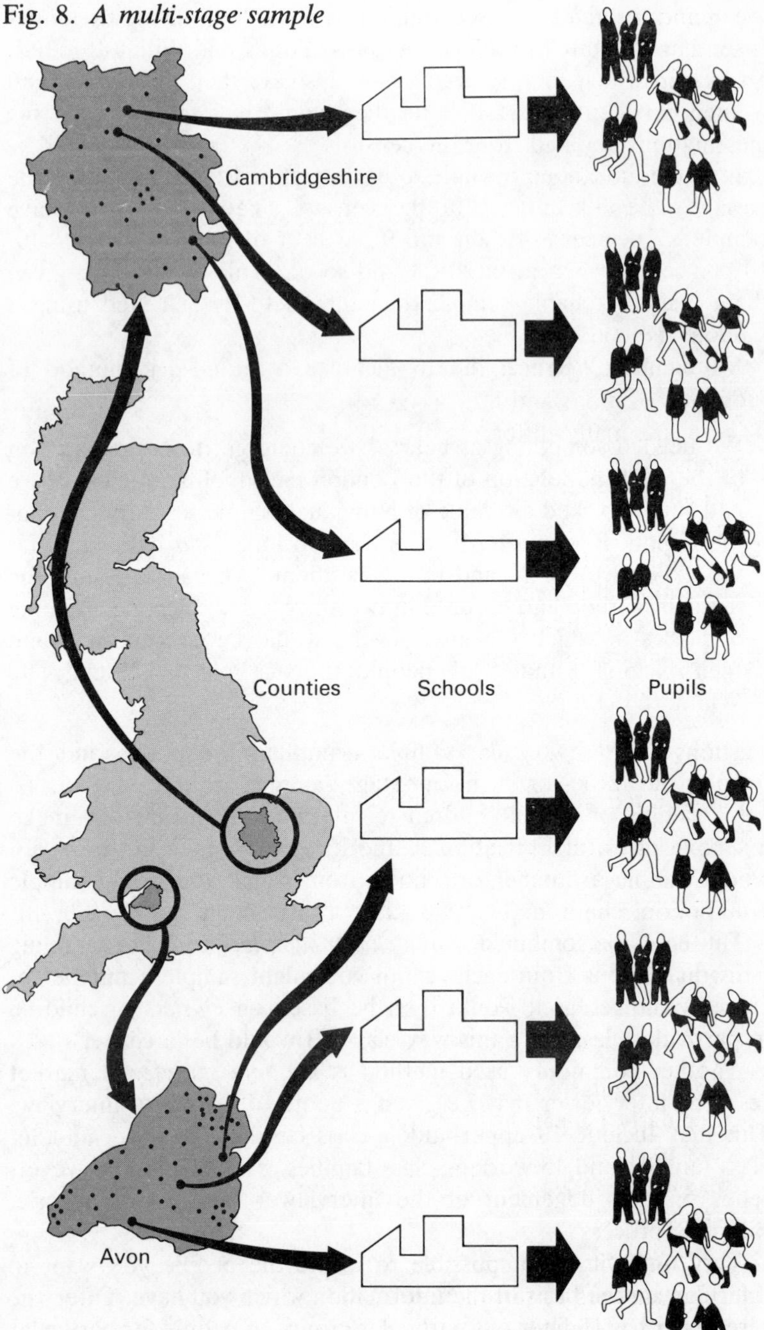

Cambridgeshire

Counties   Schools   Pupils

Avon

78

Young and Willmott used their main sample as a sampling frame to obtain a sub-sample of men and women who were aged between 30 and 49 and who were married. They later used this sub-sample as a sampling frame for a further sub-sample for active sportsmen and women.

All of these different forms of sampling are used to get as accurate a result as possible.

Asking questions

If you want to find the answers you have got to ask questions. But what questions and how do you ask them?

There are many different ways in which social researchers ask questions. The question may be printed on a form which is sent by post to all of those in the sample. They may be on a list of questions which the interviewer fills in as he or she asks the person being interviewed, or they may be questions which arise in the course of a fairly informal conversation.

Whichever method is used the aim is always the same – to get accurate and reliable answers about the topic being studied. The questions should be easy to understand, not using too many long words or an ambiguous turn of phrase. Very often a series of simple questions is better than one longer question. Instead of asking:

'Can you tell me the make, colour and age of your car?'

the interviewer should begin by finding out if the person being interviewed has a car. Then separate questions about make, colour and age could be asked. If the person has no car there is no point asking the further questions.

Just as they should be easy for the respondent (the person who answers) to understand, questions should be easy for the interviewer to ask. A question like this may be accurate but it is not easy to ask:

'Do you regularly eat ice-cream when you go out for the day – by regularly I mean at least four times out of five, assuming ice cream to include ice-cream products such as lollies but not iced drinks and meaning days out for leisure rather than going to work or school?'

Many interview schedules include 'filters' which lead from particular answers to further questions. These must be easy for the interviewer to follow.

When all of the questions have been asked the answers need to be 'coded'. If the questionnaire is well designed, coding is easy. Often the interviewer or even the respondent will mark the answers by ringing numbers on the form. These numbers can easily be transferred to a master sheet ready to be added to answers from other interviews.

Finally, the questionnaire must hold the attention of both interviewer and respondent. It should be as interesting as possible, and not too long.

A QUESTIONNAIRE

In Fig. 9 you can see some sections from a questionnaire used in a survey of housing conditions in the London Borough of Southwark. The survey was carried out by a private research agency. This questionnaire would be used by an interviewer who asked questions and then ticked off the answers on the questionnaire. Before the interview starts, the interviewer would mark off the boxes at the top of the first page. The questions would be read to the person being interviewed (the subject) one at a time in exactly the form shown on the sheet. This will help to ensure reliability when there are a number of different interviewers using the same questionnaire. In question 1a the interviewer wants to discover the name that the subject uses for the district lived in. Notice that the subject's name for the district is asked for first, if that does not fit with the coded list of districts the interviewer will ask 1b and show the subject a printed card with the list of districts on it. Why do you think the questions are asked in this order? Cards are often used when the interviewer wants the subject to choose between various alternatives. Question 2 is simpler and the interviewer just needs to code the answer on to the form. The coding makes it easier for the answers to be analysed later.

Questions 1 and 2 are *multiple choice* questions. Question 3 is different. The subject does not have to choose an answer. Instead the interviewer notes down the reply and may even probe to get a fuller answer. This is an *open-ended* question. Why do you think an open-ended question is used here?

What type of questions are used for 21a and 22a? If the subject answers NO for either of these two questions the interviewer has instructions to 'skip to Q.22 or Q.23' in the right-hand column. These questions will be specially for those who lack these amenities. This complete questionnaire, of which we have only seen one small part, contains 75 questions and would take up to 45 minutes to complete. If the interviewer is going to keep the subject's co-operation for all of this time he or she will need to keep their interest. This can be done by varying the questions and by making the subject feel that they are doing something which is going to be worthwhile.

Interview-type questionnaires such as this have the advantage that if the subject does not understand the question the interviewer can

Fig. 9. *Southwark housing survey*

SOCIAL & COMMUNITY PLANNING RESEARCH			
16, Duncan Terrace, London N1 8BZ	Telephone: 01-278 6943		

P.362 **SOUTHWARK HOUSEHOLD SURVEY 1975** April 1975	
INTERVIEW QUESTIONNAIRE (1–4)	
(5) (6)	
Household Code [ ] Card [2]	
(7) (8) (9) (10) (11)	
Ward/P.D. Code [ ][ ][ ] Serial Number [ ][ ]	
Interview Type: Head of Household [1] Time interview started:	
Household [2] WRITE IN:	

		Col./Code	Skip to
1a)	What is the name of this district you live in, that is, what do you call it? WRITE IN NAME CODE IN PRECODED LIST IF POSSIBLE, OTHERWISE ASK b) IF NAME NOT ON PRE-CODED LIST ASK b) AND THEN CODE	(12–13)	
	SHOW CARD A b) I have on this card the names of the various parts of the Borough of Southwark; in which of these do you live?	Bermondsey 01, The Borough 02, Camberwell 03, Dulwich 04, Dulwich Village 05, East Dulwich 06, West Dulwich 07, Herne Hill 08, Honor Oak 09, Newington 10, Nunhead 11, Peckham 12, Rotherhithe 13, Walworth 14	
2.	How long have you lived in .... (CODED DISTRICT NAME)?	(14) Under 6 months 1, 6–11 months 2, 1 year, but less than 2 years 3, 2 years, but less than 3 years 4, 3 years, but less than 5 years 5, 5 years, but less than 10 years 6, 10 years, but less than 20 years 7, 20 years or more 8, All my life 9	

			Col./ Code	Skip to
3.	I would like to hear what you like and dislike about living in .... (CODED NAME OF DISTRICT).			
	First can you tell me what you like about .... (CODED NAME OF DISTRICT) as a place to live?			
	PROBE FULLY, INCLUDING "Why do you say that?" AND "What else?" UNTIL FINAL "No".		(15)	
			(16)	
4.	What do you dislike about .... (CODED NAME OF DISTRICT) as a place to live?			
	PROBE FULLY, INCLUDING "Why do you say that?" AND "What else?" UNTIL FINAL "No".		(17)	

	~~bath~~ .... do you .... ~~wi~~ any other households?	~~s~~ole use Shared use	1 2	
21a)	ASK ALL Apart from a sink in a kitchen, do you have a wash-hand basin with running water?	Yes No	(48) A 1	Q.22
	IF YES AT a) — CODE A b) Do you have the sole use, or do you share with any other households?	Sole use Shared use	2 3	
22a)	ASK ALL Do you have a flush toilet?	Yes No	(49) A 1	Q.23
	IF YES AT a) CODE A b) Do you have the sole use, or do you share with any other households?	Sole use Shared use	2 3	
	c) Is the entrance to it .... READ OUT		(50)	
	.... inside your accommodation outside your accommodation but inside the building or, outside the building?		1 2 3	
23a)	ASK ALL How many bedrooms do you have, including bedsitting rooms and spare bedrooms?	NUMBER OF BEDROOMS	(51) (52)	
b)	Do you have the sole use of all these b~~..~~ ~~....~~ shared or sub-let		1	Q.24

repeat it or in some cases explain it. This is not possible with a questionnaire that is sent through the post. Postal questionnaires have to be very clear and easy to understand. They are also generally shorter than interview questionnaires. If a postal questionnaire were too long people would not bother to complete it and this would reduce the number of questionnaires that are returned. Postal questionnaires often have a much lower response rate than interview questionnaires. There is also a danger that the subjects may be 'self-selecting'. People may only return a postal questionnaire if they are interested in the subject, or feel that it is worthwhile, or have strong views on the subject. This can bias the findings of the research. It is also more difficult to detect any false answers in postal surveys. An interviewer is more likely to be able to tell if someone is telling the truth than the researcher who just receives replies through the post.

Both types of questionnaire have their advantages and disadvantages and are used for particular kinds of research.

Observation

Observation is something we all do for most of the time. We notice things that happen around us; we store the information, fitting it into our existing knowledge; we link it to our ideas of why things happen and use it when similar events occur again. Sometimes we are just observers, for example when we are standing on the touch-line watching the game, even watching it on television. At other times we are so closely involved that we get little opportunity to observe. The sociologist has a similar experience. Observation is often closely linked to participation. At one extreme is the pure observer watching the events through a one-way mirror or a television camera lens completely separated from the situation observed. At the other extreme is the participant who loses sight of his sociological task and 'goes native', joining that which he, or she, set out to study. Most participant observation research lies between these two extremes.

The evidence gained from participant observation is often very different from that provided by surveys. Surveys and questionnaires tend to produce numbers and percentages. They focus on quantity. Participant observation is more concerned with quality and produces impressions. For this reason it is sometimes called *qualitative* or *impressionistic* research.

Sociologist Howard Becker describes how he carried out a participant observation study in a medical college.

We went to lectures with students taking their first two years of basic science and frequented the laboratories in which they spend most of their time, watching them and engaging in casual conversation as they dissected cadavers or examined pathology specimens. We followed these students to their fraternity houses and sat around while they discussed their school experiences. We accompanied students in the clinical years on rounds with attending physicians, watched them examine patients on the wards and in the clinics, sat in on discussion groups and oral exams. We ate with the students and took night calls with them. We pursued interns and residents through their crowded schedules of teaching and medical work. We stayed with one small group of students on each service for periods ranging from a week to two months, spending many full days with them. The observational situations allowed time for conversation and we took advantage of this to interview students about things that had happened and were about to happen, and about their own backgrounds and aspirations. (Becker 1958)

Becker suggests that research like this goes through four stages which overlap each other. In the first stages of the research the observer will be trying to fit together a number of separate events into a framework of ideas and concepts. At this time the researcher is deciding what is important, what it means and how it can be checked. This second stage involves checking some of the hunches that arise during the first stage. Some of these may prove to be untrue and are abandoned, others may appear to have some truth in them and will be explored further. It is also likely that new theories and ideas will appear and will need to be checked out. In the third stage the researcher tries to build the information and ideas into a theory, or model, to explain the situation studied. Finally he will present his evidence to others and show that the theory is proved.

Sociologists engaged in participant observation are faced with four major problems. Firstly, they have the problem of controlling bias. How sure can anyone be that the impressions they have of a given event are not influenced by their own viewpoint? This can be prevented by regular checks on the information, accurate and regular recording and sharing the work with other sociologists. The second problem concerns the extent to which the researchers become involved in what they study. Sociologists try to remain detached from the situation they study but participation sometimes makes detachment difficult. Thirdly, there is the effect the observer has on the situation he or she observes. When some sociologists tried to study a flying saucer cult which had predicted the end of the earth they found that the members of the group interpreted their interest in the group as evidence that the prophecy was true. By joining the group the researchers gave it a reason for continuing. Finally, there is always a moral problem in participant observation research. The researcher participates because he wants to do research. The people with whom he participates may not wish to be researched, and may not agree with the findings. In some cases researchers carry out *covert* research, not telling the subjects that research is going on. When James Patrick studied a Glasgow gang he did it in secret. If he hadn't the gang wouldn't have trusted him and might have attacked him. It could be said that covert research involves a breaking of the trust between the researcher and the researched.

Interviews

Interviews are used in research involving surveys and in participant observation. They involve two people: a researcher who presents the questions and topics for discussion and the person being interviewed who is expected to respond. An interview, therefore, is a social situation involving particular individuals who are playing particular roles. Each individual in such a situation has ideas about what is happening and what it is all about. They have their own ideas about the other person and about their role and status. All of these different things affect the way the interview goes and its value as a source of information. Some interviews may be very formal affairs with printed questionnaires and clearly defined relationships. Others may be more like extended conversations. The problems, however, are very similar.

The interviewer needs to establish a relationship with the subject who is likely to get bored, or drop out altogether, if he doesn't feel that the interview is worthwhile. To keep the subject's interest, the interviewer must appear interested in the subject and make comments which show that the subject's opinions are valued. Problems arise when the subject begins to give the interviewer the answers he thinks the interviewer wants. When this happens *interviewer error* makes the results less reliable. Interviewers have other problems, too. If a number of different interviewers are working on the same survey they must be consistent so that they get similar responses.

Experiments

In a science like chemistry or biology an experiment involves two situations which are identical in every way except for the one factor which is being tested. The experimental plant grows in sunlight while its 'control' is locked away in a darkened cupboard. They differ only in the amount of light they receive. Earlier in this chapter we considered some of the reasons why this kind of approach was not common in the social sciences. However, social scientists and in particular social psychologists do conduct experiments and their results may be of value in sociology.

An American psychologist, S. E. Asch (1951), conducted a series of experiments which illustrate group pressure. Groups of students were asked to help with a test of visual perception. They were shown a series of cards with lines of different lengths drawn on them. As each pair of cards came up, each of the group in turn was asked to say which of the three lines on one card was the same length as the one line on the other card. However, all but one of the students had secretly been told to give a wrong answer every time. The one student who was not in on the deception was placed near to the end of the row. As the lines came up and the 'planted' students kept making a wrong choice, the one real subject became more and more perplexed. In 37 out of every 100 cases the individual subject actually gave in and began agreeing with the rest of the group who were obviously wrong.

One of Asch's subjects, who did not give in and agree with the others, describes the experience: 'Despite everything there was a lurking fear that in some way I did not understand I might be wrong; fear of exposing myself as inferior in some way.' Another said: 'I felt disturbed, puzzled, separated, like an outcast from the rest. Every time I disagreed I was beginning to wonder if I wasn't beginning to look funny.' The group has a very powerful influence on our attitudes.

Another kind of experiment was used to assess the value of ITA, or the 'initial teaching alphabet', in helping children to read. 'Janet and John' readers were used in a large sample of schools. In certain schools standard readers were used while in others they had been translated into ITA. The schools were carefully matched in terms of their location, pupil-teacher ratios, social class, and size, and the pupils were matched for age, sex, social class, measured intelligence and vocabulary. In this way the experimenters tried to compare like with like, with the reading schemes as the only things that varied. This kind of control matching is common in social science experiments. The experiment seemed to show that ITA worked better than traditional methods, but how reliable were the results? A number of possible sources of error could have influenced the result. It is quite likely that there were influences present in the experiment which the researchers had not foreseen and which had not been 'matched'. The schools which used the new methods may have been so pleased at being involved in what they saw as an important piece of research that they worked harder, expecting more from the children and as a result got better results. This kind of effect is usually known as 'Hawthorne Effect' after the experiments carried out at the Hawthorne Electrical Works by Elton Mayo (see Chapter 9).

Experiments can have a value in sociology but like all other research need to be treated with caution.

Conclusion

This chapter has been concerned with social research. In the end sociology depends on the quality of the research which is carried out. The methods described and the problems they involve are part of the sociologist's everyday problem of understanding social life. A chapter in a book such as this can only give a very general indication of what research is about. You can only really understand it by doing it.

6

Population

In 1815 the population of the United Kingdom was a little over 22 million people. By the beginning of the twentieth century it had risen to over 38 million and by 1982 reached 56 340 000. By the year 2001 the United Kingdom population will be over 57 million.

Estimating the future population is a very difficult task with many different factors to be taken into account. It is not surprising that

Fig. 10. *The growth of the population in England and Wales*

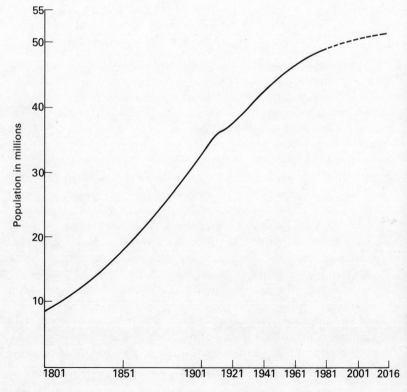

population planners often refer to their predictions as 'the best guess'.

Why has population risen in this way over the last few hundred years? There are two main influences on the level of population in any country: the numbers coming into the country and the numbers going out. It is not unlike the way the water level in your bath is determined. If you pull the plug out and leave the taps running, whether the level of the bath rises or falls will depend on the relative rates of flow of water in and out.

The main reason for the rise in population since the end of the seventeenth century has been that births have regularly outnumbered deaths. More people have come into the country than have left it. An increase in population resulting from 'natural' causes (births and deaths) is termed a *natural increase in population* in order to distinguish it from an increase (or decrease) due to migration. Throughout this period, immigrants (those coming into England from abroad) and emigrants (those going to other countries) have cancelled each other out. As many were leaving as were coming in.

It is important, therefore, to think of population in terms of 'flows' of people in and out of the country, and also in and out of different parts of the country. Migration takes place between different regions of a country as well as between different countries.

Knowing how many people there are in the country is important but it is even more useful to know how that total population divides up. If the government has to decide whether to build new schools or old people's homes it needs to know how many children there are and how many old people. It needs to know the areas of the country in which the balance of different age groups is changing, and where the population as a whole is rising or falling. Before we look in more detail at these aspects of population we need to consider the changing patterns of birth, death and migration.

Births

The *birth rate* is the number of babies born in every thousand of the total population each year. It is sometimes described as the *crude birth rate* to distinguish it from the *general fertility rate* (the number of births per thousand women of child-bearing age per year), and the *total period fertility rate* (TPFR, the average number of children which would be born per woman if the fertility rate for the age group continued throughout the woman's child-bearing life-span).

Fig. 11. *Population changes*

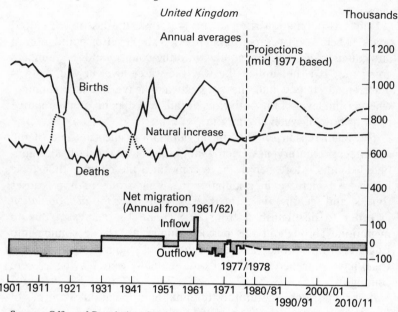

Source: Office of Population Censuses and Surveys

Within the United Kingdom there has been a considerable fall in the birth rate this century. In 1901 there were 35 children born for every thousand of the total population. By 1951 the rate had halved to 16 per thousand and by 1977 it was down to 11·6. From this very low level the birth rate rose to 13·3 per thousand in 1980, falling again in 1982 to 12·6. The fall in the number, and rate, of births since 1900 has not been a steady decline. At the end of the First and Second World Wars and in the late 1950s there were brief periods when the number of births rose dramatically. After each 'baby boom', however, the birth rate fell once again. By the 1970s the level of births had fallen below that which was necessary for the population to replace itself.

FERTILITY

The explanation for these changes can be found in the changing pattern of fertility. The number of births at any one point of time will be influenced by many things. An important factor will be the number of women who are at the age when they might have children. These women could be described as 'at risk of pregnancy'. The general decline in births has meant that the number of women 'at

90

risk' has, after a period of years, also fallen. Whether or not they are married will also affect fertility rates as will the length of the marriage, the number of previous children, the woman's plans for a career and her ideas about the size of the ideal family. Throughout this century there has been a move towards smaller families, started later in life, as well as a decline in childless families. Nearly half of the women who married in the early 1920s had one or two children, but over one in six were childless and nearly one in four had four or more children. Among the women married forty years later in the early 1960s less than one in twelve were childless and even fewer had four or more children. Two out of every five women married

Fig. 12. *Average family size*

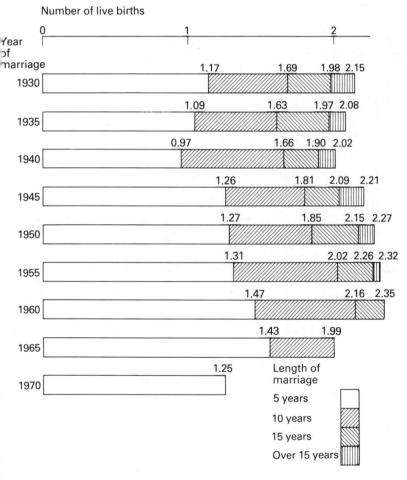

in the early sixties had two-child families. During the 1970s the gap between marriage and the birth of the first child increased from an average of 20 months to a little over 30 months, falling off slightly in the early 1980s. Average family size has fallen from between two and three children for women married in the 1920s to an average of less than two children for women married in the 1960s.

Table 14. *Distribution of family size*

Number of Children	Women married in the years:			
	1920–24	*1935–39*	*1956–60*	*1961–65*
0	16	15	10	8
1	24	26	17	21
2	24	29	39	41
3	14	15	22	23
4 or more	22	15	12	7
Average family size	2·4	2·1	2·1	2·0

Source: Lesley Rimmer 1981

In 1967 a survey of women who had been married for up to twelve years showed that for the majority three or four children was thought to be the ideal family size. A similar survey in 1972 showed that the majority of women at that time wanted less than three children whilst a 1976 survey showed that the vast majority of women wanted two children.

This deliberate move to smaller families was a major factor in the decline in fertility this century. The reasons for this change are not difficult to discover. The extension of compulsory education in the latter part of the nineteenth century kept children out of paid employment for longer. Increased opportunities led many families to concentrate their energies on providing the best that they could for smaller numbers of children. There was a greater emphasis on the quality of life and of maintaining a good standard of living. Women increasingly took on jobs and looked forward to having a career as well as a family. Couples became more conscious of the need to plan their families in order to achieve what they wanted in life. The availability of reliable contraceptives meant that family planning was possible. It would be wrong to say that the greater use of contraception was a cause of the decline in fertility. The causes

Table 15. *The ideal number of children*

Year of interview: Year of marriage:	1967 1955–62	1972 1960–67	1976 1964–71
Ideal Number of children:	%	%	%
0	0	0	1
1	0	1	1
2	23	44	65
3	22	18	17
4	42	28	11
5 and over	8	3	0
Other answers	4	6	4
Mean	3·4	2·9	2·4

Source: K. Dunnell, *Family Formation*, OPCS 1979, Table 12.4

are to be found in the ways in which people planned their lives. Contraceptives were the means whereby they gained control over their family lives.

These changes in birth and fertility rates have not been the same for all social classes nor for families in which the mother was born outside of the United Kingdom. Women in social classes IV and V are more likely to have larger families than women in classes I and

Fig. 13. *Trend in total period fertility rate, January 1973 to April 1983 England and Wales*

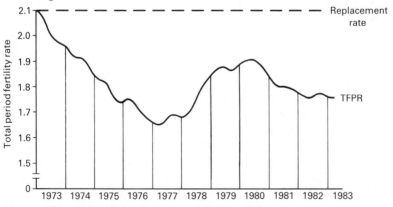

Source: Office of Population Censuses and Surveys 1983

II. Although the number of childless families and families with only one child is similar in all social classes there are clear differences in the numbers of two-child and four-child families.

Wives of unskilled workers are also likely to begin their families sooner after marriage than are women in professional families. The average gap between marriage and the birth of the first child in families of all social classes is a little over two years. In the families of unskilled workers it is little over one year whereas professional families on average delay the arrival of the first child by nearly four years. Birth rates have also been higher to women born outside of the United Kingdom.

Table 16. *Distribution of family size within social classes (for women first married between 1956 and 1965 after ten years of marriage, percentages)*

Number of Live Births	Social Class				
	I & II	III (N)	III (M)	IV & V	TOTAL
	%	%	%	%	%
0	8	7	9	9	9
1	17	15	17	18	19
2	47	42	43	33	40
3	23	26	21	24	23
4 or more	5	10	10	16	9

Source: K. Dunnell, *Family Formation*, 1979.

Life expectancy

The *death rate* is the number of deaths for every 1 000 of the population each year. Like birth rates, death rates have also been falling steadily for the past hundred years. In the early years of this century there were 16 deaths for every 1 000 of population each year, but by 1961 this was down to a rate of 12 per 1 000.

This decline in the rate of deaths per 1 000 of the population is the result of a number of factors. There has been an improvement in the overall standard of living of people in Britain. There has been no famine for over a century. We are no longer dependent on food we grow ourselves. We can import food from other countries and pay for it in exports of machinery and manufactured goods. There have been advances in medicine and in public health: cholera,

Fig. 14. *Family size and social class*

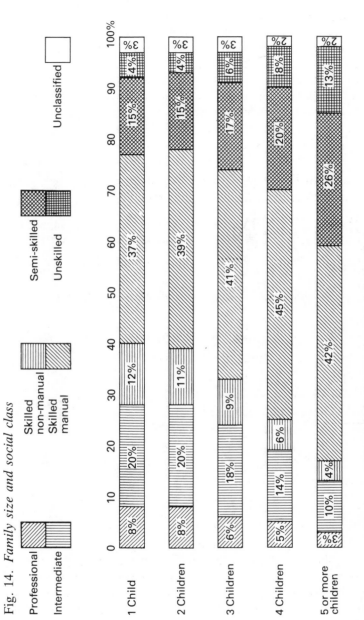

(Number of children at birth of last child by social class of husband 1976)
Source: Social Trends

typhoid and smallpox epidemics are things we read about in the newspapers, but they no longer occur in Britain. Hospital services have improved, in particular the care of expectant mothers and their babies. The *infant mortality rate* (the number of babies who die within their first year out of every 1 000 live births) is at its lowest ever.

As a result of these improvements men and women are living longer. In 1900 men on average could look forward to a life of just under half a century whilst women had a 'life expectancy' of just over the half century. A girl born in 1979, however, could expect to live to a ripe old age of 76, and a boy to 70.

The total number of deaths have been well below the number of births for most of this century. In almost every year more have been born than have died and this has been a major cause of the population increase. The gap between births and deaths has not, however, remained constant. There have been periods when births were considerably more than deaths and in the early 1980s there were more deaths than births.

Table 17. *Death Rates and infant mortality rates (England and Wales)*

| | Infant Mortality Rates | | Death Rates | |
	Males	Females	Males	Females
1961	28·4	19·3	12·6	11·4
1966	22·0	17·1	12·5	11·2
1971	20·2	15·5	12·2	11·1
1976	16·4	12·4	12·6	11·8
1979	14·4	11·3	12·5	11·7
1980	13·4	10·7	12·2	11·5

Source: Social Trends 1984

Although the death rate has remained fairly steady over the last thirty or forty years the infant mortality rate has fallen steadily.

Migration

It is clear from Figure 11 that for most of this century more people have left Britain to settle overseas than have come to live in Britain.

It was only in the period from 1931–1951, when refugees were escaping from Eastern Europe, and in the few years before the passing of the Commonwealth Immigration Act in 1962 that more people came into Britain than left. Since 1962 there have been further Acts of Parliament in 1968, 1971, 1976 and 1982 designed to tighten the control over immigration. These laws have been aimed mainly at restricting the entry of black migrants from the New Commonwealth (including India, and a number of African and Caribbean states), and from Pakistan. Immigration by white migrants and those from the Old Commonwealth (including Canada, Australia and New Zealand), and from South Africa has not been restricted to the same extent.

In passing laws which discriminate clearly against particular groups of migrants it has been argued that high levels of immigration will lead to Britain becoming 'swamped by coloured immigrants'. Such arguments assume firstly, that all black people in Britain are immigrants, and secondly, that all immigrants are black. The evidence supports neither of these assumptions. As early as 1764 it was estimated that there were 20 000 black servants in London alone, at a time when London's population was under 700 000. By the end of the nineteenth century all of the major ports in Britain had sizeable black communities. The major period of immigration was, however, in the 1950s. At this time large numbers of people were attracted to Britain from the New Commonwealth in search of work. British employers, such as London Transport, advertised for workers in the West Indies. This was also a time when former British colonies were gaining their independence and many of the white administrators and farmers were returning to Britain. One in three of those who gave their birthplace as India in the 1966 Census were, in fact, white. The period of high immigration was fairly short and by the middle of the 1960s it had been reduced to a trickle. From then on changes in the black population became a matter of natural growth and not immigration. The 1981 Labour Force Survey estimated that 37·5 per cent of the non-white population had been born in the UK, compared to 96 per cent of the white population. Because the black population is generally younger and has a higher proportion of women of child-bearing age the proportion of the black community which is born in Britain will rise. It is likely that the age-structure of the black British population will eventually resemble that of the British population as a whole and differences in fertility rates will become less. The characteristics of Britain's black population are considered in more detail later in this chapter.

MIGRATION STATISTICS

Details of the movement of population into and out of Britain are collected in a number of ways. Firstly, there are *Control of Immigration Statistics* which are collected by the Home Office. These are used to monitor immigration under the various immigration laws. They are concerned only with the inflow of migrants and do not include those people who are not subject to immigration controls. They are, therefore, principally statistics of black immigrants. A second source of information is the *International Passenger Survey* which is based on a sample survey of passengers at the main points of arrival and departure. Because its purpose is to monitor tourism and the balance of payments migrants form only a small proportion of the people sampled. As well as serving different purposes and using different methods these two sources of information also use different definitions of 'immigrant' and 'emigrant'. A third source of information is the Census of Population, (See Chapter 6) which includes a question on birthplace but does not seek information on racial or ethnic background. Whereas the earlier surveys focus on population movements the Census provides some indication of the numbers of people who were born overseas and reside in Britain on the day of the Census. The information gained from the Census is usually combined with a number of other surveys, such as the General Household Survey and the Labour Force Surveys to give a general view of migration patterns over a period of time. The collection of statistics on the black population is examined later in the chapter.

THE PATTERN OF MIGRATION

The figures for *net migration* which show that Britain has had an outflow of migrants in the thirty years since the end of the Second World War do not provide a complete picture of migration patterns. Simply subtracting the number of immigrants from the number of emigrants hides quite large movements of people in either direction. It also fails to show the countries to which migrants went or from which they came.

A typical pattern of migration can be seen in the figures for 1980–1 and 1982–3, (Fig. 15). Over this two-year period 165 000 more people left Britain than arrived. Most of the emigrants went to countries within the 'Old Commonwealth' or to the Republic of South Africa. A large proportion also went to America or the Middle East. Those countries from which more people came to Britain were mainly those on the Indian sub-continent. Migration between Britain and the Caribbean was fairly low. However in some

Fig. 15. *Net migration 1980–82*

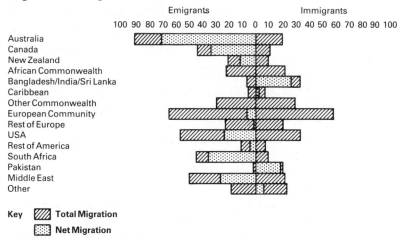

Key ▨ Total Migration
░ Net Migration

Source: O.P.C.S. International Passenger Survey 1983

cases very small *net* figures fail to reveal very large movements in both directions. For example in the net figures for 1981–2 there appears to be no evidence of migration between Britain and the smaller Commonwealth countries. In fact 29 000 people travelled in each direction. Similarly the 7 000 net emigration to countries in the European Community is made up of 65 000 emigrants and 58 000 immigrants. It is therefore important to consider the flow of migrants as well as the *net* totals.

Looked at carefully these figures show, firstly, that the total amount of movement is far greater than is suggested by the net figures, and secondly, that immigrants do not always come from the same places that emigrants go to. They also remind us that migration is not a single movement. People may move backwards and forwards between different countries. They could be emigrants to Australia who decided to return home, elderly Chinese or Indians returning to their home villages when they retire, British doctors going out to America for a year or two or British engineers returning home at the end of a period of contract work in the Middle East.

EXPLAINING MIGRATION

Although it is clear that there has been considerable migration, both in and out of the United Kingdom, during this century it is not easy to explain why. For most people the decision to pack-up and move to another part of the world is a very important one. It is not a

99

decision to make lightly. In making such a decision many factors may have to be taken into account. For some people the decision to move is made because they believe that the way of life in another country offers the prospect of a better future for themselves and for their family. They compare their present lives with what they believe about life in another part of the world. It may, however, be that their present life is so intolerable that they must get out whatever another country has to offer. Refugees, for example, often have no alternative but to leave their homes. We can describe these as *pull* and *push* explanations. For some it is the 'pull' of their belief in a bright future elsewhere in the world. For others it is the 'push' of circumstances at home. For many migrants the decision is made through a mixture of 'push' and 'pull' influences.

Migration need not, however, be a once-and-for-all decision. For some communities migration is a way of life. As a result of changes in the market for rice in the late 1950s the villagers of San Tin, on the mainland of Hong Kong, were forced either to take low-paid jobs in the city, or to emigrate. In Britain restaurants serving Chinese food were becoming popular and the young men of San Tin were easily able to find jobs, and even open their own restaurants. In the beginning, therefore, there was the 'push' of unemployment and low wages in Hong Kong, and the 'pull' of well-paid work and the chance of independence in Britain. By the early 1960s nearly 90 per cent of the people of the village worked abroad, mainly in Britain and Holland. Emigration had become a way of life for San Tin and the influence of 'push-pull' factors became less. The village changed from agriculture to a *remittance economy*, surviving on money sent from abroad. As one of the villagers commented, 'In some villages everyone grows rice for a living, but in San Tin we are all emigrants. That's what we do best.'

Migration is, therefore, a complicated process of movement of people across the face of the earth. It is often difficult to see a clear pattern in such population movements and they may be even more difficult to explain in a simple way.

The structure of the population

So far in this chapter we have looked at population from the point-of-view of the *total* population. We have viewed 'the population' as one large mass of people. If we want to understand changes in population more clearly we need to break the 'mass' down into its various parts. We can do this in five ways.

1. Where do people live and how do they move about the country?
2. How do people earn their living?
3. What is their sex?
4. How old are they?
5. What differences are there between ethnic groups?

Regional distribution

The typical Englishman is an urban, or suburban dweller. As can be seen from the map on page 102 the majority of people in Britain live in an area roughly 50 miles wide running from the Thames Estuary in the South East to the Mersey and the West Riding in the North. Within this belt live three-fifths of the population of Great Britain. Over the whole country four types of population change can be seen. In Scotland and Wales there is a decline in the population of the upland regions mainly caused by the lack of employment in these areas. There are not enough babies being born in these areas to compensate for the migration out of them. A similar situation occurs in northern England where there is overall growth of natural population but again a heavy loss through migration. In the Midlands a natural increase in population into the region in the 1970s has been replaced by a net loss. Finally, in the South even heavier inward migration adds to a high level of natural growth. The South East has often been regarded as a magnet drawing people from all over the country. In many ways this is true but it is counter-balanced by an equivalent movement of population out of the area. London, of course, is at the centre of all population movements in the South East. The population of Greater London has in fact fallen by 800 000 since 1951.

URBAN DISPERSAL

The result of these trends has been to pack people even more tightly into the already overpopulated strip of land running from the Thames to the Mersey. Within this area a process of 'urban dispersal' has been taking place. Fewer people are choosing to live in the centres of the big cities and are moving out to the suburbs and further. This is the result of increased car ownership, freeing families from the necessity of having everything within walking distance; of soaring land prices which have forced young couples to go further and further into the countryside in search of a home at the price they can afford; and of a growing desire to live in something like countryside. An advertisement for a new housing de-

Fig. 16. *Population density*

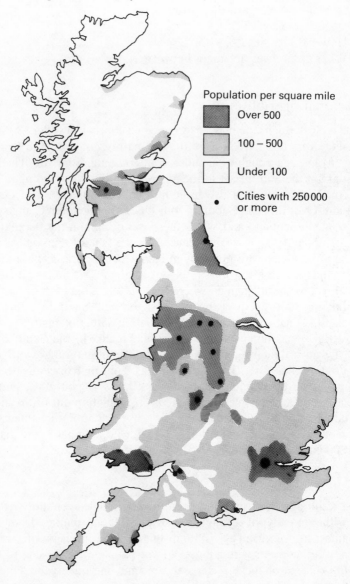

Population per square mile

Over 500

100 – 500

Under 100

• Cities with 250 000 or more

velopment in Kent enticed people to 'share the delights of a latter-twentieth-century village', complete with woods, green fields and a fast train service to London.

102

Fig. 17. *Population in the regions 1961–76*

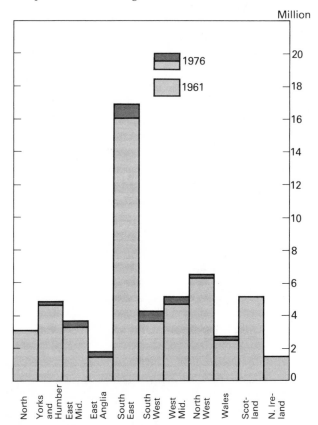

Source: *Regional Statistics No. 13* H.M.S.O.

Urban dispersal has also had the effect of reducing the amount of green countryside which is available for all to enjoy. In the late 1960s 11·6 per cent of the area of England and Wales had been built on, by the year 2000 15·2 per cent will be under concrete. A vast new city of Milton Keynes has been built on farming land in north Buckinghamshire.

This movement out of the city centres has also been influenced by the job situation and birth rates. When many older industries were established, cities grew up around them. As these industries declined people moved away to look for new jobs. New industries were more likely to be established in New Towns or in the suburbs. Young people were more likely to move to find jobs leaving only

Fig. 18. *Population in the regions 1971–76 (% change)*

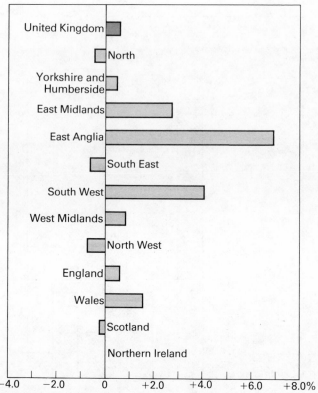

Source: *Regional Statistics No. 13* H.M.S.O.

the old. This led to a declining birth rate which worsened the situation in the older cities.

There can be no doubt that the British people are moving house more often. From the 1966 Sample Census we can see that 10·7 per cent of the population had moved house within the previous year and a third had moved within the previous five years. Much of the movement is over fairly short distances. Margaret Stacey's study of Banbury showed that nearly 15 per cent of the workers who came into the town came from within a 25-mile radius. Not quite as many (13·7 per cent) came from the surrounding industrial Midlands, 12·1 per cent from Lancashire, Cheshire and Yorkshire, 11·6 per cent from Greater London, and only 3 per cent from as far as Scotland. Population movements tend to have a 'ripple' effect moving in slowly towards the centre.

Fig. 19. *The decline of the cities 1971–76*

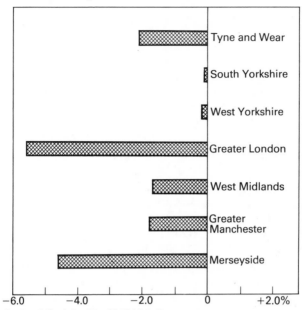

Source: Regional Statistics No. 13 H.M.S.O.

Fig. 20. *Population changes in the countryside 1971–76*

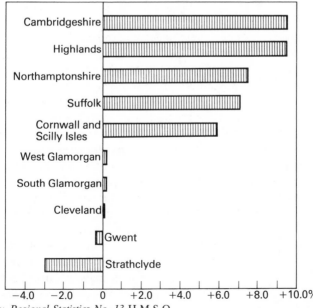

Source: Regional Statistics No. 13 H.M.S.O.

Moving house does not affect all classes in the same way as Table 18 shows.

Table 18. *Number of moves in the previous 5 years (1972)*

Socio-economic groups	Percentage of households which moved	
	No moves	2·4 moves
Professional	53	16
Employers	62	11
Intermediate	56	16
Junior non-manual	64	11
Skilled manual	66	10
Semi-skilled manual	67	9
Unskilled manual	70	9
Average number of moves for all groups	64	10

Source: General Household Survey

GOVERNMENT ACTION

Central and local government authorities are well aware of the problems created for the country as a whole by these movements of population. Incentives in the form of grants to industry and provision of industrial training have been given to the worst hit areas. Tight controls have been placed on industrial and commercial building in Central London and a number of government departments have moved away from the South East to areas of high unemployment. Local authorities have engaged in vast rebuilding programmes which have transformed city centres. Birmingham, Glasgow and London are only three of the towns which have undertaken a programme of urban renewal. New Towns have been built to provide work and homes away from the cities. Since 1944 half-a-million people have moved to New Towns and by the beginning of the twenty-first century they will provide homes for two-and-a-half million people.

The earliest government action came in the 1920s and since then there has been a succession of policies for regional development. These have involved subsidies to firms to enable them to build factories or to keep them going, subsidies towards the cost of labour in particular areas, training programmes and industrial developments and a range of legal controls. Such measures have had little overall effect and in some cases have increased problems.

The Home Office funded Community Development Projects studied a number of areas affected by the decline of particular industries. They felt that the regional policies had had a limited success but at a considerable cost.

But what about the costs of this limited success? The Exchequer has spent enormous amounts. In the ten years up to 1973 nearly £500m (at constant 1970–71 prices) was spent on regional development incentives in the northern region alone, excluding loans, factory buildings and so on. Assuming that the figure of 50 000 additional jobs created is correct, each extra job in the north costs roughly £10 000 to create and maintain over this period. It would be truly remarkable if such an expenditure of public money had not succeeded in luring a number of firms to the Development Areas in the name of regional policy.

Leaving aside the question of cost, doubts have also been growing about the type of jobs brought to the regions by regional incentives. For a long time, many people felt that any job was welcome in those areas, but slowly it dawned on them that perhaps a perfume factory, for example, was not the answer to the run-down of a coal mine. (Community Development Project 1977)

The occupational structure

In 1881 one in every eight workers was employed in a primary industry such as mining, fishing or agriculture. By 1951 only one in twenty worked in these industries. At the turn of the century 47 per cent of the population were engaged in manufacturing with 44 per cent working in service industries, such as banking or distribution. In 1978 little more than 3 per cent of the population worked in the primary sector, over 40 per cent were in manufacturing industries and nearly 57 per cent provided services. This is evidence of a major change in the economic basis of life in Britain. Manufacturing industry has lost its position as the major employer of labour in Britain and its place has been taken by service industries.

This change can be seen even more clearly in the kind of jobs people do. In 1911 manual workers made up nearly three-quarters of the working population. By 1961 they were less than three-fifths and whereas clerks accounted for little more than 4 per cent of all workers at the turn of the century, by 1961 they amounted to 12·7 per cent.

It is clear, therefore, that Britian has experienced change not only

107

Fig. 21. *The industries people work in 1982 (UK)*

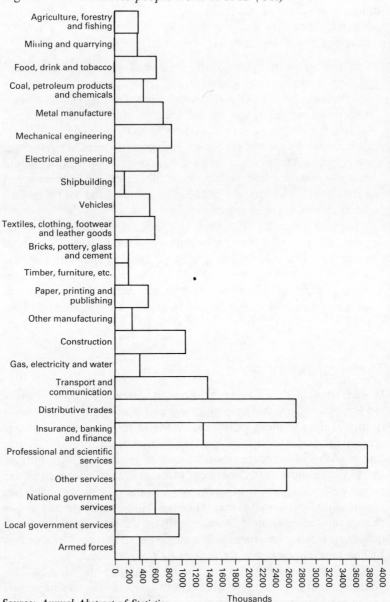

Source: Annual Abstract of Statistics

in the types of industry within which people work but also in the kind of jobs that they do. The majority of people in Britain today work in service industries at non-manual jobs.

108

Fig. 22. *White-collar workers in manufacturing industry. Administrative, technical and clerical staff as a percentage of all workers in the industry*

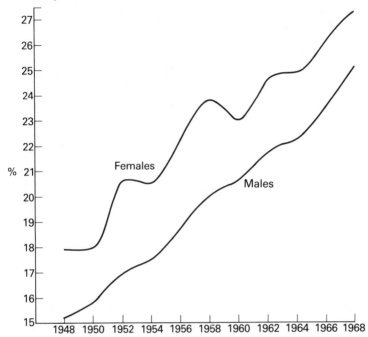

Source: *British Labour Statistics: Historical Abstracts 1886–1968*

There are a number of reasons for these changes. The twentieth century has seen a decline in manufacturing industry in Britain. Increased competition from overseas and insufficient investment at home have both had an effect. The industries which have taken their place have often been highly mechanised, often automated, and have required fewer workers. This is seen clearly in Fig. 22.

The proportion of men and women employed in 'white-collar' jobs has risen steadily since the end of the Second World War.

BALANCE OF THE SEXES

A third factor in changing population trends is the balance of the sexes at different levels. For much of this century there have been more women than men at almost all ages. At present there is a majority of men in the under 15 group, and this is likely to grow between now and the end of the century. In the 15–64 age range there are at present more women than men but by 2001 this may

109

have been reversed. For every 1 000 women in 1931 there were only 920 men. By 1965 there were 940 men and by the end of the century there are likely to be 970 men to every 1 000 women.

For most of this century more boys have been born than girls. In recent years roughly 106 boys have been born for every 100 girls, but this is not a constant rate and there seems to be no biological reason why it should be. The boys' early advantage is not maintained. Males seem to be less sturdy on the whole than females and the balance eventually shifts in the women's favour. It can be argued that men are generally in more vulnerable occupations. They do most of the dangerous jobs and are more likely to experience stress. They also suffer greater risks in war time. The dramatic decline in the ratio of men to women aged 16–44 following the First World War can be clearly seen in Table 19.

Table 19. *Sex ratio 1901–2001 (the number of males to every 100 females) (United Kingdom)*

	1901	1921	1941	1961	1981 (estimates)	2001
Under 16 years	99·8	101·4	102·8	104·5	105·9	106·2
16–44 years	92·4	87·9	97·4	101·1	103·5	104·8
45 years and over	86·6	87·7	81·9	81·1	81·5	84·1
All ages	93·7	91·5	93·3	94·1	95·2	96·9

Source: Social Trends 1979

Improvement in medicine, a greater concern for industrial health and safety and the absence of war do seem to be enabling men to hold their own for a longer period of life. It is also likely that as women gain greater equality, particularly at work, they will be prone to the same stresses and risks which have in the past affected men. However, it still seems likely that women will continue to live longer than men. The life expectancy of women at birth is about 74 years compared with 68 for men.

Age

The main trends in the age distribution of the population can be seen in Fig. 23. Britain has an ageing population. In 1901 6·2 per cent of the total population were over 65; by 2001 it is likely that 16·6 per cent will be in this age group. Improved standards of living and

Fig. 23. *The age structure of the population*

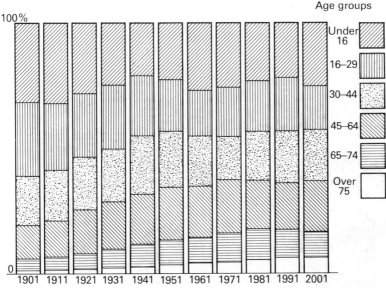

Source: Adapted from *Social Trends*.

early retirement have meant that men and women are now living longer than ever before.

The size of younger age groups show the greatest variations. At the beginning of the century nearly one-third of the population was under 16. This dropped to one-in-five in the 1940s and, as a result of the bulge in birth rates in the late 1950s, rose to one-in-four in the early 1970s. It is likely that this group will remain at about 22 per cent with the possibility of a rise early in the next century. As these different proportions move through the age groups it is possible to see some of the effects they will have on the country as a whole.

Future populations are to some extent influenced by the size of the 16–44 age group as this is the period when people are starting families.

The percentage of the total population in this age group was greatest in the first half of the century. From the 1950s it declined rapidly until the 1980s when the 1950s bulge worked its way through and seems likely to decline again in the next century.

Another important group is that from 45–64. These are people who are at the top of their careers. In 1901 only 13 per cent were in this age group. By the 1960s it was 22 per cent. This could mean that there are more people chasing a limited number of senior jobs.

111

This has been the effect of the growth of managerial jobs described earlier in this chapter.

The most important age division is based on economic activity. Those under 16 and over 65 are generally non-productive members of the society. They are either too young, or too old to work. They depend upon the work population which is mainly in the 16–44 age group. Table 20 shows the changes in the economically active and dependent groups.

Table 20. *Economically active and dependent age groups, percentage, United Kingdom*

	1901	1921	1941	1961	1981	2001
Under 16	32·5	27·9	20·9	24·7	22·0	23·3
16–64	61·3	64·0	67·3	60·7	60·3	60·1
65 and over	6·2	8·1	11·8	14·6	17·7	16·6
Total	100	100	100	100	100	100

Source: Social Trends

Since the middle of this century the size of the main 'productive' age group has settled down to roughly three-fifths of the total. At its peak in the early 1940s it was 67 per cent and it fell in 1971 to 58 per cent. However, these figures do not give the whole picture. They only show those who could work. Throughout this century there has been a trend towards a later start to the working life – because of the need for longer periods of education and training – and an earlier finish – because of early retirement. The clear result has been that the 'burden of dependency' has fallen upon a smaller working population.

In addition, whereas in 1901 only one-in-six of the dependent population was over 65, in 1981 it will be one-in-three. Old people cost the nation more than young people. Though they have contributed to the nation's wealth throughout their lives they require a greater amount of the nation's resources when they retire. Retirement pensions, for example, make up over half of all social security payments. The older people get the greater are their demands upon the health service and welfare departments. This change in the balance of young and old in the dependent population adds to the 'burden of dependency'.

Britain's black population

So far we have divided the British population in four different ways in an attempt to provide a clearer picture of how the total population is built up. By looking at age, sex, employment and location it has been possible to gain a better understanding of the overall structure of the population. There are other ways in which the total population can be divided. One of these is by racial or ethnic group. Earlier in this chapter we considered statistics on migration and recent migration patterns. Within Britain there are many people whose families originated in Asia, Africa or the Caribbean. These groups are often described as being of *New Commonwealth and Pakistan* origin (or NCWP). They make up the core of Britain's black population. In this context the term 'black' is used to describe those who are not 'white'. Defined in this way Britain's black population includes people from India, Pakistan and China as well as those whose family origins are in Africa and the Caribbean. The term 'black' is used in preference to the term 'coloured', which although still used in some official statistics is not generally acceptable within the black communities.

The collection of statistics based on race is a matter of great controversy. On the one hand there is the view that the very act of collecting statistics on the basis of skin colour or ethnic background is discriminatory and racist. There is a genuine fear that information based on racial origin might be used against black people. The alternative view is that until accurate information on the black population is available it will not be possible to remedy the injustices which currently exist. The problem is complicated by the difficulty of collecting accurate information on British citizens, many of whom are born in Britain, but happen to be black. Although there have been attempts to include 'ethnic questions' in the Census they have failed because of the difficulty of finding questions which produce reliable answers and which are also acceptable to the black communities.

It is therefore necessary to use information derived from a number of sample surveys to piece together an accurate picture of the black population. The main sources of the information are the General Household Survey, the 1977–8 National Dwelling and Household Survey and the 1979 and 1981 Labour Force Surveys. These various surveys used different methods of estimating the non-white population. If the head of the household was born in the New Commonwealth or Pakistan this was taken to mean that the household could be defined as 'non-white'. This was correct in nine out of ten cases.

113

It did not allow for white families in which the head of household was of NCWP origin, perhaps born in India or the West Indies during the colonial period, or black and Asian families in which the parents had been born in Britian. An alternative approach, used in the Labour Force Surveys and the National Dwelling and Housing Survey was to ask the question, 'To which of the groups listed on this card do you consider you belong?'

1. White
2. West Indian or Guyanese
3. Indian
4. Pakistani
5. Bangladeshi
6. Chinese
7. African
8. Arab
9. Mixed
10. Other

The General Household Survey, on the other hand, required the interviewers to assess the people interviewed as either 'coloured' or 'white'. Information on the size and composition of the black population is therefore based on estimates drawn from a number of surveys and not on Census data. These estimates show a black population of about 1·5 million in 1981 within a total population of 53 million. At a rough estimate between three and four per cent of the total population of Great Britain in 1981 was of NCWP origin.

The black population is not evenly distributed throughout the country. Different black communities are to be found in different areas. Fifty-six per cent of all people who are of Afro-Caribbean ethnic origin live in London compared to just over 10 per cent of the total white population. Whereas the Afro-Caribbean communities tend to be concentrated in Inner London the Asian communities are more likely to be found on the outskirts. There are large West Indian and Asian communities in the West Midlands and in West Yorkshire, though Leicester's black community is predominantly Asian. The different settlement patterns of different groups developed out of the early immigration. New arrivals tended either to settle near to the place where they arrived in the country or to live for a while with their fellow countrymen before finding a place of their own nearby.

In comparison to the white population the black communities contain larger proportions of young people. There are far fewer black people of retiring age, and many more under sixteen. The age pattern within particular black communities is closely linked to the number of years since the community became established in Britain. Those groups which settled fairly recently have fewer old people and more in the younger age groups. As the communities become settled the age structure becomes more like that of the white population.

Fig. 24. *Population by ethnic origin*

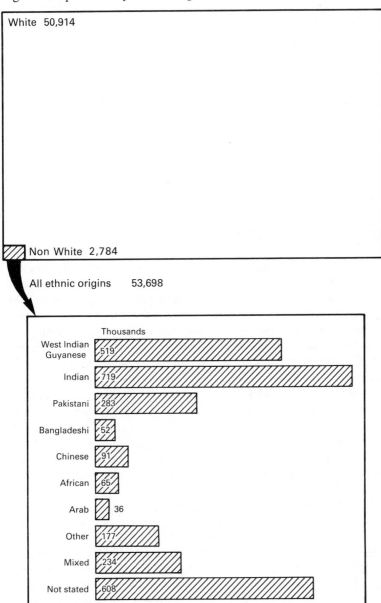

Table 21. *Population by ethnic origin and age Great Britain 1981*

Ethnic Origin	Age				
	Under 16	16–29	30–44	45–59/64*	60/65+*
	%	%	%	%	%
White	22	21	20	20	18
West Indian	31	28	20	18	2
Indian	33	29	21	14	3
Pakistani	45	25	17	12	1
Bangladeshi	48	22	13	17	1
Chinese	33	32	22	9	3
All ethnic origins	23	21	20	20	17

Source: 1981 Labour Force Survey

(* ages refer to different retirement ages for men and women.)

In Britain as a whole there are roughly equal numbers of men and women. The black population, however, has a larger proportion of men. As with the age balance the longer a particular group has been settled in Britain the closer the balance of men and women will come to the national average. In the early stages of migration the majority of the migrants are men. When they are established their wives and families are able to join them. Amongst the fairly small Arab community there are 169 men to every 100 women. In the Pakistani groups the ratio is 122:100 and with the Bangladeshis 119:100. The West Indian community has 96 men for every 100 women, very close to the white ratio of 94 to every 100. This unequal ratio of men to women among the Asian communites has often meant that the men have to return to India or to Pakistan to find brides. Since the early 1970s a large proportion of immigrants have been women coming to join their husbands.

In 1982 there were just under 626 000 live births in England and Wales. Of these 81 303 (13 per cent) were to mothers who were born outside of the United Kingdom. Eight per cent of these births were to mothers who had been born in the New Commonwealth or Pakistan. This does not tell us very much about the birth rates within the black communities. Some of these births would have been to white women who had been born overseas and many mothers of Afro-Caribbean origin would themselves have been born in the United Kingdom. The fertility rates of Afro-Caribbean and Asian women do, however, tend to be higher than those for white women. This is partly because the black population is found mainly in the

Fig. 25. *Fertility rates*

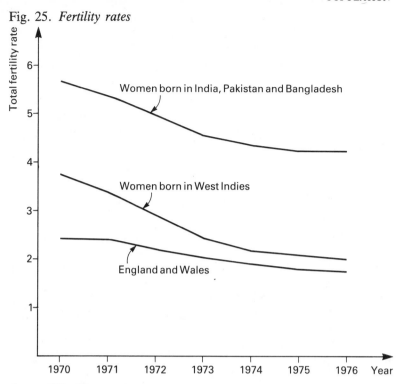

Source: Iliffe 1978

manual social classes, which tend to have higher fertility rates than the predominantly white middle- and upper-classes, and also because there is a higher proportion of women of child-bearing age within the black community. The decline in fertility which we have already considered in relation to the overall population has, if anything, been greater for the black population.

Death rates for people born in the New Commonwealth and Pakistan are considerably lower than the overall death rate for the United Kingdom. This is to be expected when you consider the smaller proportion of old people in the black population. There are, however, important differences within the black population. For the population of NCWP origin the death rate is six per thousand compared to twelve per thousand for the United Kingdom population as a whole. For those born in India, Pakistan and Bangladesh the death rate is nearer to nine per thousand compared to only four per thousand amongst those born in the West Indies. There are also higher perinatal mortality rates (deaths of infants under one week per thousand live births). The rate for mothers born within the

117

United Kingdom was 21·3 in 1970, for mothers born in the West Indies it was 23·1 and for Asian mothers it was 31·7.

Although there are clear differences in the population structure of different groups within the United Kingdom these differences are tending to get less as groups become established within British society. Differences in the average age, the sex ratio, birth rates and mortality rates come directly from the experience of migration. Within two generations the population structure of any migrant group will move close to that of the wider society.

The future

How will population change in the future and what will the consequences of these changes be? We have already discussed in this chapter the problems of predicting population growth. Official estimates of the size of the population in Great Britain in the year 2051 vary between 60 million and 116 million. The gap between highest and lowest estimates made in 1971 for the 1991 population was 4 million. If such estimates are so unreliable why do people still bother with them?

The real answer is that government and industry must have some basis on which to plan ahead. Even unreliable predictions are better than no prediction at all. The size and structure of the population is so important in every area of planning – housing, schools, hospitals, jobs, etc. – that some idea of future trends is essential.

In the past the greatest concern has been that population growth will get out of control. An eighteenth-century clergyman, Thomas Malthus, wrote one of the first books on population.

In his *Essay on the Principles of Population* Malthus wrote that while food supplies would grow in arithmetical progression, population would increase geometrically, and that soon population growth would outpace the available food supply. Then, he claimed, 'vice, misery and poverty' would cause the population to fall back to a reasonable level. Malthus urged 'moral restraint' as a means of holding back the population and so preventing misery and starvation. His fears seemed to be unfounded. The Industrial Revolution, development of new sources of food in Canada, Australia and Argentina, improved agricultural methods at home, all made possible an increase in population far greater than Malthus could have considered possible.

An alternative theory of population, the optimum theory, sees the total population of a country in terms of the number of workers needed to produce goods for the market and the number of people who are needed to buy them. The 'optimum' level of population is that which allows the economy of the country to function most effectively. The role of the government is to enforce measures which keep the population at its optimum level. There may be some justification for this in conditions of full employment but population levels cannot be controlled 'on demand' like the output of electricity. Attempts to relate the growth of the economy to a population policy since the Second World War have not met with much success.

The difficulty is that industrial and economic changes take place much more quickly than changes in the population. It will take seventy years or more for the 1950s bulge in the birth rate to work its way through the system. In that time men have stepped on the moon, computers will have taken over many jobs and the new technology of the silicon chip will have entered every area of life. To add to the problems no one really knows what causes changes in fertility patterns and birth rates which have a major effect on future populations. The sociologist, therefore, must do the best that is possible with the information that is available and should approach any prediction with a certain amount of caution.

7
The Family

It is difficult for us to imagine life without families. Families are important both to us as individuals and to the wider community within which we live. The family is the close social group within which we spend much of our early lives. Important family events are marked by celebrations. The family is a part of our system of laws and a focus for the activities of the state. In recent years there has been much public concern within the mass media about the 'quality of family life'. The family is often held to be responsible for lack of discipline among young people and for educational success or failure. An understanding of the family is, therefore, important for a full understanding of our society.

What is a family?

What is a family? This may seem a strange question to ask. Why should we need to define something that is so obvious? You might find it useful at this point to write down your own definition of the family. The problem of definition arises when we try to put into words something which in everyday life is so varied. If you ask any group of people who belongs to their family you will get many different answers. There is a danger that by taking too narrow a definition we will begin to think of those families that fit the definition as 'real' or 'proper' or 'normal' families and the rest as in some way inadequate. The American sociologist, G. P. Murdock, writing in 1949, gave the following definition:

> The family is a social group characterised by common residence, economic co-operation and reproduction. It includes adults of both sexes at least two of whom maintain a socially approved sexual relationship and one or more children, own or adopted, of the sexually co-habiting adults. (Murdock 1949a)

At first reading this seems a useful definition. It does, however, present certain problems. It does not allow for families with only one parent. It assumes that families only begin at the birth of children to a marriage. The idea of a 'socially approved sexual relationship' is very vague. How do we know when a relationship is 'socially approved'? Does this mean that if a relationship is not socially approved there can be no family? Another definition by E. W. Burgess and H. J. Locke defined the family as:

> a group of persons united by the ties of blood, marriage or adoption, constituting a single household, interacting and communicating with each other in their respective social roles of husband and wife, father and mother, brother and sister; creating a common culture. (Burgess and Locke 1953)

Is this a better definition? Does it cover all of those groups which we might reasonably describe as families?

Most attempts to define the family are based on one or more of the following features:

1. The *structure* of the family, in other words who the members of the family are and the different roles that they play, e.g. father, mother, son, daughter.
2. The *functions* carried out by the family, that is, what the family does both for those who belong to it and for the wider society.
3. The kind of *relationships* that hold the family together, including marriage, birth and adoption.
4. The *location* of the family members and in particular whether or not they live together or in the vicinity.

Instead of a single definition of the family we need to examine carefully the variety of family life. Sociologist Peter Worsley suggests that there are three key features of families. He pictures marriage, residence and parenthood as three overlapping circles (Figure 26).

Using Worsley's diagram it is possible to identify seven different families. We often regard Family 1, in the middle within all three circles, as the typical family. It is the family which we see in advertisements and in the mass media. Some people have described this as the 'cereal packet family' because it is the family shown in advertisements for breakfast food. This is also what some people think the family ought to be like. Moving out from the centre of the diagram, however, we can see that other family patterns are just as likely. Family 2 combines marriage and parenthood but does not have a shared home. This could be a family that has separated or in which the children have grown up and moved away. It may be that the breadwinner has to go away to find work. Family 3 has marriage and residence but no parenthood, in other words a child-

Fig. 26. *Family patterns*

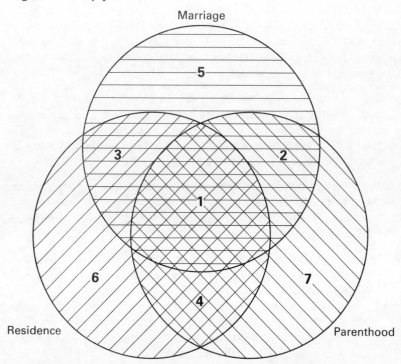

Source: Adapted from *Introducing Sociology*, second edition 1977

less couple. Family 4 has a shared residence and parenthood but no marriage. This could be a 'common-law marriage' or a single parent. On the very outside of the circles are groups which have much less claim to be considered as families. These include separated childless couples, childless couples 'living together' and illegitimate children living apart from their parents. Each of these groups could claim, however, to be part of 'a family'. Worsley's approach enables us to see how different patterns of marriage, residence and parenthood lead to different types of family.

So far, however, we have focussed entirely upon the close family made up of parents and children. We would describe this as the *nuclear family*. When two or more nuclear families are put together we get a *composite family*. In some tribal societies composite families would include all of those nuclear families descended from a single headman or chief, all living within a single compound, or collection of huts. In Britain the composite family is most likely to be an *extended family* made up of three generations.

Fig. 27. *Families: nuclear and extended.*

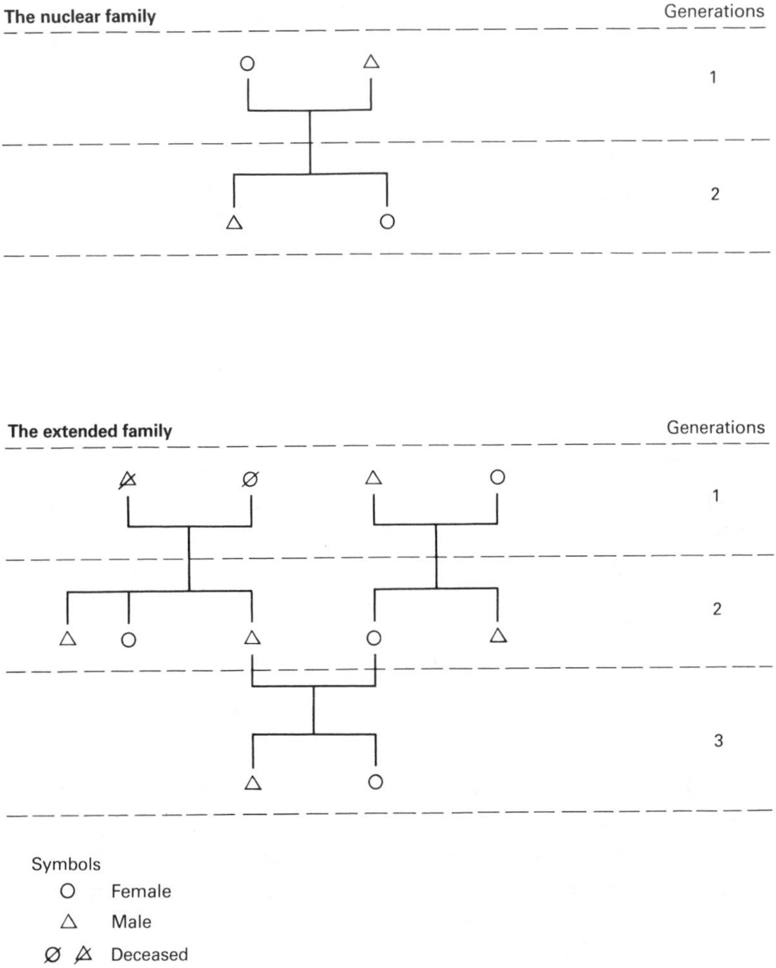

The nuclear family   Generations

The extended family   Generations

Symbols

    O   Female

    △   Male

    Ø △̸   Deceased

EXTENDED FAMILIES

Nuclear families seldom exist in total isolation. They are usually surrounded by a network of relatives – grandparents, aunts, uncles, cousins and perhaps more. These make up the kinship group of which the nuclear family is one part. Where this wider group of kin are particularly close, living nearby or keeping in regular touch, we would describe them as an extended family. In established working-class communities like Banbury's One End Street most people would live their lives within such a kinship group. Middle-class extended families have been just as important though less close. Instead of

123

living 'round the corner' they keep in touch by telephone and regular visits. However, it has been the extended family of the urban working-classes that has been of particular interest to sociologists. Willmott and Young's studies of 'Family and Kinship in East London' showed the importance of the extended family in the 1950s.

In Figure 28 we can see the extended family of a man living in East London thirty years ago. He regularly sees many of his relations, most of whom live within a few miles. The rebuilding of city centres and the decline of traditional industries has led to the disappearance of extended families such as these. People lost touch with their close relatives when they moved out into the suburbs, or to other parts of the country in search of work. The pattern of family life changed. The nuclear family became more isolated and more dependent upon its own resources. It has become *privatised* and concerned with its own affairs rather the wider family network. These changes had implications for women in the family. Gavron (1970) conducted a survey in the early 1960s into the ordinary lives of ninety-six mothers with young children living in North London.

There were equal numbers of middle-class and working-class wives in the group studied. They were asked questions on a number of topics: the home, marriage, equality in the marriage, children, the organisation of family life, leisure, social contacts, and work. Housing was especially a problem for the working-class wives, 71 per cent of whom shared houses with other families. The two major problems were that the wife was left at home with the children for most of the day and often felt cut-off from other people, and that it was difficult to find a safe place for the children to play. The middle-class wives were less affected by these two problems. They were usually more able to make social contacts within the area and thus overcome boredom and loneliness and as most middle-class homes had their own gardens there was little problem in finding play-space for the children.

When they had first got married, wives in both groups felt that it gave them more freedom. With the arrival of children many of the wives felt that marriage was becoming more like a prison. Some of those who had children almost as soon as they got married felt that they had hardly tasted the freedom. When asked about equality it was obvious that the wives had differing views of what the word meant. The middle-class wives took it to mean 'independence', whereas the working-class wives understood it as 'sharing'.

The greatest event that affected any of the families was the birth of the first child. The impact of this event was greater even than the impact of the marriage itself. All the mothers felt that this marked

Fig. 28. *Kinship in Bethnal Green*

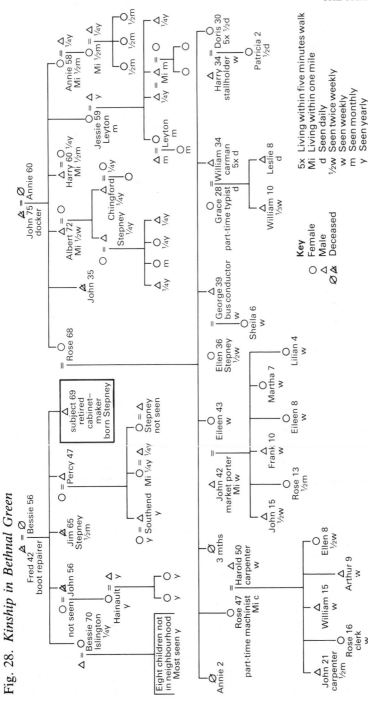

Key

○	Female
△	Male
∅ △	Deceased

5x Living within five minutes walk
Mi Living within one mile
d Seen daily
½w Seen twice weekly
w Seen weekly
m Seen monthly
y Seen yearly

Source: P. Townsend 1957

125

the real break with a working life. The middle-class mothers, however, had a greater sense of 'child-rearing' as an interruption in a career, rather than the end of the career. In nearly all cases husband and wife shared in the task of running the home; for some this amounted to a sharing in decisions as well as sharing the jobs of the home, such as washing up and putting the baby to bed. Leisure was a problem for many families. The working-class wives were not keen to have baby-sitters whom they did not know well, which usually meant that they relied on relatives. Often husband and wife had to take their leisure separately. One would stay in whilst the other went down to the pub or to the pictures. Very often the middle-class wives were more aware of the danger of becoming 'house-bound' and took steps to prevent it. Whereas the middle-class wives had friends, the working-class wives had relatives.

Marriage

It is often very difficult to separate ideas about the family from ideas about marriage.

In our society a wedding is an important social and legal event. It is socially important because it states in public, in a ritual fashion, that two individuals have accepted certain social conventions and obligations. It is important legally because the law, at marriage, recognises certain rights and duties. Once legally married the status of the marriage partners changes. They cannot become *un-married* without the agreement of the law. The marriage partners also have certain rights in law. Increasingly, however, many of the rights, and the obligations, involved in civil marriage are being applied to those who are 'married' in every respect but without the legal ceremonies. Couples are often said to be 'living together', or in official words are 'cohabiting'. Frequently the relationships of these couples are as strong and binding as those found in so-called 'proper' marriages. Often they are even stronger. Such marriages are termed *common-law marriages* and may be recognised by the law where it can be proved that they are well established.

Since the early 1970s there has been an increase in the proportion of couples who are cohabiting. As well as those couples which have a long term commitment, often with children and shared finances, and who regard themselves as married, there are an increasing number of couples who see 'living together' as a short-term arrangement which may eventually lead to marriage. A study by the General Household Survey in 1979 showed that 20 per cent of those married since 1975 had previously lived together, compared to only 3

Fig. 29. *Marriage and remarriage*

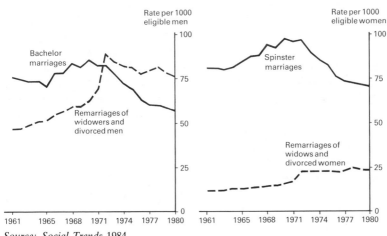

Source: Social Trends 1984

per cent of those who married a decade earlier. The increase in cohabitation is one explanation for the overall decline in the number of marriages in recent years. The delay in getting married has also led to the increase in the average age of marriage. Teenage marriage is now much less likely than it was twenty years ago for all social classes. At the same time as the decline in the number of first marriages there has been an increase in the number of remarriages. One-third of marriages which took place in 1980 involved at least one partner who had been divorced, compared to one-fifth in 1971. Although marriage shows no sign of disappearing in Britain, with over 80 per cent of men and women aged between 25 and 60 married in 1980, the general trend is for marriages to start later and to end earlier.

Marriage may be organised in a number of different ways. There are differences in the choice of marriage partner, including both how the choice is made and from whom; differences in the number of partners any one individual may marry; differences in patterns of inheritance and in where the married couple live.

Marriage in Britain is *monogamous*. It involves one husband and one wife. To marry more than one person would make you guilty of the crime of *bigamy*. There are many societies in the world where it is quite usual for someone to have more than one marriage partner. In these societies marriage is *polygamous*. If a man has

127

more than one wife it is termed *polygyny*. For a woman to have a number of husbands is *polyandry*. There are also differences in rules and customs concerning whom one may marry and the handing-down of property and titles. In some societies the choice of wife or husband must be made from within a particular group such as a tribe, clan or caste. Marriage *within* a group is said to be *endoga-mous*. Hindu marriage, for example, is endogamous because it is usual to marry someone from the same caste. In other societies it is customary to marry *outside* of the group. These marriages are described as *exogamous*. There are also differences in the reckoning of *lineage* or *descent* and the ways in which property or position in society are handed down. In Britain you may inherit from either of your parents, though you normally would take your name from your father. Within the British monarchy the succession to the throne is through the male line in the first instance. Inheritance through the male side of the family is described as *patrilineal* whereas inherit-ance through the female line is *matrilineal*.

For most young people in Britain 'falling in love' is considered to be the only real reason for marriage. It is thought to be far more important than whether the prospective partner has a good job, or prospects for promotion, or even whether or not the parents agree. However, in many communities, both in Britain and elsewhere in the world, 'romantic love' is thought to be something that will develop after marriage. It is not something that is looked for before it. In such communities marriages are *arranged*, either by the parents of the bride and groom or by a specialist match-maker. In these societies marriage is considered to be something which

Table 22. *Patterns of marriage: a summary*

Choice of Partner	Exogamy	Endogamy	
	Arranged	Free Choice (Romantic Love)	
Number of Partners	Monogamy	Polygamy	
		Polygyny	Polyandry
Reckoning of Descent	Patrilineal	Matrilineal	
Residence	Vivilocal	Matrilocal	Neolocal

concerns the whole extended family. Marriage will introduce a new member into the family home and could affect the inheritance of the family land and property. It is, therefore, expected that the leaders of the family should have the right to say who joins the family.

Following marriage the couple may either live with the husband's family, with the wife's family or set up a new home of their own. If it is the custom for the newly-weds to live with, or close to, the wife's people the society would be described as *matrilocal*. If instead they live with the husband's family the society can be said to be *vivilocal*. In Britain it is normal for a couple to find a place of their own as soon as they can afford it. We would, therefore, say that in our society residence is *neolocal*.

These differences in marriage patterns can be seen in Table 22.

FAMILY AND MARRIAGE AMONG THE BARABAIG

Differences in patterns of marriage can be seen more clearly when we examine marriage in other societies. The Barabaig are a community of cattle-herders in Northern Tanzania. They were studied by an American anthropologist in the late 1950s. The traditional way-of-life was beginning to change but many of the old ways still survived. The hump-backed zebu cattle of the Barabaig were the main means of subsistence and an important focus of social life. Wealth was calculated by the size of a man's herd. A wealthy tribesman would have enough cattle to support a number of wives and their children. They would provide the help he needed to look after the herd.

Marriages were arranged though it was not unusual for a young man to suggest to his parents the name of a girl he wished to marry. Before a marriage could take place there would be a careful investigation into the girl's family. Barabaig society is divided into a number of *clans*, each descended from a different ancestor. In all there are about sixty clans varying in size from one family group to several hundred members. Marriage between two people from the same clan is forbidden as is marriage to a girl whose mother, grandmother or great grandmother came from the proposed husband's clan.

The marriage itself would be marked by gifts of cattle from both families. Some of these would take the form of 'bridewealth' given to the girl's family by the father of the bridegroom, or by the groom himself if he is marrying a second wife. The payment of bridewealth gives the groom's family rights over the children of the marriage. Should a marriage end in divorce the wife will return to her own family although her children will not. Descent is through

129

the father and the children therefore belong to him. After the marriage the bride will go to live with her husband's family unless he decides to establish a new homestead for himself and his new wife. When a man has more than one wife he will often divide his herd and establish two or more homesteads in order to protect the cattle from drought or disease which might affect one part of the territory.

For the Barabaig, therefore, their arranged marriages are determined by rules of exogamy; descent is patrilineal; residence is patrilocal and for the more wealthy members of the tribe marriage may also be polygynous.

Is the family universal?

In the previous section we looked at marriage in a tribal society in East Africa. This was one example from thousands of different patterns of family life. By now it should be clear that there is no common pattern of family life that is found everywhere in the world. There are many different types of family. This does, however, raise another important question. If families are so different do we need families at all? In other words is it possible to have a society without families? Is the family, in fact, universal? This immediately runs into the problem we considered earlier in the chapter: what do you mean by 'the family'? Generally the basic family unit is taken to be the nuclear family, although some anthropologists would argue that it is the mother-and-child which is fundamental to all families.

Two main approaches have been taken to this question. Firstly, there is the view that the family is a universal social group if it can be shown to exist in every society. Secondly there is an approach which claims that the family satisfies important human needs and provides certain social functions. The family would, therefore, be necessary to the continued existence of human society.

There are two main types of society which appear not to have some form of nuclear family. Firstly, there are traditional tribal societies such as the Nayar of Northern India. For the Nayar the basic social group is made up of all of those descended in the female line from a common ancestress. At birth a child joins the group of the mother. Following initiation in their early teens the women may have sexual relationships with any men they wish. There is no formal marriage and no nuclear family. The children are not recognised as being the offspring of any particular partner and are cared for by the mother and her relatives.

The second type of 'family-less' societies is more recent in origin.

These are communities established in the late nineteenth and twentieth century with the clear intention of abolishing the family. Some were part of wider social and political revolutions, as in Israel and the Soviet Union, while others were smaller settlements and communes.

The leaders of the Russian Revolution regarded marriage and the family as features of the capitalist oppression they sought to overthrow. Both were abolished. Divorce and abortion became available on demand. The Soviet experiment lasted until 1935 when new laws were introduced making parents responsible for their children. In the following year stricter laws for marriage and divorce came into effect though even today marriage and divorce are far simpler in Russia than they are in Britain.

When the modern state of Israel came into being following the Second World War the Kibbutzim were established as an alternative to the traditional closely-knit Jewish family. Within the Kibbutz the rearing of children was to become the responsibility of the community and women gained equal status to men in the new society. Children grew up within special Children's Houses under the care of a trained nurse or metapalet. They saw their parents for only a few hours each day. Over the years the separation of parents and children has been relaxed with children spending more time within their parents' home. In the newer Kibbutzim different approaches to child-rearing developed.

The second approach to the problem of the universal family looks at what the family does instead of how it is organised. It considers human needs and social functions rather than family structure.

Within human society there are a number of basic social and biological needs. Among these are the need to reproduce and to satisfy sexual drives, the need to provide food and warmth and the need to care for and to socialise children. Providing for these needs is an important function of the family. However, because families normally meet these needs does not mean the family is the only way in which they can be met. Sexual needs, for example, are often satisfied outside of marriage, and have been done so throughout history. Children can be cared for in other ways. We have already seen how the Kibbutz makes it possible for children to be brought up by the community and not directly by their families. Psychiatrists like R. D. Laing and David Cooper have suggested that these alternatives may be far better than the family. Instead of providing the foundations upon which children develop they believe that the family is basically destructive, preventing people becoming individuals.

Changes in the family

The family in Britain today is very different from the family of two hundred years ago. Many of the changes that have taken place in British society have had an effect on the family. Economic changes have been a particularly important influence on patterns of family life.

We can think of the economy as two basic activities: production and consumption. Things are produced in order to be consumed. In peasant societies the family is involved in both production and consumption. The family produces food both for itself and for the market and also manufactures goods which can be sold to increase the family's income. The way of life of the modern Navaho Indians is typical of this type of economy. Although many of the Navaho work for wages outside of the Indian territory agriculture and craft industries are still important.

> Men do most of the work in the fields, look after the horses, wagons, saddles, and cattle, and haul wood and water . . . When the lambs are being born every able-bodied member assists. At other seasons responsibilities are distributed according to who is available and to arrangements within the extended family, but herding tends to be the duty of youngsters and the old. Women spend their spare time in weaving, and occasionally making baskets or pots. Some men are silversmiths and women are also beginning to participate in this craft. (Kluckholm *et al.*, 1962)

Within industrial societies, however, production for the market has been removed from the home. The family has become a unit of consumption. This does not mean that the family's involvement with production disappears completely. Productive work still takes place within the home, for example through housework and DIY, but it is no longer production for the market. Instead of being involved 'as a family' with the production of goods and services the family devotes most of its efforts to supporting individual members of the family who go elsewhere to work as, for example, in this description of a miner's family in Ashton in the 1950s:

> Nowhere does one find luxury; instead there is cosiness (a combination of warmth and comfort), tidiness, and above all cleanliness, achieved through hard work on the part of the housewife. Working people in Ashton regard these as the basic requirements of a household, which must provide a sound and comfortable place to eat and sleep for parents and children . . . and, very important, a haven for the tired man when he returns

from work; here he expects to find a meal prepared, a room clean
and tidy, a seat comfortable and warm, and a wife ready to give
him just what he wants – in fact the very opposite of the place he
has just left, with its noise, dirt, darkness, toil, impersonalism and
no little discomfort. (Dennis *et al.*, 1950)

The position of women within the family has also changed
considerably. With smaller families and greater life expectancy
women can look forward to a considerable period of their lives when
they will not be concerned with child-rearing. Children are today
more likely to be seen as an interruption in a woman's career rather
than a reason for not having a career.

Changes such as these have led some writers to suggest that
a new modern type of family has developed. The separation of roles
that we saw in the example from the study of Ashton is thought to
have been replaced by a more equal relationship between husbands
and wives.

The roles of husband and wife within the family are described as
conjugal roles. In families in which husband and wife have clearly

Fig. 30. *Changes in the pattern of women's lives*

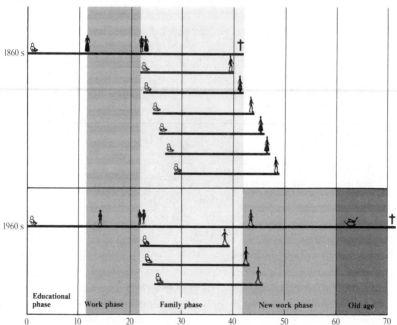

Source: Adapted from A. Myrdal and V. Klein 1968

133

distinct roles, as in Ashton, conjugal roles would be described as *separate*. Where the roles are shared, with the husband taking on baby-care and the wife also going out to work, the conjugal roles are said to be *joint*. Elizabeth Bott has suggested that the change from closely-knit extended families to the more isolated and independent nuclear families has led to a greater emphasis on joint conjugal roles. Michael Young and Peter Willmott have described families such as these as *symmetrical families*.

In Chapter 2 we considered some of the methods used in Young and Willmott's *The Symmetrical Family* (1973) and in Oakley's *Sociology of Housework* (1974). It will be useful here to consider some of their conclusions. Young and Willmott traced family life through three stages. Stage 1 can be seen in Britain before the Industrial Revolution. At this stage the family is the unit of production. In an agricultural society all of the family must work together to make a living. The second stage is the 'stage of disruption' when the unity of the family is broken. The husband becomes a wage-earner, the wife runs the house, or works elsewhere, the children go to school. This stage comes in with the Industrial Revolution. Stage 3 begins early in the twentieth century. These families are 'home-centred'; they share much of their lives; they are more 'nuclear' than 'extended'; roles have become similar but separate; and, above all, they depend upon technology.

> Gas light and electric light were inventions as crucial as piped water; at least husbands could see the faces of their wives after dark without too great an expense. The miniature electric motor was another key invention, powering home laundries, home ice-makers, tiny cold stores, floor cleaners and cooking aids. The average housewife has been given 'about the same amount of mechanical assistance (about two horsepower) as was used by the average industrial worker around 1914'. These inventions have, perhaps, done more for the wife than the husband. But he has been just as absorbed by the machines which have brought entertainment into the home, starting with the gramophone and ending (so far), with colour television, and more so than she by the new style of do-it-yourself handicraft production with its power tools and extension ladders and stick-on tiles and emulsion paint. (Young and Willmott 1973)

At stage 3 we can see the appearance of the symmetrical family. These three stages follow from one another but also overlap so that within modern Britain families at each of the stages exist side-by-side. Young and Willmott's slightly rosy view of family life in modern Britain has not gone unchallenged. Ann Oakley in her study *The Sociology of Housework* questions the whole idea of a 'symmetrical family'. Her evidence suggests that in a number of very important areas of family life roles are far from equal. Women's lives were firmly based in the home carrying out domestic tasks and looking after children. The involvement of the husbands in these activities varied considerably.

Table 23. *Husband's participation in housework and child-care.*

Husband's participation in housework	working-class %	middle-class %
low	85	35
medium	5	45
high	10	20
	100	100
Husband's participation in child care		
low	50	40
medium	40	20
high	10	40
	100	100

Source: Oakley 1974

Ann Oakley comes to the conclusion that:
1. Only a minority of husbands give the kind of help that is evidence of real equality in modern marriage.
2. The pattern of husband's participation differs between social classes.
3. Men are more likely to take part in child-rearing than in housework.

It is very difficult to speak generally about family life in Britain. Every family is different and the common patterns are not always clear. Ann Oakley also reminds us that most sociologists are men and this may influence the way in which they look at changes in the family.

How true is it that the modern family is more separated from its kin and from the extended family than at any time in the past? The evidence does not fully support this kind of view. Historians such as Peter Laslett have shown that the single nuclear family was far more common in the period before the Industrial Revolution than many writers had supposed. It would also be wrong to suggest that the extended family has vanished completely. Many families still live only a short distance from many of their relatives and rely upon them for help and support, especially with child-minding. Even families which do live at a distance from their kin depend upon the extended family for help at times of illness or bereavement and for financial assistance when needed.

The functions of the family

Although the family continues to provide help and support many basic human needs are met outside of the family. Functions which were once provided by the family have become part of the network of services provided by local authorities, by the state and by voluntary organisations. This can be seen in the ways in which the traditional role of the family in caring for the very young and the very old has been taken over by the state. In the past a young mother would turn to her own mother for help and advice. Today that advice and help is available from health centres and child welfare clinics. Many old people depend not upon their family but upon day centres, sheltered housing, home helps and meals-on-wheels services provided by the local council. Education and the training for employment are provided by schools and training centres rather than by the family. There is, it is argued, hardly one aspect of family life which has not come under the influence of either the state or some other organisation. This has led some writers to claim that the family has been stripped of its functions. Against this view it has been argued that only those functions which are non-essential have been lost and that the state, in fact, supports the family in carrying out essential functions. These essential functions of the family can be grouped under four main headings: reproduction, socialisation, maintenance and social placement.

REPRODUCTION

Marx once wrote that the society which did not reproduce the conditions of production at the same time as it produced would not last a year. By this he meant that a society must produce more than just goods and services, it must also reproduce the means by which those goods and services are themselves produced. A factory owner, for example, must spend some of his resources on replacing the machines that are needed to produce the finished product. Because human labour is an important part of production the society must also reproduce labour power. This reproduction has traditionally taken place within the family. In Britain the number of children born outside of marriage has been steadily increasing. In 1979 10 per cent of all children were born outside of formal marriage. Increases in the number of children in single parent families also suggest that the nuclear family is not the only basis for reproduction, though it is still the main one.

SOCIALISATION

As well as reproducing the working population the family also reproduces attitudes towards society through socialisation. We saw in Chapter 3 how the family prepared children for adult roles. The preparation for economic and political roles is an important part of this. Within the family children learn respect for authority, they learn that it is important to work hard, to be honest and punctual. Within the family children learn many of the basic attitudes whch will be important when they eventually go out into the wider society. It is within the family that children begin to acquire the roles appropriate to different sexes. They come to know which are men's jobs and which jobs are thought suitable for women. From about the age of seven boys and girls tend to be led into different types of behaviour. The girls are more likely to spend time within the home helping mother and engaged in more passive activities. The boys, on the other hand, are more likely to be out of doors playing with other boys and being far more independent. These differences are part of the way in which boys and girls are prepared for male and female roles within the economy. Primary socialisation is therefore an important function of the family.

Table 24. *Eleven year olds' participation in household duties*

Duty	Boys	Girls
	%	%
Washing up	40	63
Indoor housework	19	44
Miscellaneous dirty/outside jobs	36	8
Going on errands	39	21

Source: Newson, J., and others, 1978

MAINTENANCE

Within any society individuals have to find ways of providing food, warmth, clothing and shelter. It is often necessary to provide for workers and for the young and the old. Within economic systems

based on slavery, the employer takes responsibility for the maintenance of the worker. In the Israeli Kibbutz it is the responsibility of
the community. In most western societies, however, this function
falls upon the family. It is not a function which the family performs
without help. Here again the state supports the family in performing
its functions. Benefits such as Family Income Supplement and Child
Benefit are intended to help the family maintain its members.

SOCIAL PLACEMENT

The fourth function of the family is social placement. The family
plays an important role within the system of social stratification. As
we saw in Chapter 4 most people end their lives in a social class
position not very different from where they began. It is not just a
matter of being born into a particular family within a certain social
class. The family, through patterns of socialisation, also passes on
the attitudes, beliefs and knowledge which are typical of that social
class. This may consist of political attitudes as well as particular
knowledge and ways of behaving. Family background also influences
the other social groups to which the individual will belong including
sport and recreational activities, religious affiliation, and political
parties.

Although the role of the family has changed considerably in recent
years, and is still changing, the family still performs important functions for the wider society.

One-parent families

In 1971 single-parent families made up 8 per cent of all families with
dependent children. By 1981 the proportion had risen to nearly 12
per cent. The greatest increases occurred among those families in
which the parents were divorced and in the families of unmarried
mothers. Statistics of the number of single-parent families which
exist at any one point of time give a false impression of the real
effect of single parenthood. Such figures 'freeze' the action at a
single moment. They do not show the continuing sequence of
events. It is important to consider the single-parent family as one
stage in a wider process of family change.

There are many reasons why someone brings up a family on their
own. It is often a period between the ending of one marriage, either
through death or divorce, and the beginning of another. The
changes which lead to the formation and the ending of one-parent
families are shown in Figure 32. Being a single parent, or being part

Fig. 31. *One-parent and two-parent families (families with dependent children)*

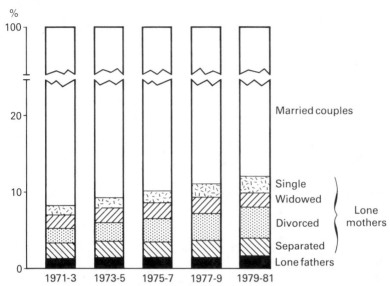

Source: *General Household Survey*

of a single-parent family, is something that many people pass through during their lifetime. The statistics do not show this 'moving picture' at all clearly. In sociological terms we would say that there is a lack of 'time series data', that is information which shows how families change over a period of time. It is, however, likely that as many as one in three children are likely to experience living with only one parent at some stage in their lives. It is important, therefore, to consider single-parenthood as one stage in a complicated process of beginning and ending families.

Although the majority of single parents are lone mothers there are an increasing number of lone fathers. On average lone fathers are older than lone mothers and they are more likely to be caring for older children. Whereas the average age for lone mothers is thirty-six the fathers are, on average, nearly ten years older. One third of lone mothers have a child under five years old compared to one in twenty of the lone fathers. This makes it more likely that lone fathers will be able to take on a full-time job. Their working hours are, in fact, similar to those of fathers in two-parent families.

In Figure 33 we can see some of the differences between single-parent families and families with two parents. Single parents tend to have fewer, and older children than two-parent families.

Fig. 32. *One-parent families*

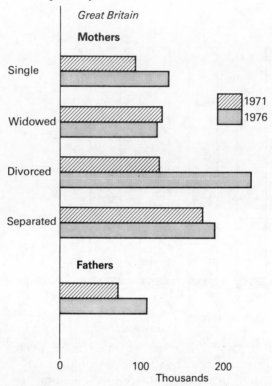

Great Britain

Source: Office of Population Censuses and Surveys

Single-parent families are more likely to be living in poverty, and the parents, particularly lone mothers, more likely to take lower paid work. One in two of lone mothers are likely to go out to work, slightly less than the proportion for married mothers, but they are more likely to be in full-time, rather than part-time jobs. In 1979, however, earnings were the main source of income for only 48 per cent of one-parent families compared to 95 per cent of two-parent families. Single parents are more likely to be dependent on state benefits. Although one-parent families make up only 12 per cent of all families they take up 40 per cent of Family Income Supplement.

Their housing conditions tend to be poorer with fewer amenities and are more likely to be overcrowded. Often single parents can only find suitable housing in the inner cities. In some inner London Boroughs one in three families are headed by a single parent. One in ten of lone mothers and one in three of unmarried mothers live

Fig. 33. *Beginning and ending one-parent families*

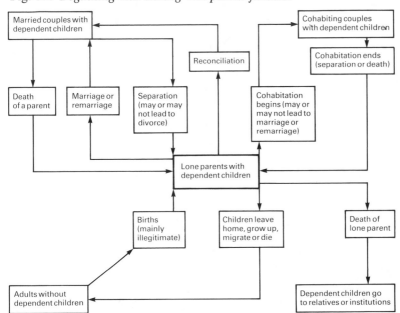

Source: R. Leete, *Population Trends 13*, 1978

with their own parents upon whom they often depend for child-minding in order to be able to go out to work.

Divorce

Before 1857 it was only possible to get a divorce by Act of Parliament. After the Matrimonial Causes Act of that year it was still only the husband who could petition for divorce, and then only on the grounds of his wife's adultery. A further Act of 1878 gave the wife the right to apply to the courts for a separation order on the grounds of her husband's cruelty but it was not until 1923 that husband and wife could sue for divorce on equal terms. In 1937 the grounds for which a divorce could be granted were extended to cover desertion and insanity as well as adultery and cruelty. In 1943 the first Divorce Court outside London was established.

CHANGES IN THE LAW

Immediately after the Second World War the demand for divorces rose rapidly. So great was the rise that special arrangements had to

141

Fig. 34. *Children in families*

(a) Number of children (%)

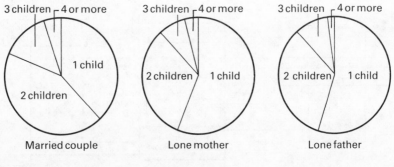

(b) Age of youngest child (%)

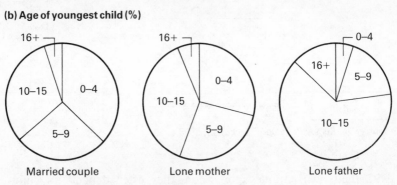

Source: General Household Survey 1981

be made to revise Divorce Court procedure and clear the backlog of cases. This took place in 1946 and 1947. The Matrimonial Causes Act of 1950 gathered all of the previous legislation under one Act of Parliament, and in the previous year, 1949, the Legal Aid and Advice Act had allowed the cost of divorce to be borne by the state under Legal Aid. By 1950 a divorce could be obtained anywhere in the country, by men and women of all classes on equal terms.

During the 1960s however, there was increasing concern about 'the grounds for divorce'. It was felt that if a marriage had obviously 'broken down', and there was no hope of a fresh start being made, a divorce should be granted whether or not adultery, cruelty, desertion or insanity were involved. This led eventually to the 1969 Divorce Law Reform Bill which gave 'irretrievable breakdown' as the only reason for granting a divorce.

This occurs when the couple have lived apart for at least two years and both agree to a divorce, or five years apart if only one partner

142

Fig. 35. *Divorce*

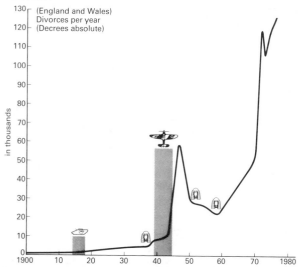

wants a divorce, in which case the court has to ensure that a divorced wife is adequately provided for. If the respondent has deserted the petitioner, without cause, for two years before the petition, or if, as the result of some action on the part of the respondent (including adultery), the petitioner can no longer be expected to continue living with the respondent, then a divorce would be granted. The courts are required to make every effort to get the husband and wife back together before granting a divorce. Courts are also able to ensure that proper arrangements are made for the care of any children of the marriage. As we can see from Fig. 35 the rise in divorces has not been smooth. A high level of divorces was reached at the end of the Second World War and it did not reach that figure again until the mid-1970s. A divorce trend such as this does not support the view that marriage as a whole is breaking down. Divorce rates are more closely tied to changes in the law, social upheavals and changed attitudes to divorce itself. When the Divorce Law is changed it is because society has changed its view of how unsatisfactory a marriage must become before the partners are allowed to part.

Marriage is, however, more popular than ever. People are marrying younger and more are choosing to get married. Combined with increased expectancy of life this means that there is more 'marriage' going on today than ever before. People expect more of their marriages today. Films, television, books, and magazines

143

increasingly tell people what they should expect from their marriage. Mass media provides a yardstick against which couples can measure the success of their marriage. It is not surprising that more decide that they have made a wrong choice.

Fig. 36. *Divorce by length of marriage 1981 (percentage)*

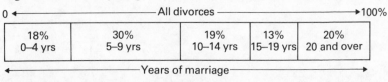

Source: Social Trends

Very often the increase in the number of divorces is used as evidence of the breakdown of family life in Britain. Such statements need to be looked at carefully: firstly very few divorced couples remain unmarried for very long. Re-marriages, after divorce or widowhood, made up nearly one-third of all marriages in 1976 and, as Fig. 29 shows, the proportion is rising. Divorce tells us more about a person's desire to have a good marriage than about any wish not to be married at all. Secondly, though most divorces do involve children, two out of every five do not involve children under the age of 16.

The greatest risk of divorce is within the first ten years of marriage and people who marry while they are still in their teens are

Fig. 37. *Children and divorce 1982*

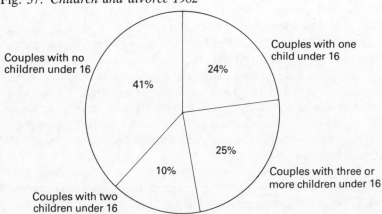

Source: Office of Population Censuses and Surveys

especially at risk. In 1977 12 per cent of all women married ten years earlier had divorced but for women who were married before their twentieth birthday it was closer to 19 per cent.

An increase in divorce rates indicates the greater strain put upon marriage today and people's desire to have a happy marriage even if it means a second or a third attempt.

8

Schooling

In Britain just about everybody spends some part of their life in school. It hasn't always been like that and it is not like that in every part of the world. Although there were schools in Britain long before the Industrial Revolution schooling as we know it today is a direct result of the development of industry and the growth of towns in the nineteenth century.

At first schools placed an emphasis on 'elementary' education which taught the basic skills of 'reading, writing and arithmetic', often known as the '3 R's'. The teaching of religion and moral values was also important. By the end of the nineteenth century elementary education was available for all children. It was free and compulsory. Secondary education, which developed more specialised knowledge and skills, was not available for all children until after the Education Act of 1944.

Schooling and education

We often confuse the words 'education' and 'schooling'. Although they are closely related they do not always mean the same thing. Education is a far broader concept than schooling. It refers to all of those experiences through which people learn. The family provides an important part of education, as do churches, youth clubs, evening classes and a whole range of other activities. Education need not even be confined to organised ways of learning. It would be quite reasonable for someone who has just returned from holiday to say that visiting another country was 'an education in itself'. Schooling on the other hand is concerned with a particular form of organised education. It is what goes on in institutions called schools. Sociologists use the word 'schooling' because it more accurately describes the main form of institutional education in industrial societies. Some people would say that education and schooling are quite different things. Deschoolers, like Paul Goodman and Ivan Illich, argue that what goes on in schools can never be real education. Illich has written that the school system rests upon the illusion that 'most learning is the result of teaching'. 'Teaching', he continues, 'may contribute to certain kinds of learning under certain circumstances. But most people acquire most of their knowledge outside of school'.

WHY DO WE HAVE SCHOOLS?

We can approach this question in three ways. Firstly, schools have a technical function within society and within the economy. The 'technical function' approach sees schooling as a bridge between the family and adult life, providing a training in the skills and attitudes necessary for employment and participation in a democracy. As well as providing the skills that are needed for people to start out on a career schools also provide qualifications and certificates which enable people to be directed into particular kinds of employment.

A second view focuses on the role of the school for the development of the individual. This is best seen in the 'progressive' approach to education which sees schooling as a time when the individual's true capabilities will develop. The headmaster of a primary school adopted this approach in an interview with some sociologists.

Care and concern shown to individual children . . . We are concerned as a general principle with trying to develop each child, and we would use Mathematics, or what could loosely be described as English, Art and everything else, to do this . . . You see, the aim is trying to develop a child and help him to mature and become a person rather than that he should be a good user of adjectives and a doer of multiplication sums . . . (Sharp and Green 1976)

These two approaches – the *technical function* view and the *progressive* view – are alternative ideologies of education. The ideological character of these two approaches is criticised by Marxist writers who see schooling as the way in which industrial societies pass on particular values and skills to each new generation and in so doing ensure the reproduction of capitalist modes of production. Marxists see schooling as an important part of the operation of the capitalist economy.

147

The development of English education

The history of schooling in England is the history of two types of education which grew up alongside one another throughout the nineteenth and twentieth centuries. One pattern of schooling developed for the sons of the middle- and upper-classes while a different pattern developed for children of the working-class. There had been schools in the Middle Ages but they were mainly monastery schools which trained priests. With the growth of towns in the fifteenth and sixteenth centuries schools were founded to serve the needs of the local merchants and businessmen. From the seventeenth century tutors and small private schools also provided an education for the sons of the middle-classes. For the children of the working people there were no such schools. Children learned in the home and on the job. A young man would learn a trade directly from a craftsman. Girls would learn from their mothers. At a time when the family was the main basis of production, either through farming or cottage industry, schools were not necessary. It is not until the very end of the eighteenth century that we can see the beginnings of mass schooling as we know it today. Whereas the first schools for the middle-classes were the local grammar schools which the middle-classes provided for themselves, the earliest schools for the working-class were Sunday Schools and schools provided by educational charities.

Robert Raikes, who founded the first Sunday Schools, was concerned at the mobs of young people who roamed the streets on their only 'day of rest' from the factories of Gloucester. Apart from keeping hooligans off the streets it was thought that such schools would also civilise the rabble by teaching morals and religion. The schools set up by the National Society and the British and Foreign Schools Society combined religious and moral education with training in work habits suited to factory industry. Discipline in these schools was firm. They were sometimes compared to 'grand intellectual factories'. The churches were at the centre of the spread of mass schooling in the early years of the nineteenth century. Although the State had provided financial help from the 1830s, schools were not provided by local School Boards, separate from the churches, until after the 1870 Education Act.

By 1925 the 'Board Schools' provided an elementary education for the majority of children. Some of the more able working-class children gained scholarships to local secondary grammar schools where they joined the children of those parents who could pay the fees. Finally, some children went to the separate fee-paying pre-

Fig. 38. *The tripartite system*

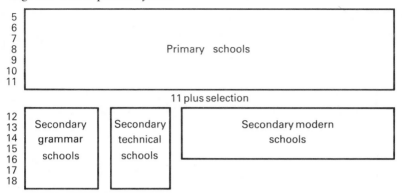

paratory schools and from there to the independent 'public' schools.

The separation of working-class and middle-class education continued into the tripartite system set up by the 1940 Education Act which established secondary education for all. The secondary modern schools and the secondary technical schools developed from the senior classes of the former elementary schools, now renamed primary schools, and from the central schools which had grown up in some areas. New secondary grammar schools were set up on the lines of the earlier grammar schools but without fees. Scholarships were replaced by the 11+ examination which became the basis for 'selection' to each type of school.

Private education in 'independent' schools continued. Many of the old 'grammar schools' remained outside of the state system and were now rather misleadingly called 'public schools'. The independent pattern of schooling consisted of preparatory schools taking children from 8 to 13. For the under 8's there were pre-preparatory schools. At 13+ children transferred to an independent secondary school or to a public school.

The comprehensive debate

Not everyone viewed the 1944 Education Act with approval. Some education authorities regarded the tripartite system as unsuitable for both practical and educational reasons and devised alternative schemes for their areas. Anglesey, for example, lacked both resources and children to provide three different types of secondary school, and instead introduced a system based on one 'comprehensive' school.

Fig. 39. *Comprehensive education*

(a) 11–18 comprehensive schools

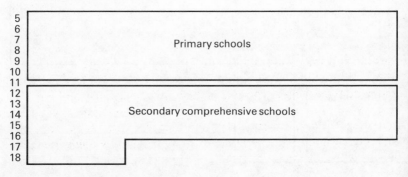

(b) Two – tier comprehensive schools

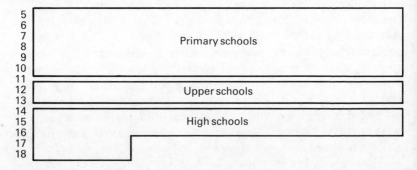

(c) Middle school system

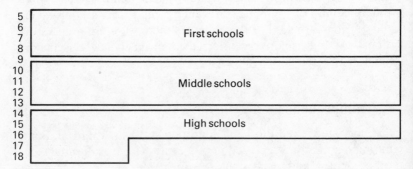

London, on different grounds, also rejected the tripartite system and produced a long-term plan for 'All-through' (11–18) schools. Leicestershire in 1957 introduced a further alternative form of 'comprehensive education': children went from the primary school, at eleven plus, to a high school, with the option of transferring to a grammar school if they wished at fourteen.

These alternative approaches to the problem of providing a secondary education suited to each child's age, aptitude and ability grew out of criticisms of the principles of the 1944 Act and the experience and evidence which was built up by sociologists and educators in the 1950s and 1960s. This resulted in the continuing debate about the best structure for secondary education. On one side were those who advocated 'comprehensive schools' and on the other were those who pressed the claims of the grammar schools. Because education is a matter for the state, involving large sums of government money and centralised administration by a government department, affecting the whole future development of British society, this debate has become an important issue for each of the main political parties.

The Conservative Party, on the whole, favours the arguments of those who wish to see grammar schools remain alongside other types of secondary school. The Labour Party, on the other hand, feels that it is wrong to divide children in this way and that the needs of society are best met by having one school, providing equal opportunities for all children of the same age.

The argument over the best way to organise schooling is a long and bitter one. The great majority of children today are educated in comprehensive schools of one type or another but a number of local education authorities still maintain their grammar schools.

Those who favour comprehensive schools point to the lack of precision in the process of eleven-plus selection. There is considerable disagreement among psychologists about the true meaning of 'intelligence', and as a result doubt arises whether it is possible to measure it. Similarly there is some doubt whether success or failure at eleven-plus has any bearing on how a child will develop. Many comprehensive schools can point to 'so-called' eleven-plus failures who did well at school and even went on to college or university, some to get first class honours degrees.

A third criticism concerns the unequal chances of children in different areas of the country. A survey by J. W. B. Douglas showed that one out of every three to four children living in Wales had the chance of a grammar school place compared to one in eight in southern England. There has also been criticism of the social effects of an education system which deliberately divides pupils.

On the other side those who wish to see grammar schools retained point to the academic record of such schools which they fear would be lost if they were merged into new 'non-selective' comprehensives,

151

to the need for the nation to educate the really able to be its leaders and innovators, to allow parents an element of choice in sending their children to school, and to allow local authorities to decide on the type of schooling best suited to the area without pressure from central government. The argument in favour of grammar schools is, at heart, an argument in support of tradition and the pursuit of excellence, both thought to be features of the grammar school system.

Education and equality

Those who favoured comprehensive schools, especially those who were within the Labour Party, expected that the end of the tripartite system would give more opportunities to working-class children and would end the 'wastage of talent'. The rapid spread of comprehensive schools in the 1970s did not achieve this goal. Working-class children continued to do less well at school and few went on to higher education.

The lessons to be learned from the development of comprehensive schooling are many. Although comprehensive schools, in some form

Table 25. *Staying on*

Occupation of Father	Percentage of 16-year olds at school	Percentage of 18-year olds in 6th form or Further Education
	%	%
Professional and Managerial	5	20
Intermediate	18	40
Skilled non-manual	10	12
Skilled Manual	39	18
Unskilled and semi-Skilled Manual	19	8
Others and don't know	9	2

Source: Adapted from D.E.S. '*16–18 year olds attitudes to education*', 1976.

or another, provide for the majority of children, there is no part of the country with schools that are fully comprehensive. All schools are 'creamed' in some way, either by parents choosing to send their children to private fee-paying schools, or by selective schools which compete with the comprehensive schools.

It has also become clear that changes in the organisation of the school system will not on their own lead to greater equality, either of opportunity or of outcome. Even where selection for secondary education has been ended there has been a continuation of selection within the secondary school. Streaming has been used to divide pupils into classes based on apparent differences of ability. It has not been unknown for comprehensive schools to have ten or more 'streams', each class supposedly more able than the one beneath. 'Banding' avoided the problem of separating pupils into many finely graded 'streams' by grouping classes into 'bands'. When this happened the top 'band' followed the more academic courses while the bottom band provided 'remedial' education. Many schools did, however, prefer to develop mixed-ability teaching in the lower years and in those subjects which did not require all pupils to progress at the same pace. 'Setting' is used to divide pupils up on the basis of their ability at a specific subject.

A comprehensive system of education could not work unless it was part of a society which was relatively equal. As long as there were different expectations of schools within different groups in society, or differences of opportunity for children with different backgrounds, the comprehensive system could not achieve the ambitions of those who fought for it. As Professor Basil Bernstein put it in 1969 'Schools cannot compensate for society'.

This debate over the best pattern of organisation of education is only one aspect of a far larger debate concerning equality within the educational system.

There are a number of different ways of using the word equality when considering education and schooling. One important area of concern has been with equality of opportunity.

In brief, the problem of equality of opportunity is how to provide every child in the country with an equal chance of going as far as his or her ability allows. In theory the 1944 Education Act provided an education suited to 'aptitude and ability' in which any child who had the ability could get to the top. Within ten years doubts were growing about the accuracy of this idea. The Early Leaving Report of 1954 showed that when working-class children were placed in the top ability group at grammar school they ended up doing, on average, less well than their middle-class classmates. They tended

153

either to leave before their exams or to do less well than would have been expected from knowledge of their abilities. In addition it was found that the higher up the education ladder a working-class child went the more were the odds stacked against him.

Interest centred on the relationship between social class and the education system, the extent to which 'education' is a middle-class activity and the way working-class children are denied opportunities to succeed.

An American sociologist, Ralph H. Turner, pictures the English system of education as a sort of private club. Those who are in a position of power in the club (Turner calls them an 'elite') choose those people who will be invited to join. Each new candidate needs to be sponsored and to possess the personal qualities which the 'elite' think new members ought to have. Turner compares this system to the American education system which is more like a race. Everyone starts off from the same point and runs until he can get no further. Those who have stayed in until the end are the winners. There may be rules of 'fair play' in the race but winning is open to all on the basis of ability and achievement. In the race or 'contest system' everyone knows the rules and the 'prize' is obtained by the contestant's own efforts. No one can hand out success in life. It has to be won. In the 'sponsored system' Turner believes that certain groups have the power to hand out success to people who possess certain qualities not connected with ability or achievement.

Turner's view looks at inequalities of access to different kinds of outcomes. There are also inequalities in what people bring with them into schooling, and inequalities in what is provided for them when they get there. It is wrong to think that schools are being fair if they treat everyone equally. Justice often involves treating unequals unequally. If a child has difficulty in learning to read you would expect the school to provide extra help. It would be wrong to consider inequalities of outcome without also considering inequalities of background or of provision. Tyler (1977) has listed types of educational inequality.

1. Inequality of achievement – which is based on how well you do at school.
2. Inequality of background based on your home, neighbourhood or culture.
3. Inequality of aptitude or ability based on those things that you are good at.
4. Inequality of school environment caused by differences in the resources provided.

5. Inequality of credentials occur when qualifications have different values.
6. Inequality of life chances brought about by differences in access to future possibilities.

The education debate

The development of comprehensive schooling is only one of the issues that have been at the forefront of educational debate within the last twenty years. The introduction of new teaching methods, raising the school leaving age, cut-backs in educational expenditure have all provoked fierce debate. The mass media has had an important role within such debates, often determining the key issues and shaping public opinion. The role of the media was central to the Great Debate initiated by Labour Prime Minister James Callaghan in his Ruskin College speech in October 1976.

In 1972 the Conservative government published a White Paper on Education. Its title 'Framework for Expansion' summed up the main educational concerns of the 1950s and 1960s. These had been times of growth and expansion. Rising birth rates had meant more and more children coming into the schools. People expected more from the schools and there was a general feeling that better education was essential if the nation was to succeed in the world. Increased national expenditure on education was seen as an investment in the future. The 1972 White Paper, however, marked the end of an era of educational expansion, not the beginning.

As education took up increasing amounts of the national wealth politicians began to question whether or not it was money well spent. Was the high level of expenditure leading to higher standards and better qualifications? In particular there was anxiety about progressive teaching methods and school discipline. These anxieties were brought together in a series of Black Papers published by the right-wing opponents of the current trends. The key themes of falling standards, poor discipline and the dangers of progressive, or child-centred, teaching methods were picked up by the mass media in headlines such as 'Infant muggers' and 'Crisis in the Classroom'. Each new item of educational news was made to fit these dominant themes. If the evidence did not support the media's views it was scorned as being 'out of touch with reality' or it was used selectively to support a particular belief. The important 1975 Bullock Report on the teaching of English was described by one newspaper as 'whitewash' which 'shrouded reality in trendy pieties'. In a similar way the research by Neville Bennett into the effects of different

155

styles was used to support the general view that progressive teaching was educationally unsound. A view not supported by the research itself.

The so-called crisis reached a peak in 1975 with the events at William Tyndale Junior School in London. The teachers at William Tyndale had adopted a style of teaching which aimed at allowing the children as much freedom as possible in organising their own learning. This led to a direct conflict with some of the parents, with the school managers and eventually with the Local Education Authority. The national press saw these events as further confirmation of the crisis which, it was claimed, affected the nation's schools.

Whether or not there was such a crisis was, in the end, not particularly important. The fact that people believed there was a crisis and that the mass media kept telling them that there was one was quite enough to force the government to take action. This led the Labour government under James Callaghan to respond to the popular pressure by calling for the 'Great Debate' on education and by publishing a consultative Green Paper on 'Education in Schools'.

By the end of the 1970s the major issues in education had changed considerably from those of the 1960s. The political pressure of the 'Great Debate', a growth in youth unemployment, falling birth rates and cut-backs in government expenditure on education combined to produce a new set of educational issues. 'Standards', 'account-ability', 'parental choice' and 'firm discipline' were established at the centre of educational discussion. Government policies reflected these concerns. The 1980 Education Act allowed for greater parental choice of schools. The publication of examination results created a pressure on schools to justify their performance. Increased state help was given to independent schools through the Assisted Places Scheme. At each stage educational policy was justified by reference to 'what everyone knows about the problems in our schools'. Yet what everyone 'knew' about the schools was shaped by the mass media, often on the basis of very limited evidence.

Pupils and teachers

So far in this chapter we have considered education in terms of the organisation of schooling. A 'macro' view has been taken looking at education on a large scale. Sociologists are also interested in 'micro' issues in schooling. Instead of looking at schools as a whole, they examine what happens in classrooms when teachers and pupils interact. If you were a stranger who had never seen a school class-room before the first thing you would notice is the number of people crowded into it. An infant classroom may contain as many as forty children and a number of adults. A secondary school classroom would normally have between twenty and thirty people in it. Coping with crowds is a fact of life for the teachers. They employ all sorts of strategies to help them cope. Their problem is that they have not only to control the crowd but also teach them something. There are many strategies that teachers use and as many pupil strategies also. Humour is a strategy used by both teachers and pupils. Pupils appreciate teachers who can share a joke but they can also use jokes as a way of getting at the teacher. When Peter Woods asked a non-examination group about their likes and dislikes they grouped teachers into four categories:

1. Those that keep you working.
2. Those you can laugh and joke with.
3. Those you can work and have a laugh with.
4. Those that just don't bother.

Anne, Jane and Deidre gave an example of the difference between teachers in categories 1 and 3:

> Anne: Oh yeah, they'd do anything to make him laugh. He puts them into the report book and everything. They don't care.
>
> Deidre: He put one girl in twice in one day. They do it on purpose. If he was more friendly with them like Mr. Lennox is, 'cos he'll have a laugh with you.
>
> Jane: You see, he won't smile and have a laugh wth you like Mr. Lennox will.
>
> Deidre: 'Cos we can have a joke with him can't we?
>
> Jane: Yeah, and we work as well, but in there they play about and don't do any work.
> (Woods, P. 1976)

There are many other strategies teachers use in order to control the crowd and get them to learn and many strategies pupils use to disrupt the process. However, sociologists are not only interested in how teachers and pupils behave. Their attitudes and the way in which they view schooling are also important.

TEACHER EXPECTATIONS

An important part of the interaction that takes place in classrooms is the expectation that teachers and pupils have of one another. What teachers expect and how they 'label' pupils can have an influence on behaviour and learning. This was examined by Rosenthal and Jacobson in their study of 'Pygmalion in the Classroom'.

The children in an elementary school in San Francisco were given an intelligence test. Following the test the researchers drew up a list of pupils who, they claimed, were likely to make the greatest progress over the next eight months. This list was given to the teachers. In fact the names on the list had been chosen at random and there was no evidence to suggest that the children were any different from their classmates. At the end of the eight months all of the pupils were re-tested. Those on the list did better than the other children.

This research led to claims that the teachers' expectations were the main cause of the different levels of achievement. Later research showed that it was not quite as simple as Rosenthal and Jacobson thought. It has been shown that teachers treat pupils differently if they think they are clever. Teachers also treat girls differently from boys, working-class pupils differently from middle-class pupils and black pupils differently from white pupils. A teacher asks different kinds of questions, encouraging some pupils to think out reasons while others are only expected to remember a right answer. Some pupils may be asked more questions or given more help with the answer.

It would be wrong, however, to think that teachers have complete control over who learns. Pupils do not have to accept labels given them by teachers nor will they always respond in the same way. Labels are more likely to be accepted if the pupil accepts the teacher as a person whose opinions are to be accepted and if the labelling occurs frequently. A label is more likely to be accepted if others – friends, other teachers and parents – also support the labelling and if the labelling is done publicly. There is no reason why a particular label should lead to particular kinds of behaviour. A pupil may be labelled a 'trouble-maker' or a 'dunce'. That labelling could lead to more trouble-making or lower achievement. It may, however, lead the pupil to change his or her ways, to stop causing trouble or to work harder and achieve more. It is also possible for the pupil to ignore the labelling, to claim that 'it doesn't really matter'.

Schools can influence the pupil's pattern of achievement in other ways than by labelling. Each individual's school life is marked by a number of decisions: which school to go to?, which subject to take?, which exam?, to leave or stay on? Sometimes these are open decisions with any number of alternatives. Sometimes the decision is limited by the options available. Very often the school provides 'guided choice' in which the teachers can influence the final decision. The selection of option choices in the fourth year of the secondary school is an example of an occasion when such decisions are made. Studies of option choices show that choosing is fairer for some pupils than others. For an able child there is a choice of subjects that he or she could do, or may want to do. For the less able it is often a matter of rejecting those subjects that he or she can't or doesn't want to do. The advice of teachers will often direct pupils into particular pathways. This directing of pupils into or away from particular subjects is based on ideas of 'appropriateness'. Stephen Ball in his study of Beachside Comprehensive (1981) quotes the Head of Human Studies:

> There are three sink subjects, Creative Arts and Crafts, Human Studies and Modern Applications of Science which are eight periods each week, which attract the remedials; they only skim the material, which is all they can manage really; they are now open to other pupils but most of them are remedials. (Ball 1981)

Cicourel and Kitsuse in their study of this process at work in an American High School referred to it as 'tracking'. Pupils are directed towards particular tracks and once there their future choices are more limited.

The problem of knowledge

Knowledge and schooling are often tied together in our minds. If anyone asked you what school was for, you would probably say something about 'knowing things' or 'getting knowledge'. But what is the knowledge we get at school, what use is it and who decides it should be there?

The world is full of knowledge and it grows more every month and every year. The encyclopaedias in a library are packed full of knowledge and there is even more knowledge which cannot be squeezed into them. In universities there are even bigger libraries with even more books packed full of even more knowledge. If you went to school for every day of your life you could never hope to learn everything that there is to know. The knowledge you get at school is a selection from that vast stock of knowledge in the world. School knowledge is not only selected, it is also organised. Encyclopaedias have a way of organising knowledge. They do it alphabetically, starting at 'A' and going through to 'Z'. In schools knowledge is organised into subjects. This organisation of subjects in a school is known as 'the curriculum'. Fig. 40 shows you a typical fourth year curriculum in a secondary school.

159

Fig. 40. *A school curriculum*

A 3 classes	English	Mathematics	French or German or History	Physics or Biology or Economics	Chemistry or Geography or Biology	Art or Metalwork or Home Economics or Sociology	Latin or Chemistry or Music	Period Education		PE
B 3 classes	English	Mathematics	French or History or Social Studies	Science or Business Studies or Technical Drawing	Geography or Commerce or Rural Studies	Art or Metalwork or Home Economics	Woodwork or Needlework	Tutorial	Religious	Games and
C 2 classes	English	Mathematics	Social Education	Office Skills or Rural Studies or Catering	General Science or Art	Woodwork or Metalwork or Home Economics	History or Geography			

(Time scale across the top: 0 2 4 6 8 10 12 14 16 18 20 22 24 26 28 30 32 34)

In school the organisation of knowledge can be seen in the school timetable. The timetable gives a certain amount of time to each subject. If you look at the timetable you will see three things: Firstly, it does not include every possible subject. Few schools would include pharmacology or archaeology on their timetables though bits of them may be squeezed into other subjects. Secondly, different subjects do not receive equal amounts of time in the week. For example, English and mathematics usually receive more time than music and history. Thirdly, some subjects are taken by everybody, and are therefore compulsory, while others are only taken by some. This selection of who-takes-what may involve choice on the part of the student or it may involve decisions by those who run the school.

Your school timetable may also show some areas where subjects are not kept apart, where the boundaries between subjects are blurred. Integrated studies or Humanities are examples of the breaking down of subject boundaries. You may also notice that the amount of choice and compulsion, the type of subjects taken and the amount of time spent on certain subjects differs between different groups.

Some of these differences can be seen in Fig. 40 which shows a secondary school curriculum. This is not a timetable. It only shows the subjects available and the amount of time given to them. It does not show when pupils will study these subjects during the week. This school's fourth year is arranged in three blocks. The cleverest children are in block A. The slowest in block C. Each block has certain subjects of its own. Only block A has German, Latin or physics, block B has business studies and commerce and block C has social education. The block A subjects are more 'academic' and have clearer boundaries whereas block B and C have 'practical' subjects and more integration. In general terms block A has more of the 'high-status' subjects – French and German, Latin, physics, chemistry and biology – while block C gets 'low-status' subjects. For example block C has 'office skills' where block A has 'economics' and 'general science' instead of separate physics, chemistry and biology. Fig. 40 gives us a very simplified picture of the school curriculum. Your school may use a far more complicated pattern. The main features of Fig. 40 are likly to be found in many schools.

1. School subjects can be divided into high- and low-status subjects. High-status subjects are:
   (a) more specialised
   (b) more academic or theoretical
   (c) more traditional

   Low-status subjects are likely to be:
   (a) more general
   (b) more practical
   (c) vocational, or 'job-centred'.
2. There is a wider choice and less compulsion in the more able 'blocks'.
3. Pupils placed in particular blocks are directed towards certain careers or occupations.

To get an even better view of school knowledge you can look at the syllabuses for particular subjects. For example you could compare G.C.S.E. Social Science with G.C.E. A-level Sociology. How far are the differences between them based on differences in their difficulty rather than differences in the kind of knowledge they contain?

It should by now be clear that we cannot consider the selection of knowledge to be taught in schools separately from matters of status and power in schools. School curricula and syllabuses are the result of decisions made by individuals who have the power to make such decisions. They are also decisions which affect the way others learn, and in the end affect how they see themselves and the world. We have already seen that such views can be termed ideological because they support particular groups who have power. Decisions about school knowledge are, in the last resort, political decisions.

THE POLITICS OF SCHOOL KNOWLEDGE

Who decides about school knowledge and what influences their decision? Obviously teachers are involved. Although the teachers plan what happens in the lessons it would be wrong to assume that they have complete control. Schools have a number of levels of authority – heads of department, faculty-heads, curriculum co-ordinators, head teachers and their deputies – each having some influence over areas of the school's work. Beyond them are the local inspectors or advisers, the school governors, the Education Officer and the local Education Committee. In addition there are the civil servants at the Department of Education and Science in London and Her Majesty's Inspectors (H.M.Is.) As well as this network of authority there are examination boards, teachers' unions, parents and employers, newspapers and television each influencing what goes on in school in some way.

The question 'who decides what and why?' is therefore difficult to answer. The teacher or the headmaster who is at the centre of all of these influences has to decide, but the decision is likely to be affected in some way by wider social pressures. In society there is general agreement among most of these groups about what school should be doing. It is only when these groups disagree that conflict results. When the teachers at William Tyndale Junior School tried to change the way children learned and challenged the generally held views about schooling they were suspended and eventually dismissed. In nearly all schools, however, there is agreement about what schools should do and what knowledge is important.

Of course, this agreement is not always shared by everyone, as Fig. 41 shows. Eighty-nine per cent of the parents of 16-year-old school leavers interviewed said that to get a young person 'as good a job or career as possible' was an important aim for the school. Only 28 per cent of headmasters agreed. Ninety-six per cent of headmasters claimed that 'personality and character' were important whereas only 56 per cent of parents agreed with them. Parents, however, probably have less influence over schools than anyone and their views do not carry so much weight as those of headmasters and inspectors. The kind of schooling we have does depend on some sort of general agreement, or consensus. Without it schooling would be almost impossible. It affects not only what is taught but how it is taught and it provides reasons for 'why it is taught'. However, even though there is agreement amongst those who have the power to influence what happens in school, it does not answer our basic question of why certain things are taught in certain ways. Why is it that certain types of knowledge are more highly valued than others? The reasons are partly historical. The basis of the present day education system was laid over a hundred years ago at a time when English society was very different. The 'high-status' subjects of today are

Fig. 41. *What parents and headmasters think is important at school*

(a)

Parents of Boy 15 year old leavers

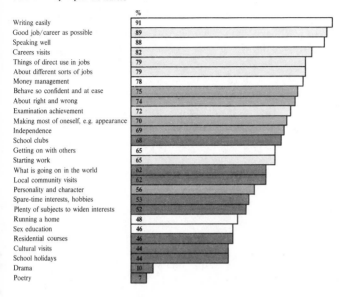

	%
Writing easily	91
Good job/career as possible	89
Speaking well	88
Careers visits	82
Things of direct use in jobs	79
About different sorts of jobs	79
Money management	78
Behave so confident and at ease	75
About right and wrong	74
Examination achievement	72
Making most of oneself, e.g. appearance	70
Independence	69
School clubs	68
Getting on with others	65
Starting work	65
What is going on in the world	62
Local community visits	62
Personality and character	56
Spare-time interests, hobbies	53
Plenty of subjects to widen interests	52
Running a home	48
Sex education	46
Residential courses	46
Cultural visits	44
School holidays	44
Drama	10
Poetry	7

(b)

Headmasters

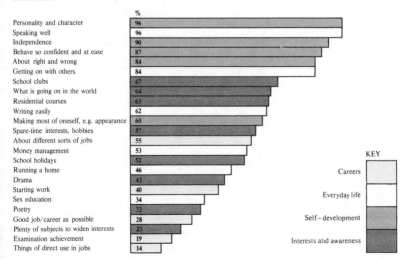

	%
Personality and character	96
Speaking well	96
Independence	90
Behave so confident and at ease	87
About right and wrong	84
Getting on with others	84
School clubs	67
What is going on in the world	64
Residential courses	63
Writing easily	62
Making most of oneself, e.g. appearance	60
Spare-time interests, hobbies	57
About different sorts of jobs	55
Money management	53
School holidays	52
Running a home	46
Drama	43
Starting work	40
Sex education	34
Poetry	32
Good job/career as possible	28
Plenty of subjects to widen interests	23
Examination achievement	19
Things of direct use in jobs	14

KEY

Careers

Everyday life

Self-development

Interests and awareness

Source: Schools Council Enquiry One: *The Young School Leaver* (H.M.S.O. 1968)

those which were found in the universities and public schools of the late nineteenth century.

The differences in the curriculum of blocks A, B and C in Fig. 40 are very close to the differences between the education provided for the aristocracy, for the merchants and industrialists; and for the factory workers a century ago. Ideas about what schooling ought to be like are very firmly rooted in people's minds. Schools have a habit of reproducing themselves in each generation. Remember that today's teachers were yesterday's pupils. This does not mean that schools do not change but that they change very slowly. But it is not enough just to say that schools teach the things they do teach because they have always done the same. That is not the whole answer. Schools teach particular subjects in particular ways because that is what society at large expects. School knowledge is the knowledge that people in society have come to expect schools to be handing on.

Education for girls

We can see how schools reflect the ideas and values of the wider society if we look at the education of girls. On the surface girls are educated in much the same way as boys. They go to the same, or similar, schools, have the same teachers and much the same choice of lessons. This measured intelligence is very similar yet out of these basic similarities important differences appear.

Girls take different subjects from boys. They do less well at things like maths or science. They go into different jobs. In 1970 42·3 per cent of boys took apprenticeships leading to skilled jobs. Only 7·1 per cent of girls did the same and most of these went into basically female-oriented occupations like hairdressing and tailoring.

Women were also less likely to make a career in any of the professions except for jobs like teaching and nursing which are thought to be women's jobs.

Girls are, throughout their lives, expected to behave differently to boys. A fourteen-year-old girl described it in the following way in a social studies lesson:

Children learn how they are different from one another by the way their parents and friends talk about them: Example – 'Oh what a sweet little girl you have and so pretty, does she help you round the house?' 'What a rascal of a son you have, always getting into mischief. Oh well I'd worry and think there was something wrong with him if he didn't.' (Sharpe 1976)

Fig. 42. *Exam subjects*

Subjects dominated by girls (each sex as % of total entry, 1982)

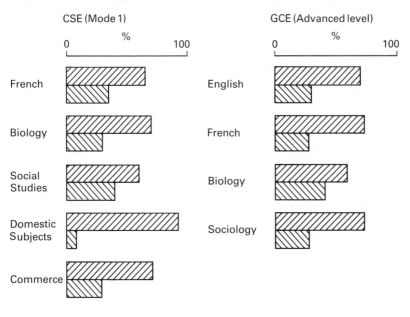

Subjects dominated by boys

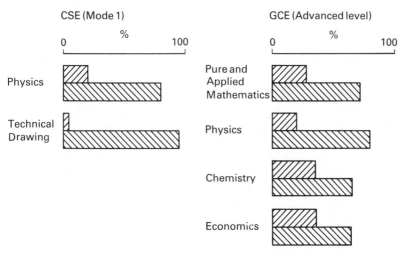

Key

Girls Boys

Source: Education Statistics 1983

165

Table 26. *Women in the professions*

	% of all in profession.
Architects (1973)	5·8
Chartered accountants (1976)	2·3
Solicitors (1975)	5·2
Professional engineers	0·5
University professors	1·7

These different expectations are continued in advertisements which show women as fun-loving, always smiling, always beautiful and perfectly groomed to please their men; in comics which portray Dr John and Nurse Susan; in children's reading books and on films and television. This view of women which puts them second to men in nearly everything that matters has in the past reflected in official statements about girls' education.

The Newsom Report in 1963 stated:

The domestic crafts start with an inbuilt advantage. They are recognisably part of adult living. Girls know that, whether they marry early or not, they are likely to find themselves making and running a home.

In a slightly different way a Schools Council booklet on the needs of disadvantaged children suggests that self confidence can be developed:

when older secondary school girls (and why not sometimes boys?) are involved in the care of pre-school children. (Schools Council 1970)

Statements like these can be supported in two ways. The first argument stresses the biological differences between males and females. Differences in achievement between boys and girls and differences in the education they receive are, it is claimed, caused by innate differences between the sexes. This point of view sees girls as being in some way limited by their sex. Rarely is it suggested that it might be the boys who are limited. The argument breaks down when differences between girls as a group and boys as a group are compared to differences between individual boys or girls. The differences of ability between different boys and between different girls are far greater than differences between the sexes. If differences are 'biological' then we would expect them to be shared by all females of the human species throughout the world – and they are not. In other countries women do all of the jobs that men do in Britain. This is not to say that males and females are not biologically different but the differences are not important when it comes to education or jobs.

The second argument stresses differences in the life styles and careers of girls. Differences in what women do at home and at work now are used as reasons for continuing to educate girls to do those jobs in the future. This point of view fails to recognise the need for women's roles to change. These two points of view lead to a pattern of schooling which either sees girls as (a) lacking something that boys have got and therefore in need of special treatment to make them more equal or (b) a different kind of human being in need of a different kind of education. A third approach to the education of girls is to see boys and girls as having similar needs, similar hopes and aspirations and similar opportunities.

The problem for the sociologist is to discover how far this third alternative is being achieved. There are some signs that girls are catching up. In school subjects like mathematics, physics, chemistry and economics where boys have been the majority of G.C.E. 'O' level candidates, the increase in the number of girls gaining passes has been greater than the increase of boys. But important differences still remain and though most schools recognise the need for equal opportunities there is still a strongly held belief that girls need to be educated differently. Such a belief is not confined to the schools. It is often shared by employers, parents and the girls themselves. When boys leave school they expect to have a good job or a career to go into. When girls were asked about their careers they replied,

'It's a bit hard to combine a career and marriage'.

'A person who does full time . . . I don't think should have children anyway as it would interfere with her career'.

'Career girls are girls who don't want to get married'.

'I think men should have careers. If girls want to they can but I think it suits men really'. (Sharpe 1976)

The problem of changing the way girls are educated is not just a problem for the school. The way girls are educated reflects the dominant attitudes towards women in the wider society. In considering the question – Why do schools do what they do? – we cannot separate schooling from the attitudes and beliefs of society as a whole.

9

Work and Industry

To the economist work is part of the process of production and the creation of wealth within society. To the sociologist, however, work is viewed as an activity which has an influence on social life. How people earn their living forms the basis for differences of class, status and power. It is also linked to differences in attitudes and social behaviour. People do not only go to work to earn a living. Work gives people status and provides an important part of their daily lives. Asking a child 'What do you want to be when you grow up?', or saying to someone 'What do you do?' indicates the importance we attach to work. To be unemployed means more than just not having a job. People who are unemployed often feel that they are in some way failing to contribute to society, as though there is something morally wrong in not working. This *work ethic* is an important part of our culture and is closely linked to our ideas about ourselves, our roles and status in society.

Before the Industrial Revolution it was much more difficult to separate that part of our lives we might call 'work' from that part that we might call 'home' or 'family'. We have already seen how people's work and family lives were closely linked within domestic economy. The coming of the factory at the end of the eighteenth century separated work from other areas of life. With the development of factory industry people had to leave their homes and 'go out to work'. The factory workers became employees. They sold their labour power to the factory owners in return for wages. The factory workers could not work at home because they no longer owned the machinery that was needed to produce the goods. Work became an activity which occupied separate amounts of time for which the worker was paid a sum of money. With this money he, or she, was able to buy those things necessary to live. As we saw in Chapter 7 the family changed from a *unit of production* to a *unit of consumption*.

The coming of the factory also changed the character of work.

Within domestic economy the worker would follow the process of production through from the earliest stages to the finished product. In the factory the worker was very unlikely to have very much contact with the finished article. The workers could no longer see the results of their labour. They were separated, or *alienated* from the end-results of their labour. Work came to be seen as something that you did to earn a wage.

The changing economy

During the last fifty years there has been a number of very important changes in the British economy. Firstly, there have been changes in the types of industry within which people work. Many of those industries which were important at the end of the nineteenth century declined and new industries took their place. Coal, iron and steel, shipbuilding and textiles, for example, had all begun to decline by the early part of the twentieth century and their place was taken by new industries such as motor vehicles, electrical engineering and chemicals.

Secondly, although the new industries very often took the place of the older industries they did not need as many workers. Whereas the old industries had tended to be *labour intensive*, in that they used large numbers of workers, the new industries were *capital intensive*, using machines which were part of the *capital* of the industry. A third development was the decline in importance of manufacturing industry and the expansion of tertiary industry. Primary industry produces raw materials through argriculture or by mining. Secondary industry is concerned with the production of manufactured goods – such as motor cars and television sets – from those raw materials. The third area is described as *tertiary industry* and is concerned not with producing goods but with providing services. The tertiary sector of the economy includes banks, shops, cinemas, roadsweepers, school teachers and many other aspects of daily life. In the last fifty years there has been a steady growth in the tertiary, or service, sector of the economy. An important part of this rise in the importance of services has been the growth of the public sector, that is those services provided by the state and by local authorities. Employment in public services rose until the late 1970s and then began to fall.

A fourth change in the economy has been the increase in the size of firms and businesses. The major part of the British economy is privately owned. The shares in the ownership of these firms may be bought and sold on the Stock Exchange. Large firms will often buy

Fig. 43. *Employees in major industries (UK)*

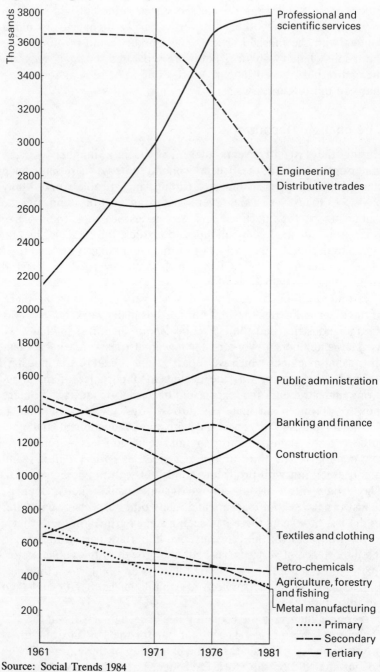

Source: Social Trends 1984

170

the shares in a smaller or weaker firm in order to gain control. Such mergers and take-overs have meant that the number of small, often family-run, businesses has declined and there has been an increase in the number of very large firms. Very often these larger firms had interests which extended far beyond the initial concerns of the business. Firms have tended to *diversify* as they moved into new areas of activity which enabled them to spread their interests and become involved in a number of different markets.

These larger corporations are less likely to be controlled by family interests and more likely to be run by professional managers. The process of amalgamation also meant that there was an increase in the average size of the plant in which people worked. Many industries are, or have been, state owned. These industries too were involved in this process of amalgamation.

Table 27. *The size of manufacturing plants 1979*

Factories employing:	*Number of factories*	*Total number of employees per factory (thousands)*	*Average No. of employees per factory (thousands)*
less than 20 people	80 921	553·7	6·84
20–49 people	16 847	515·8	30·61
50–99 people	8482	594·0	70·30
100–199 people	5821	814·7	139·95
200–499 people	4339	1330·1	306·54
500–999 people	1408	968·6	687·92
more than 1000 people	908	1969·5	2169·05

Source: Adapted from *Annual Abstract of Statistics* 1984

A fifth change has been the increase in the speed of the development of new technology. This has led not only to completely new industries but also to completely new methods of production within the existing industries. Fully automated production lines, robots, word processors and, above all, computers have changed the shape of industry throughout the world, having an effect on social as well as economic aspects of life.

Unemployment

In the United Kingdom unemployment has been rising since the 1960s. The period following the Second World War was a time of unusually high employment. In the early part of this century a shortage of jobs was often hidden by the effects of war and the high unemployment of the 1930s only came down with the beginning of the Second World War. The rise in unemployment from the 1960s began slowly. Figure 44 shows how at first there was a period of rises and falls with the peak of each rise and the trough of each fall being a little higher than the one which preceded it leading to the sharp rise in unemployment in the 1980s.

CAUSES OF UNEMPLOYMENT

Rises in unemployment can be caused by a number of things. There are always some people who are out-of-work while they are changing jobs. This is called *frictional* unemployment and probably provides no more than 2 per cent of the total. Other workers are unemployed at certain times of the year. There are many jobs which are only required in the summer months, or around Christmas. Fewer workers are required in the building trade, for example, during the winter months when it is more difficult to work outside.

Fig. 44. *Unemployment in Britain 1901–1984*

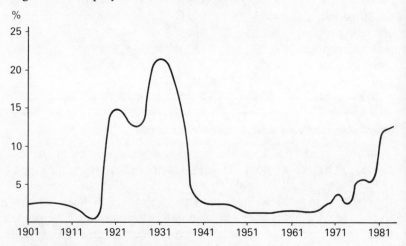

(Note: The method of calculating unemployment statistics changed in 1983 reducing the total of recorded unemployment after that date)

Sources: European Historical Statistics 1750–1970, Annual Abstract of Statistics 1984, Economic Trends October 1984

This is *seasonal* unemployment. The third type of unemployment is caused by changes in the level of activity within the economy over a short period of time. Production, trade, output, spending and other economic factors do not remain at the same level for very long. They change; sometimes rising, sometimes falling. This is sometimes known as the 'trade cycle'. Downturns of the trade cycle are the cause of *cyclical* unemployment. The final cause of unemployment is change in the structure of the economy. This is termed *structural* unemployment. The changes brought about by the development of new technology lead to structural unemployment.

Production

The earliest forms of production were based on individual craftsmen. These skilled workers would carry out all of the processes that would turn the raw materials into the finished article. A potter would shape a pot on a wheel, decorate it, glaze it and probably even sell it to the customer. Craftsmen are still important in many trades today. Traditionally, the craftsman carried out his trade with the simplest tools. A modern craftsman uses machines to produce the finished article. This is, however, different from the way machines might be used in other forms of production. The factories which developed during the Industrial Revolution used machines in a different way. They used machines to do many of the things previously done by the craftsman. The machines were faster, producing more than was possible with craft methods and they could be operated by people who were less skilled. Gradually the machines came to replace the craftsmen.

MASS PRODUCTION

Machines provided a basis for the beginnings of *mass production*. They made it possible to produce very large numbers of identical items more cheaply than was possible through craft methods. In machine production the various stages in the manufacture of a product would be separated and each would be done by a different machine. The various components would eventually come together to be assembled.

Assembly can take place in various ways. It can be organised around a stationary product which is gradually built up from the various parts. Ships and airliners, racing bicycles and car gearboxes are built in this way. In modern mass production the various processes are often laid out in a line and a conveyor belt moves the

173

Fig. 45. *Layout of a car assembly plant*

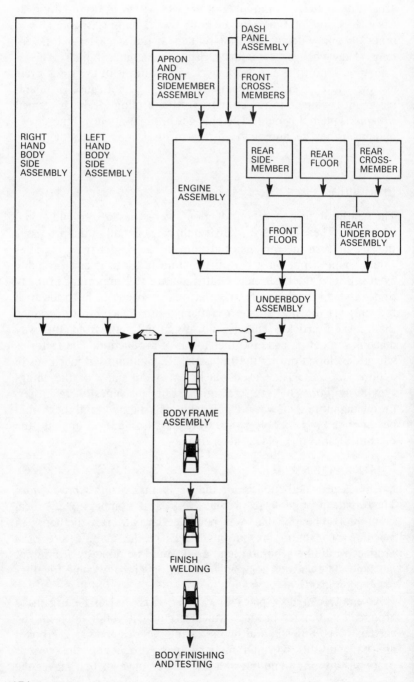

product along from stage to stage. This is the basis for assembly line production.

Assembly lines are used to make anything from chocolate biscuits to fork-lift trucks. Huw Beynon describes the Ford Motor Company's assembly line at Halewood:

> Working in a car plant involves coming to terms with the assembly line. 'The line never stops', you are told. 'Why not?' . . . 'don't ask. It *never* stops'. The assembly plant itself is huge and on two levels, with the paint shop on the one floor and the trim and assembly departments below. The car shell is painted in the paint shop and passed by lift and conveyor to the first station of the trim assembly department. From this point the body is carried up and down the 500-yard length of the plant until it is finally driven off, tested, and stored in the car park.
>
> Few men see the cars being driven off the line. While an assembly line worker is always dealing with a moving car it is never moving under its own steam. The line – or 'the track' as some . . . refer to it – stands two feet above the floor and moves the cars monotonously, easily along . . . This is the world of the operator. In and out of the cars, up and over the line, check the line speed and the model mix. Your mind restlessly alert, because there's no guarantee that the next car will be the same as the last. (Huw Beynon 1975)

Assembly line production is used when a fairly standard product has to be built up from a number of different parts. In modern assembly lines the 'putting together' is done by robots rather than people. When using assembly line methods the manufacturer needs to be able to produce very large numbers of similar products. When this is not possible 'batch production' may be used with a 'batch' of one product being produced before switching to a batch of another product. Another method of production is used when raw materials are transformed into a finished product through a continuous process. Turning crude oil into petrol, or sand and potash into glass, can best be done through some form of process production. These processes are often carried out automatically within machines in giant processing plants which require very few workers. Men and women are only required to supervise and control the process and to maintain the plant.

AUTOMATION

Modern factories use computers to control production. Robots carry out the various tasks previously performed by human beings. An

175

article in an American trade magazine describes how the production of components for aircraft can be totally automatic.

Your first impression when you view the McDonnell Douglas parts fabrication plant in St. Louis is the sheer size and loneliness of it all. Some two dozen acres of milling machines noisily grind grooves, slots, and intricate patterns in airframe parts to a tolerance of 0.0025 inch. The machines for the most part, work alone – watched only by a few men who glance occasionally at a control panel or sweep the cuttings.

Nor are these men in charge here. The machine tools are directed by numerical controllers, which are in turn directed by a whole hierarchy of computers presided over by a master computer. This 750 000 sq. ft aircraft parts plant is among the most advanced computer-aided manufacturing factories in the world. But it is far from unusual. Highly automated plants elsewhere in the US, Japan, and Europe turn out automobiles, engines, earthmovers, oilwell equipment, elevators, electrical products and machine tools. These plants are well on their way to evolving into what has been a dream for two decades: the automated factory. (Neil Ruzic 1978)

To understand why technology changes we need to understand why people produce things. Factory owners produce goods which can be sold in order to make profits. We would normally call the producer a firm or a business. Production is based on four 'factors of production'. These are land, labour, capital and enterprise. Land can mean the land upon which the factory is built or, more importantly, the raw materials used in production. Labour is the effort applied by workers, the labour force, in order to produce goods from the raw materials. Capital is those things, such as factories and machines, in which the owners of the business have invested their money so that they can produce the goods. Enterprise is the means whereby the firm is organised and directed.

Firms produce goods at lower prices than their competitors in order to make greater profits. The price of a product depends on the price paid for the raw materials, to which must be added the costs of labour and capital, in the form of factories and machines. There will also be distribution costs, costs for advertising and profits for the retailers. The cost of labour is a large part of the manufacturer's total costs. If the costs of labour can be reduced then the firm can reduce the price of its product and compete more effectively.

As the employer cannot normally cut wages in order to reduce the price of the product other ways of reducing labour costs must be found. One way would be by increasing *productivity*. This means that each worker must produce more goods in the same time while receiving the same, or only slightly more, in wages. A second way of reducing labour costs would be to reorganise the way the job is done so that it can be carried by less skilled workers who can be paid less. Instead of one worker making a complete article the process of production will be broken down into a number of stages. Each stage will be given to a different worker who becomes skilled at performing just that stage in the process. This is known as the *division of labour*. We have already seen that in modern industry the division of labour is very considerable. The division of labour often involves *deskilling* and the replacement of human power with machine power. Machines produce goods with fewer workers and carry out the more difficult jobs which would previously have been done by skilled workers. The managers of the firms expect to control the way work will be done. The struggle to reduce the cost of production is often closely linked with the struggle to maintain control. The introduction of technology may have important effects on the struggle to reduce costs and maintain control.

Technology in the office

We can gain a clearer understanding of the social effects of these changes if we consider how technology has influenced office work. The development of new technology affects every aspect of the firm, the office as well as the factory. The most important development in office technology in the nineteenth century was the invention of the typewriter. This speeded up the process of producing copies of letters and documents and replaced the clerks who had previously copied them by hand. The typewriter increased productivity tremendously. It was also seen to be a suitable form of employment for young women who were paid less than men. The development of 'typing pools' in which all of a firm's typing could be done under the supervision of an office manager meant that the work could also be more closely controlled. Secretarial work provided many advantages to female workers. Working conditions were usually good and the work itself brought young women into contact with the men who ran the firm. The good secretary was more than just an efficient typist. She would normally be expected to carry out other tasks which were closer to woman's traditional role in the home. Making tea, watering the plants, going to fetch sandwiches, or to organise birthday or anniversary presents all helped to create the role of 'office wife'.

This widening of the secretarial role to include forms of 'domestic' work was often to the advantage of the secretary, making it possible for her to gain considerable control over the way she spent her time at work and increasing her job satisfaction.

> Because conventional typewriters rely on the control of the typist, she can adopt any number of methods to cease working: she can pretend to look busy yet have a chat; she can drop a paperclip in the typewriter and wait around for the mechanic to come; she can run out of stationery and meet someone on the way back from the stationery office; if the work is late, then 'the ribbon got stuck' or she had to phone a company to get Mr. So-and-So's correct title and 'it took ages getting through'. Duties which are auxiliary to typing, such as filing, also enable her not to be tied to the typewriter all day. (Hazel Downing 1980)

The typewriter remained the main form of office technology until the middle of the 1970s when it began to be replaced by the word processor. Based on computer technology the word processor makes it possible to type words into a keyboard so that they can be viewed on a small television screen. They can then be corrected or altered and sent to a printer which produces them as a finished letter or document. Often the typist has no control over the layout of the finished article and may not even see it printed. Instead of being typed out, placed in an envelope and put in the post a letter may be transmitted directly to another office where it is printed or viewed on a screen. Copies of documents may then be stored in the computer's memory, removing the need to file away large amounts of paper.

Word processors do more than change the way information is communicated. Firstly, they move control of the work process away from the typist and into the machine. The speed of work is now determined by the word processor and not by the typist. Secondly, the typist's traditional skills of layout and design, along with the sense of pride in producing a well-typed letter, are no longer required. The computer does it all for her. Finally the word processor makes it possible to achieve increases in productivity. The benefits of word processors to the employer are brought out clearly in the advertising of one of the leading manufacturers.

> System 30, a visual word processor, requires minimum operator training for maximum productivity. Such operational features as operator screen prompts and automatic word wraparound assist the operator in producing final documents in one quarter of the

time it would take with most conventional typewriters . . . a built-in reporting system helps you monitor your work flow. (Hazel Downing 1980)

The introduction of the electronic office changes the character of office work. The 'social office' with its combination of secretarial and domestic roles is replaced by a far less flexible form of office work centred on the machine. The typist is no longer able to organise how she spends her time. Office technology enables the employer to gain increases in productivity using less highly trained workers while increasing control over the work routine.

Why do people work?

The most obvious answer to this question is that people need to work in order to survive. An economist would say that people go to work to earn money with which they can buy the goods they need to live. Work is seen solely as a way of gaining an income. This is not a completely satisfactory answer. It does not explain why individuals may prefer to take on lower paid jobs when they could earn more elsewhere, or why they may do extra work without being paid for it. Work, therefore, is important for other reasons than just providing people with an income.

JOB SATISFACTION

There are two kinds of satisfaction that people gain from work. Firstly, work can be interesting and satisfying in its own right. Going to work, doing the job, gives the individual a sense of achievement or a feeling that the job is worth doing. The satisfaction gained from work is *intrinsic* to the job. This means that work is valued for the things we gain from the job itself. Secondly, work provides things other than intrinsic rewards. People go to work for money. The money enables them to do all manner of things *outside* of work. These rewards are *extrinsic*. Many jobs provide both intrinsic and extrinsic rewards and different individuals may see the same job in different ways. It is not always the easiest and most comfortable of jobs which provide a sense of achievement. Even the hardest jobs may bring a sense of satisfaction and individual pride. In the following description of a steel-works the writer describes the excitement to be found in working at a furnace.

I was in a modern steel works . . . and that first day I liked very much what I saw there. I'd no sooner stepped on a furnace than

179

the melters concentrated on it in communal fashion, and I knew enough to realise that the steel would soon be tapped from it. The heavy hammers, two of them, were rising and falling in unison as they smashed the long iron bar up the taphole. Then the men who had wielded them stepped back as the metal sparkled from the furnace into the ladle waiting below. There was drama in it, in the flowing steel, and in the noise, and in the blast furnaces away to the right where the hot iron was filling in the sand beds. Drama too in the nearby rolling mill where the strips of steel became longer and longer and faded slowly from a white glow to a dull red. Drama even in the tanned sweating melters, who I saw were at peace in the midst of all the confusion, and I liked that . . . I don't think I was more than a week in that place before I knew that I could never leave steel. There was a something about it that was almost hereditary. It had thrilled my father under far harsher conditions, and although it still was nobody's paradise it thrilled me. There were things that I hated, and the night work was one of them, but nothing drove me away. (Patrick McGeown 1969)

When the work itself is satisfying sociologists say that it has an *expressive* meaning. When work is seen simply as a means to an end, and is not valued in its own right we would say that it has an *instrumental* meaning.

APPROACHES TO WORK STUDY

People's attitudes to work vary. Sociologists and social psychologists have tried to discover what people think of their work, and what can be done to enable them to work better. In many of the early studies of attitudes to work and work behaviour the main aim was to find ways of making people work more efficiently in order to increase profits. The earliest research was carried out in the 1920s by an American engineer, F. W. Taylor, who developed an approach to work which he called 'scientific management'. Taylor believed that there were three principles which employers should use in order to get the work done in the most economic way possible. Firstly, find the best men for the job. Secondly, teach them to do the job in the most efficient way and with the least possible effort. Finally, pay them good wages as an incentive. In an early experiment Taylor applied his ideas to unloading iron-ore from railway wagons. By watching the men carefully and timing their actions he was able to devise a pattern of work which enabled one worker to move four times as much ore as the average. Taylor's methods of timing workers, noting down their movements and then replanning the

Fig. 46. *Work satisfaction*

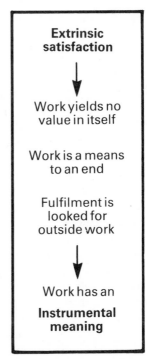

Source: Adapted from Watson, T. J., *Sociology, Work and Industry*, RKP 1980

work process became known as 'time and motion study'. One of the effects of this was to make it possible for employers to reduce the cost of labour by getting the same amount of work done by fewer workers. 'Speedy Taylor' as he was known became one of the most hated men in America.

ELTON MAYO

Later studies caused social scientists to change their ideas of how people worked best. The *scientific management* approach of F. W. Taylor gave way to the *human relations* approach to the study of work. Scientific management looked for the working conditions which produced the best possible results. They sought the correct temperature or level of lighting, for the worker, experimenting by altering conditions and then measuring changes in productivity. Each man was viewed almost as a machine only needing the right working conditions to function properly. Such ideas were overthrown by the work of Elton Mayo and his research at the

181

Hawthorne Works of the Western Electric Company in Chicago between 1924 and 1927. The Company, which provided generous sick pay, pension schemes and recreational facilities, called in Mayo to investigate a general feeling of discontent amongst its 30 000 employees.

The team of research workers began by experimenting with the levels of lighting in two similar workshops. They assumed that there must be something wrong with the working conditions in the factory. Too little light, or too cold, perhaps too hot or too noisy. They started with the lights. In one workshop lighting levels were increased. In the other they remained the same, as a control group. Observers noted the changes in attitudes and output in each group. As expected, the work output increased with each new rise in the level of lighting in the experimental workshop. The problem seemed to have been solved. But, in the other workshop, where the lighting remained the same, output also rose. And when the lighting in the first workshop was reduced, output did not fall, it rose. When lighting in both workshops was reduced, output rose yet again. In the end, lighting in both workshops was back to its original level and output had doubled. The level of light was not in this case linked to the efficiency of the workers.

A second experiment was set up. Six girls were selected to work at assembling telephone relays. The finished relay was dropped into a chute at the end of the bench and could easily be counted. The girls set to work, and their daily output was recorded. In the first week each girl produced 2 400 relays. Sitting with them at the bench for the five years of the experiment was an observer who noted what went on, answered the girls' questions and listened to their complaints. Every few weeks a change was made in the girls' working conditions and the changes in output were recorded. Extra rest breaks were introduced and then taken away. Free meals were provided, they clocked off at 4.30 p.m. instead of 5 p.m. Piece work was introduced. They were sent home at 4 p.m. instead of 4.30 p.m. Eventually the girls were put back to the working conditions they had had at the start. At every change the girls' output had risen until at the end the girls each produced 3 000 relays a week under the same conditions as when they produced 2 400.

How were such results to be explained? Elton Mayo came to the conclusion that the main influence on the girls' output was the attention being given to them. The girls felt important because they had been chosen for the experiment. They appreciated having someone who would keep them informed about what they were doing, who would listen to their complaints. As a result they worked harder.

The girls felt that they were valued members of the firm and no longer cogs in a machine. The very fact that they were being studied led to changes in their behaviour. Social scientists still refer to the 'Hawthorne effect' when describing how the very activity of investigation has an effect on the subject investigated.

Elton Mayo's research at the Hawthorne Works led to a revolution in the study of work. When workers were treated as individuals who needed to feel appreciated instead of just 'cogs in a machine' to work, and get paid, they responded by working better.

The human relations approach, like 'scientific management' before it, has been criticised for being biased towards the concerns of the managers of the firms and for ignoring the fundamental conflicts of interest that exist between employee and employer.

Alienation

We have already considered the idea of alienation as the separation of the worker from the results of his or her labours. Sociologists also use the term to describe the way many people experience work.

Jason Ditton describes work in a mass production bakery:

> For them (the bakery workers) work means a lifetime of waiting at machines where attendance is necessary but full attention is not. For the bakery workers, the continuous and unchanging production process, a literally never ending stream of bread pouring from the ovens, is broken up by . . . periodic 'runs' of different sorts of bread. But the perpetual repetition of these runs year after year means that they become part of the sameness of work . . . When I last returned to the bakery . . . nothing, or so they told me, had happened in the three months I had been away. (Jason Ditton 1972)

Blauner suggests that the view that workers have of work is in some way linked to the technology that is used. Workers, he argued, can experience alienation in four ways. *Powerlessness* occurs when the worker experiences a lack of opportunity for control over the work situation, when he or she is not able to make decisions about the way the work is done. *Meaninglessness* arises when the individual worker is unable to relate the particular task to the end product of the production process. *Isolation* from other workers often results from the noise or the organisation of machines within the work-place. *Self-estrangement* is the inability to gain any sense of personal fulfilment out of work. When Blauner used his four

183

Fig. 47. *Blauner's inverted 'U' curve*

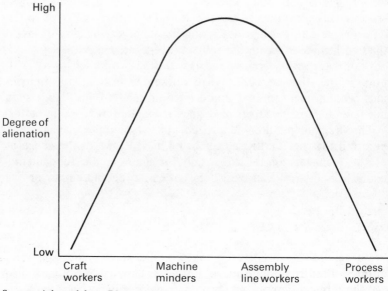

Source: Adapted from Blauner 1964

categories in the study of workers in different types of factory he found that alienation was least in those areas which were based on a craft technology and greatest in assembly line work. Workers in process production, on the other hand, showed relatively low levels of alienation. This led him to suggest that levels of job satisfaction could best be explained in terms of an 'inverted U curve'. As technology increases in complexity levels of alienation begin to rise, reaching a peak with assembly line working, and then falling as the work becomes easier and machines take over many of the more unpleasant tasks.

THE AFFLUENT WORKER

In the 1960s a team of British sociologists led by John Goldthorpe and David Lockwood carried out a study of workers in three factories in Luton. Their sample included craftsmen, process workers and machine-setters. They found that the workers who were most satisfied with their work were the machine-setters. In terms of the technological approach the machine-setters should have been the least content. Goldthorpe and Lockwood found that many of these men had worked their way up from jobs as machine minders to the more skilled job of machine-setter. Because they had come up from the machine-floor and could look back on times when they stood all day 'minding' machines they were more inclined to find greater satisfaction in their new job.

In their 'Affluent Worker' studies Goldthorpe and Lockwood consider three possible approaches, or orientations, to work. The first of these, the *instrumental* orientation, has already been considered. Work is not central to the individual's life and there is little commitment to job. The worker's approach is 'calculative' in that work is only about the size of the pay-packet at the end of the week. There is no direct connection between work and activities outside of work. The second orientation is *bureaucratic* and has strong moral elements. The worker has a commitment to the organisation and looks forward to gaining promotion within the firm in return for his loyalty. Thirdly there is a *solidaristic* orientation in which the first loyalty of the worker is towards his mates within the firm. The social relationships which exist within the work place are important and these workers are likely to spend a major part of their free time in activities linked to the firm. Goldthorpe and Lockwood suggest that instrumental orientations are more likely to be found among affluent blue-collar (manual) workers, whereas the white-collar (non-manual staff) are more likely to adopt a bureaucratic orientation. The solidaristic orientation is thought to be typical of the older generation of blue-collar workers and particularly those from more traditional working-class communites.

A major criticism of Goldthorpe and Lockwood's approach to workers' attitudes has been that they fail to show how different orientations may arise in different situations. W. W. Daniel points out that when workers are pushing for better pay and conditions, what he calls the *bargaining context*, they are more likely to have instrumental orientations. In the *work context*, however, the main issues are the satisfaction to be gained from doing a particular job and the social advantages of working with a particular group of 'mates'.

HOUSEWORK

Ann Oakley's study of housework (Chapter 4) looked at an activity which is seldom thought of as *work*. She found, however, that many of the features of factory work or office work also applied to housework.

The most valued feature of housework was the freedom it gave to the housewives to plan their own time. They valued their autonomy and felt that the best thing about being a housewife is that 'you're your own boss'. This freedom was, however, seen to be limited by the fact that housework had to be done and there were strong practical and moral pressures to get it done.

> Why do I clean the kitchen floor twice a day? Well, it's because she's all over it, isn't it? I mean it's not nice for a child to crawl on a dirty floor – she might catch something off it.
> Even though I've got the option of not doing it, I don't really feel I could not do it, because I feel I ought to do it. (Oakley 1974)

Housework was seen as monotonous and as never-ending.

> Housewives tend to be busy all of the time but they're not really doing anything constructive, are they? Well, I suppose it is constructive in a way, but you never really see anything for it and it's all routine. (Oakley 1974)

Many of the housewives felt that housework was a very lonely occupation and looked forward to going out shopping in order to get away from the isolation of the house. It was also seen to be a job which, for many women, failed to give them any real interest in life. Many feared that they might become 'cabbages' and refused to even think of themselves as housewives, preferring to write 'secretary' on official forms.

Ann Oakley's study shows that housewives experienced housework in many different ways but that for many their work was alienating in the ways described by Blauner. They often experienced a sense of powerlessness in the face of never-ending cleaning, washing and ironing. Many of the daily tasks involved were meaningless and the housewives often felt isolated and in danger of becoming 'cabbages'.

Table 28. *What is best about being a housewife?*

Best thing	Number of answers mentioning
You're your own boss	19
Having the children	9
Having free time	5
Not having to work outside the home	4
Having a husband	4
Having home/family life	3
Housework	1
Other	2
Total	47

Table 29. *Worst things about being a housewife*

Worst things	Number of answers mentioning
Housework	14
Monotony/Repetitious/Boring	14
Constant domestic responsibility	6
Isolation/Loneliness	4
Must get housework done	3
Being tied down	3
Children	2
Other	2
Total	48

Source: Oakley 1974

Work and non-work

In everyday life we often make a distinction between that part of our life we call 'work' and that which we call 'leisure'. It is often very difficult, however, to be sure whether any one activity is 'work' or 'leisure'. Imagine a crowd of people watching a football match. For most of them it is a leisure activity. They are clearly not at work. But what about the team's coach, or the sports photographers, or the groundsmen? They are at work, but they are also watching the match and enjoying it as is everyone else. The idea of leisure suggests activities which are in some way the opposite of work, as though work and leisure were alternate sides of a coin. This is clearly not the case. What we call 'work' and 'leisure' may be very similar. For these reasons sociologists use the term 'non-work' to describe activities which take place outside of work. This still leaves us with the problem of defining work itself. If the same activities, such as watching a football match, can be work or leisure how do we know which they are?

For some people there is a very clear division between work and what they do outside of work. We can see this division in terms of both time and place. Many people have set times within the week when they 'go to work'. However, for some the division is less clear. Many people work at home, either taking in work from outside on a part-time basis, or by running a business from home. Their 'work' may be something which they also do for their own enjoyment. It may not be possible to separate points of time when they are actually working from those when they are 'not working'. If we cannot separate work and non-work on the basis of time or place we are only left with a separation in terms of intention or motive. Those activities carried out for a financial reward can be considered as work whereas those which lead only to personal satisfaction are non-work.

We must also consider how the work that you do relates to what you do outside of work. Stanley Parker has suggested that there are three ways in which an individual's work relates to activities outside of work. People who have jobs which allow them a large amount of personal freedom and responsibility, are often well educated and gain personal satisfaction from work find that their work *extends* into their leisure. There are no clear dividing lines and often work and leisure are seen as one. Most doctors come into this group. They are seldom able to prevent work activities imposing on leisure time.

Another group adopt leisure activities which have very little to do with their work activity. We would say that their relationship between work and leisure is *neutral*; their leisure is seen as relaxation. Clerical workers and others with little freedom at work often fall into this group.

The third group of workers are those who get little personal satisfaction from work, who often find work dull and tedious. Leisure to them is an escape. They seek leisure activities which add colour to their lives, activities which are in *opposition* to the activity of work.

Within the last fifty years hours of work have been growing shorter. With increased automation they are likely to continue to do so in the future. Most people have more leisure time; they are also better off. They have more money to spend on more leisure. This has led to many changes in leisure activities. Because the working-class groups have benefited most from this it has meant that leisure activities whch were once for the rich alone are now enjoyed by all. Leisure has become more democratic. Mediterranean holidays are now within the reach of the vast majority of the population. An Adriatic beach in August will quite likely contain mill-workers from Burnley, clerks from Birmingham and bus-drivers from Bristol.

Leisure has become an industry with its own magazines, multi-million-pound budgets and television programmes. Bingo halls, yachting marinas, do-it-yourself shops, wildlife safari parks, evening classes and 'holidays in the sun' are all part of our 'leisure explosion'.

Occupations

There are two questions that we often ask about someone's work: Where do you work? What do you do?

What someone does is often as important, in some cases more important, than where he or she does it. To be a carpenter, a solicitor, a nurse or a lorry driver is more of a way of saying who, or what, you are than saying that you 'work for Bloggs and Co.' People see themselves as having an occupation. Very often having an occupation is even more important than working for a particular employer. As people move through their lives they may change from one employer to another but they are likely to stay in the same occupation, or something similar.

There is an important distinction, however, between 'having an occupation' and 'belonging to an occupation'. To say that someone has an occupation is to say that they have certain skills or qualifications which enable them to do certain kinds of work. A craftsman might say that he has 'a trade', meaning that he has served an apprenticeship, has learned the skills, and has gained the qualifications necessary to be recognised as a skilled worker. In this sense 'an occupation' is something you possess.

For many people, however, occupation means more than simply having skills and qualifications. It also involves belonging to a group. Sociologically we would use the term 'occupational communities' to describe these groups. They may be very highly organised, formal, groups which have precise rules for membership and their own forms of training and qualification, or less formal groups which only share certain common attitudes and values and have very little in the way of organisation. The professions and the craft unions are examples of the more formal type of occupational community.

An important purpose of occupational communities, whether they be professions, such as medicine or law, craft associations like printers or engineers, or marginal groups such as prostitutes or safe-breakers, is to defend their members against outside interests. Their most important need is to maintain their own position and to prevent others from setting up in competition. All occupational groups try, in some way, to establish a monopoly in the provision of certain skills and services.

Among the earliest occupational communities were the medieval guilds. Power in the guilds was in the hands of the master craftsmen who controlled entry into the trade through the system of apprenticeships. The masters employed those craftsmen, or journeymen, who were qualified but could not afford to become masters in their own right. As the power of the masters grew the opportunities for apprentices and journeymen to move up to become masters became less. The journeymen remained as paid employees of the masters while keeping their status as skilled workers. In the Industrial Revolution the masters became part of the industrial upper and middle classes whilst the skilled craftsmen, or artisans, became a 'labour aristocracy'. It was from this group of workers, needing to defend their position as a community of skilled workers, that the first trade unions developed.

The feeling of belonging to an elite group of skilled workers was very important to the craftsman. It gave him an identity which separated him from other groups of workers and which survives until the present day, as can be seen in this description of an engineering tool-room.

One day about a month after starting work I found myself in a small shop where men sat at work before large benches covered in hand-tools. None of the usual heavy machinery was present; the men did not wear boilersuits but instead were clad in clean brown dust coats. I soon understood that these men shaped and fashioned things with their hands much as a carpenter does. I leaned against a tubular rail and watched them. But not for long; the foreman had walked up behind me: 'What are you doing, kid?' he demanded. 'Just watching,' I replied, to which I quickly added, 'it looks a difficult job,' knowing that foremen, as other mortals are not averse to flattery. The rest was easy for I had touched upon his pride at being a craftsman. He not only allowed me to watch but even explained some of the mysteries of the work to me. He told me that the place was called a 'toolroom' and that the men were toolmakers. They were among the most highly skilled men in the manual engineering trades.

The toolroom was a very different place from the unskilled 'shop' I had first been sent to on starting work. It contained about forty men, all of whom had served apprenticeships. There were only four apprentices, of whom I was the youngest. The atmosphere, while still being informally friendly, had a faint air of professionalism about it. Right from my first day there it was made clear to me that toolmakers were craftsmen and as such superior to all the other workers except for a few other small and highly skilled trades.

The ethos which has been described as 'the aristocracy of labour' was very present. At the centre of this ethos lay a strict adherence to very high standards of workmanship. The importance of the toolmaker's place in the scheme of things was explained to me by many of the men I worked with. It was obviously a source of much contentment and status. And since each man made a complete tool, jig or punch and die by himself he was able to lavish much self-satisfying effort upon it. (Jack Pomlet 1967)

Within this account of the toolroom we can see four important features of the occupational community of skilled craftsmen. Firstly, the craftsmen have a status which is higher than that of workers in other parts of the factory. Secondly, there is a clearly defined training process (called apprenticeship), much of which takes place 'on the job'. Thirdly, there is very strong emphasis on high standards of workmanship combined with a pride in the job, and finally a sense of solidarity and community among the workers.

The professions

Certain occupations are described as *professions* and the people who work in them are called *professionals*. In everyday terms we think of a professional as someone who is not 'amateur'. That is someone who gets paid for doing things which others do for nothing. A professional photographer is paid for the pictures he takes whereas an amateur takes them solely for his own pleasure, as a hobby. A professional athlete is someone who competes for money. This is not the way in which the term 'professional' is used in the study of occupations. The professions are a particular type of occupation. In the past the great professions were the law, medicine, and the church. Today there are many more occupations which claim to be 'professions'. Traditionally the professions have held considerable status within society. Members of professions have generally been well paid and have enjoyed favourable working conditions. During the last 100 years there has been a gradual process of *professionalisation* as new occupations claimed professional status. There have often been debates about whether these new groups are 'real' professions. This debate occurs because there is no single definition of what a profession is. Instead there are a number of features shared by most of those occupations which are accepted as 'professional'.

A central feature of all professions is a claim to a particular knowledge. Unlike the knowledge possessed by the craft worker which is a practical knowledge of how to make things the professional's knowledge is largely theoretical. It is knowledge which is acquired both through an extensive education and through learning 'on the job'. Thus a solicitor will have to have a good general education and be 'articled'. A doctor needs a long academic training combined with periods as a junior 'on the wards'. At the end of the period of training the new entrant to the profession needs to 'qualify' before he or she can become a full member of the profession. Qualification may mean that the new member of the profession is formally 'licensed', 'registered', 'articled', or 'chartered' and can take up employment. 'Membership' can actually mean becoming a member of the professional association with the right to use the association's initials after your name. In many professions there are a number of stages through which people have to pass before they reach full membership.

As well as maintaining control of entry and qualification the professional association may also have a duty to maintain the standards of the profession as a whole. Any member who does not uphold the code of conduct of the profession may be removed from

Fig. 48. *Characteristics of a profession*

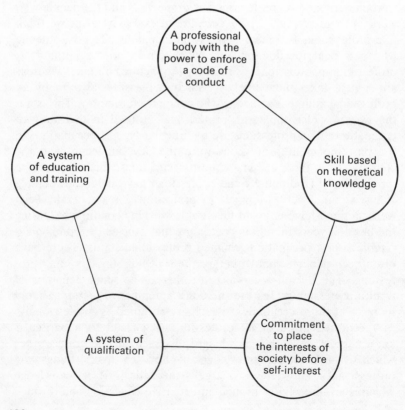

membership and unable to continue to work in that occupation. This power of control over the standards of the profession is often granted to the professional association by Royal Charter. Underlying the commitment to professional standards is a belief that the first duty of the professional is to the public good and that this is more important than any personal gain. The status of the profession combined with a strong sense of public duty and high moral tone can be seen in an architect's view of his profession:

> I had been led to believe that I was joining a profession, admired by the public, whose members were gentlemen first and foremost, then artists; men who possessed individuality and power, men who ruled their clients as they ruled the site operatives, men who were arbiters of taste and who never stopped to criticise their colleagues. It was understood that the prime object of the architect was to build to the glory of God and that the rewards were sufficient compensation for this privilege, beside which gentlemen did not lower themselves to haggle over money nor involve themselves with the sordid world of commercialism. (Christopher Gotch 1967)

In the past those who worked in the professions were largely self-employed, receiving work from their clients on an individual basis. With the growth of professions and the need for professional skills in areas as different as law, accountancy and civil engineering most professionals today are employed within private businesses or public corporations. The state and local authorities are major employers of the professions.

Organisations

An important feature of work in our society is that it needs to be organised. This means that for most people it takes place within an *organisation*. Organisations which are concerned with the economy, work and industry are only one type of social organisation. Schools, football clubs, religious bodies and secret societies are examples of others. Many aspects of our lives are 'organised', however, without being within 'organisations'. You don't need an organisation, for example, to organise Sunday lunch or a game of snooker. In the study of work and industry sociologists are particularly concerned with that type of organisation we might describe as a *formal organisation* in order to separate them from informal organisations such as mobs and queues.

WEBER

Much of our understanding of how organisations function comes from the writings of Max Weber. Weber was interested in the ways in which different types of social organisation were justified. In pre-industrial society the justification (or *rationality*) came from religious and magical beliefs. Industrial societies developed a new *rationality* based on ideas of efficiency and economy. It is this form of rationality which forms the basis for formal organisations. Weber went on to describe what this 'rationality' would look like in practice in its most perfect form. He used the term *bureaucracy* to describe this 'ideal type'. Weber was not saying how organisations should be organised, or even how they were organised in practice. He was merely describing the way a particular set of principles would look if they were found in the real world.

In Weber's 'ideal type' of bureaucracy the organisation would be made up of a number of clearly defined roles, or offices, arranged in a hierarchy. There would be managing directors and senior managers, junior managers and supervisors, charge-hands and operators. Power and authority would be given to those at the top of the hierarchy and they would pass it down to those on the lower levels. Each role within the organisation would have a clearly laid down set of duties and responsibilities and individuals would be appointed to those roles on the basis of their ability to do the job, and with a written contract of what is expected of them. Bureaucracy draws a clear division between 'business' matters and 'personal' affairs. These need to be kept quite separate. The tools required by the workers in the organisation are, for the most part, not the property of the employees. In return for their labour the workers within the organisation receive a wage or salary. While you may recognise many of the features of actual organisations in Weber's ideal type it is important to remember that his main aim was to describe the principles which formed the basis for organisations in general.

FORMAL AND INFORMAL

In real-life Weber's 'ideal type' is changed very considerably. In principle the division of the organisation into a number of offices with precise duties and clearly defined procedures is intended to enable the organisation to function more efficiently. In practice it may do the opposite. The rules and procedures may become ends in themselves. Individuals may develop a 'bureaucratic' attitude which prevents them from using their initiative or from devising imaginative solutions to work problems. The organisation as a whole may find it difficult to cope with uncertainty. This is what people mean when they describe bureaucracy as 'red tape' or 'standing in the way of progress'. When the rules and procedures of the organisation prevent it from functioning properly they are said to be *dysfunctional*.

In some situations the informal organisation of the workplace may be more important than the formal structures. The managers may permit a certain amount of 'rule-breaking' to go on when they see that it enables workers to produce more, or when it leads to improvements in morale.

In a clinic there are clear rules about the order in which patients were seen by the doctors. The receptionist used a set procedure to allocate patients to each doctor in turn. For a patient to be re-allocated to another doctor disrupted the system and involved other patients 'losing their turn'. If a doctor spent too long with one patient, however, other patients would be delayed. This presented problems for the receptionist who had to cope with a build-up of angry patients. In order to reduce pressure on her and to maintain a smooth flow of patients through the clinic the receptionist would break the rules by re-allocating patients to other doctors who were not as busy. This 'rule-breaking' was permitted because it helped to keep everyone happy and the place running smoothly.

In a similar way bus-men establish informal rules which enable them to keep control of their work routines and over their passengers in particular.

As a workgroup, bus-men have formulated a loose code of ideal passenger conduct to protect their status. They don't like the public trying to undermine it. Thus, a waiting passenger should halt a bus at a stop with a modest gesture of the outstretched arm, made in 'good time'. Working class teenagers who make no arm gesture, or stick a foot out instead are 'missed', or made to 'run for it', by the driver pulling up well past the stop. The middle class, who flag the bus down with an up-and-down movement of the arm, or substitute an object, especially an umbrella, even in good time, are equally resented for their unnecessary, ostentatious display of assumed authority. (Joel Richman 1969)

Organisations, therefore, depend upon both formal and informal procedures for them to operative effectively.

10
Government and Politics

Politics is about the use of power. We can see power being used in many situations. Teachers exercise power when they set homework or keep a class in order. Parents exercise power when they require their children to be in bed by a certain time. Referees exercise power when they enforce the rules in a game of football. In all of these situations we can see people in authority making decisions which have an effect on other people. Although social scientists are interested in the use of power and authority in situations like these the main emphasis in the study of politics is on the use of power within the state.

The state

The modern state has three main features. Firstly, it usually covers a particular area of land. The state exercises power and authority over the people who live within that area of land. We can think of the land and the people making up a *nation*, though this may not always be true where nations have been dispersed by war or by persecution or where a state includes people of a number of different nationalities. A second feature of the state is that power is centred on particular groups or institutions. In all modern states power is centralised in this way. Some people will have more power and will be able to make decisions which influence other, less powerful, individuals. This is another way of saying that within the state we will find governments, leaders and rulers. Thirdly, the state is organised on some sort of rational basis. This does not mean that governments always behave reasonably but that their actions take place within a more or less clearly defined system of government.

There are many different systems of government. For much of Britain's past power has been exercised through the *monarchy*. The nation has been ruled by one person who inherits the position of king or queen through birth. In the past the monarch has had considerable power. The French monarch, Louis XIV, once claimed 'l'Etat c'est moi', 'I am the state', and had power of life and death over his subjects. In a *dictatorship* power is also in the hands of one person, though that person is likely to be a president rather than a monarch and will have gained power through force rather than through birth. Some states are ruled by a small group of people and this would be called an *oligarchy*.

Although there are many monarchies, dictatorships and oligarchies in power throughout the world the most important form of government for our purposes is *democracy*. This may take many forms. The American system of democracy is very different from that found in Britain or in the Soviet Union. People who live under one particular system are likely to claim that their's is the only true form of democracy and that other systems are not democracies at all. Democracies have a number of features. There is usually some system of elections. Every few years the leaders will have to go to the people to get them to vote on their policies and on the ways in which they have carried them out. It is usual for each voter to have an equal say in who is elected and for all adult citizens to have the right to vote, though some democracies may only permit candidates to be chosen from a published list or may restrict the rights of certain groups of people to vote.

Most democracies are based on the principle of representation. The individual voters elect *representatives* who form a parliament, or legislative chamber, to which the government, or executive is responsible. There is often a 'separation of powers' with a separate *legislature, executive* and *judiciary*. The legislature makes the laws, the executive carries them out, and the judiciary decides on whether or not they have been carried out legally.

The British system of government

The centre of government in Great Britain is Westminster. Clustered around Parliament Square and Whitehall in London are most of the key institutions of government. The Palace of Westminister, or Houses of Parliament, contains the House of Lords and the House of Commons, made up respectively of Peers of the Realm and the elected representatives of the people. Every five years, if not before, the British people have the right to go to the polls to elect members of Parliament. The Leader of the Party which gains the most 'seats' in the House of Commons is asked by the Queen, in her position as Head of State, to form the Government. As Prime Minister he chooses his 'Cabinet' of leading MPs. From his supporters in Parliament the Prime Minister chooses men and women to lead the various departments of government, or ministries.

The House of Lords is not elected. In the past its members were the hereditary aristocracy and the right to sit in 'the Lords' was passed on from father to son. Today more and more of the active peers are appointed by the Government in recognition of their ability or service to the country. These are 'life peers' and only hold the title of 'Lord' or 'Lady' for their own lifetime. They cannot pass it on to their descendants. Life peers are chosen from all walks of life; but also in the House of Lords are twenty-four Bishops, the Archbishops of Canterbury and York and the Lords of Appeal, or Law Lords, who are High Court judges and act as the final Court of Appeal.

Debates in the House of Lords are presided over by the Lord Chancellor who sits on 'the Woolsack' – a reminder of the one-time importance of England's wool trade. Meetings of the House of Commons are presided over by the Speaker. He sits at one end of the House with the 650 or so MPs on either side of 'the Chamber', in front of him. On his right-hand side are the Government seats. The Prime Minister and Cabinet colleagues sit on the 'front bench'. Opposite them on the Speaker's left is the Opposition, with the Leader of the Opposition and his 'shadow ministers' on the 'Opposition front bench'. Behind the leaders of the two parties are their 'backbench' MPs. At the far end of the Chamber are the 'cross benches' where the members of the smaller parties and the independent members sit. Directly in front of the Speaker at the other end of the House of Commons is the 'Bar of the House'. It is from here that Black Rod, the Queen's representative, summons the House of Commons to hear the 'Queen's Speech' at the State Opening of Parliament.

The Queen cannot enter the House of Commons, instead the Commons go along, through the Central Lobby, to the Bar of the House of Lords from where they will hear the Speech from the Throne. In the Queen's speech the government lay down their policies and plans for action in the coming session of Parliament. It is, in fact, the Government's speech which the Queen reads.

The Queen is a symbolic Head of State, having limited power.

THE PROCESS OF LEGISLATION

Once the ceremony and ritual of the State Opening is out of the way the two Houses get down to the business of running the country. Parliament's job is to legislate, to pass laws. The job of the Cabinet, assisted by the civil service, is to 'execute' the policies approved by Parliament. Parliament is therefore 'the Legislative' and the Cabinet and civil service – the Executive. The Law Courts, including the Lords of Appeal, make up the 'Judiciary'.

Acts of Parliament begin life as 'Bills'. It is usual for the Government to introduce a Bill, though 'private members' and individuals and organisations outside Parliament can do so. Once the Bill has been introduced (first reading) it is written out in its proposed form and then discussed in detail by the House of Commons (second reading), and by a Committee of MPs (committee stage), before it gets its third reading, and is 'sent upstairs' to the House of Lords. Here the process is repeated and eventually the Bill is ready, having been amended and approved by both Houses. It then receives the Royal Assent, the Queen's signature, which makes it an Act of Parliament. Voting in Parliament is called 'a division'. When a vote is to be taken the division bells are rung and MPs hurry past 'the tellers', who count the votes, into the lobbies, before returning to their seats to hear the result. Debates in Parliament are published daily in the publication known as *Hansard*, and the Government's proposals for new Bills are included in White Papers.

Much of an MP's time is spent working on committees. Many of these are 'Standing Committees' concerned with the details of particular bills which are in the 'Committee Stage'. There are also a number of Select Committees which examine the work of individual government departments.

Although the state centralises the use of power it does not keep that power entirely to itself. The central government hands over some its power to other groups. These may be elected councils, known as Local Authorities, which are responsible for running services in the local area, or appointed bodies, often referred to as *Quasi-Governmental Agencies*, (abbreviated to QGAs). The Arts Council, which co-ordinates government spending on the arts, and the Atomic Energy Authority, which supervises the nuclear power industry, are examples of QGAs. While QGAs are usually under the direct control of the central government local authorities are responsible to local people who elect councillors in the same way that they elect MP's. Sometimes people refer to separate *tiers* of government. The central government is the *top tier* of government whilst the local authorities are the *second tier*.

Fig. 49. *How a government is elected*

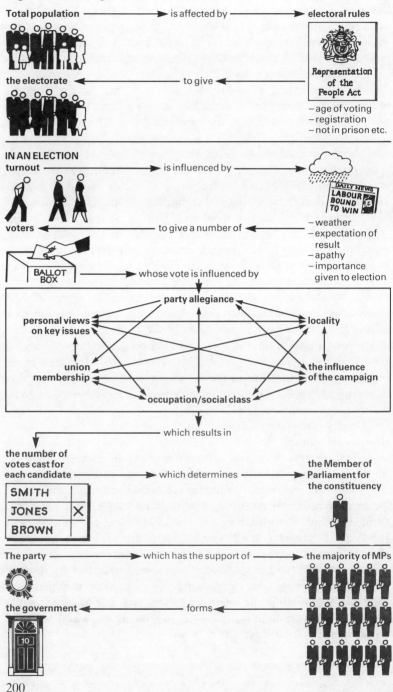

Elections

General elections are held every five years, unless the Prime Minister asks the Queen to dissolve Parliament earlier. This might happen if a Government cannot maintain its majority in the House of Commons. A by-election is held in any constituency where the MP resigns or dies.

The proclamation of an election marks the beginning of a three-week campaign by each of the parties to capture as many of the votes as possible. But though we talk of 'an election campaign', it would be more accurate if we viewed it as four campaigns, each overlapping the others, each aimed at a different audience and having different aims.

THE LOCAL CAMPAIGN

First, there is the local campaign, carried out by party workers over a small area with only a few thousand voters. The local campaign consists largely of handing out literature, usually a printed election address from the candidate; canvassing as many as possible of those whose names are on the Register of Electors in order to find out who the party's supporters are; and going round on polling day reminding them to vote. In 1964 nearly one million people, or 3 per cent of the electorate, took part in local campaigns and 34 per cent claimed to have been canvassed. The importance of the local campaign lies in its encouragement of people to vote and the morale-boosting effect it has on the local party workers.

THE CONSTITUENCY CAMPAIGN

At the next level there is the constituency campaign. At its centre is the candidate. He may have been the constituency MP in the previous Parliament. He may be a local man or someone sent by the national office of the party. Whoever he is, and however hard he and his helpers work, he is unlikely to get his name across to everyone. In the summer of 1963 only 51 per cent of a sample of electors interviewed by Butler and Stokes could name their MP. Even fewer could remember the names of other candidates. A survey in 1966 showed that hardly more than a quarter of a sample of electors knew their MP's view on key issues and on some issues this fell to one-eighth. Voters voted for parties, not for the men and women who represented the parties.

THE NATIONAL CAMPAIGN

The third campaign is the national one. At this level the party leaders do battle through the mass media. It is a campaign of Press conferences and manifestoes, party political broadcasts and party images. As many as 92 per cent of the electorate have claimed to follow the campaign on television and in the newspapers. The mass media are able to take elections right into people's homes. Despite this, most people's views remain as they were in the weeks before the campaign began. Advertising, television and the Press do not seem to have a great influence on voting behaviour during the campaign. More important is the 'image' of a party, or of a government, which people have built up during the previous years.

There have been suggestions that elections are won or lost by the actions of advertising agencies who try to 'sell' a party leader as they might sell soap powder. Richard Rose (1967) comes to the conclusion that whilst advertising politicians may be a useful way of passing on information, it does not really change attitudes. In any advertising campaign you cannot get away with selling a bad product for very long. In an election the 'product' is a party or its leader. If the voters have endured years of incompetent government and poor leadership they are not likely to be persuaded by an advertising campaign which offers them a 'new improved product' or 'dynamic leadership'. Advertising can never be better than the product it seeks to sell. A government's success in office is more important in winning an election than is three weeks of window dressing.

INFORMAL PRESSURES

The final type of campaign is very different. The local, constituency, and national campaigns are formal campaigns run by political parties and their helpers. This fourth campaign is an informal one. It has no organisation and is made up of ordinary people discussing the election as they go about their daily lives. In 1964 only 3 per cent of the Butler and Stokes sample had been actively involved in a formal campaign, but 12 per cent had tried to persuade someone to vote for a different party and 59 per cent had discussed the campaign. This informal campaign may be quite important in influencing the way people vote.

The voters

In Britain roughly 36 million people are eligible to vote. That is, they are British citizens over 18 years of age, not in prison, not certified insane, nor members of the Royal Family and are on the Electoral Register for the constituency in which they live.

Table 30. *Voting in general elections (in thousands)*

Year	Conservative	Labour	Liberal/Alliance	Other
1959	13 750	12 216	1 639	255
1964	12 002	12 206	3 093	349
1966	11 418	13 065	2 328	453
1970	13 106	12 141	2 109	900
1974	11 891	11 596	6 019	1 602
1979	13 698	11 506	4 305	1 711
1983	13 012	8 457	7 780	1 420

Not everyone turns out to vote in an election. In the General Elections held in Britain since 1945 the average turnout has been around 80 per cent, going as high as 84 per cent in 1950 and as low as 73 per cent in 1945.

From these figures it would seem that 20 per cent, or two out of every ten voters, do not bother to vote. Is this in fact the case? It is likely that the proportion of electors who deliberately don't vote is less than this figure of 20 per cent. Electoral Registers are made up in October and come into force the following February. They are always a few months out of date. In that time people may have moved too far away to vote, some may have died, or left the country. People who are away on business, have moved, or are sick can vote by post, but many fail to do so in time for their vote to be counted. Possibly 8 per cent of the electorate are affected in this way, leaving only 12 per cent of deliberate non-voters.

At the end of the election campaign all of the votes are counted and the candidate with the most votes is elected to represent the constituency in Parliament. The political party which gains the support of the majority of Members of Parliament is then able to form the government. It is clear from Figure 50 that it is possible for a government to be formed by a party which did not receive the majority of votes cast in the election.

VOTING PATTERNS

What makes people vote for a particular party and what makes them change how they vote? The first question is about political stability, the second is about political change.

Supporting a political party is often referred to as *partisanship*. From the end of the Second World War until the early 1970s British politics centred on two parties, Labour and Conservative. The Conservative Party, often known as the Tory Party, came into exist-

Fig. 50. *Shares of the votes and seats in Parliament, 1983 general election*

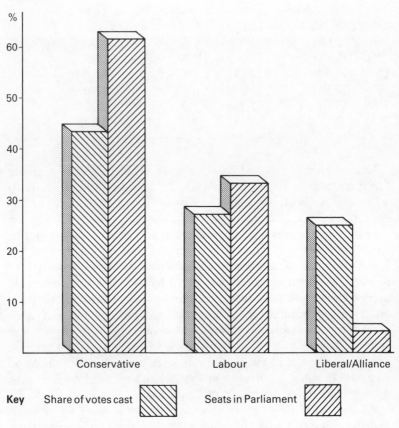

ence towards the end of the nineteenth century as the party of the aristocracy and middle classes. The Labour Party grew up in the early part of the twentieth century as the party of the industrial working class. A third party, the Liberal Party which had once been the main opposition to the Tories, declined after 1920 and gained only a small share of the votes in all elections held after 1945. It was not until the 1970s that other 'third parties' began to gain seats in Parliament. Many of these were nationalist parties, such as the Scottish National Party, Plaid Cymru and the Northern Ireland parties. In 1981 a group of Labour MPs broke away to form the Social Democratic Party which, together with the Liberals formed the Alliance.

Partisanship can be considered in both the long and the short term. The short term can be as short as just marking your vote on the ballot paper. Long term political allegiance can last a lifetime. Many people *identify* themselves with a political party and vote for them at every election.

Political socialisation

For many people their political awareness begins during adolescence. Young children do not have a great understanding of political issues, seeing things mainly in terms of personalities and political leaders. It is from the mid-teens that politics comes to be seen in terms of parties and issues. Political attitudes within the family will have an important influence. People often vote in the same way that their parents voted. The strength and direction of parental influence varies from family to family. Politically active families are more likely to have an influence than a family which is apathetic about politics. Where the parents vote for different parties the offspring are more likely to follow the mother.

Table 31. *Party preference and parents' politics*

	Parents' Partisanship		
Own party preference	Both Parents Conservative	Parents Divided	Both Parents Labour
	%	%	%
Conservative	75	37	10
Labour	14	49	81
Liberal	8	10	6
None	3	4	3
	100	100	100

Source: Adapted from Butler and Stokes, *Political Change in Britain*, 1969

The influence of the family does not always remain strong throughout the lifetime of the individual voter. Butler and Stokes have compared it to a photograph which is clear and sharp when first taken but which gradually fades as it gets older. When people first vote their parents' views are likely to have a very great influence. As they get older and mix with different groups, becoming exposed to different ideas, the family influence fades. In voting at their first election 90 per cent of Butler and Stokes' sample voted in the same way as their parents voted. In Table 31 you can see that some years later only 75 per cent of voters whose parents had voted Conservative still followed their parents along with only 81 per cent of those whose parents had voted Labour.

Butler and Stokes' study has been criticised because it relied upon people's memories of how they thought their parents had voted some years earlier. Their memories may not always have been very accurate. It is also difficult to separate the influence of the family from a number of other influences. Political attitudes, like any beliefs or opinions, depend upon what we know. Our knowledge of political issues or policies depends on our sources of information. We build up our knowledge of politics over many years and through many different sources of information. We may gain political ideas and values from the mass media, through our schooling, or from within the local community. The social contacts people make at work may be important, especially if they are active in Trade Unions. Together these influences form a basis for our *political socialisation*.

These influences may be particularly important when someone is approaching their first opportunity to vote in an election. Butler and Stokes speak of *political generations* of voters which are influenced by political beliefs at one point of time. This is often used to explain why older people are more likely to vote Conservative. They come from a political generation which grew up in a period of Conservative rule when the Labour Party was in the minority.

Social class and voting

Many of the influences on voting behaviour are linked to social class. There are, however, a number of widely held myths about social class and voting behaviour. It is often thought that people vote solely on class lines with the working classes voting for the Labour Party and the middle classes voting for the Conservatives. This means that anyone who votes for the party of the other class is a 'deviant voter'. This view assumes that each party has a solid core of support from within each social class.

Such a view of voting behaviour is far too simple. It would be impossible for the Conservatives ever to win an election if all manual workers voted Labour. If this myth were true Labour would always win elections. It is clear that far from being 'deviant voters' the working-class Conservative may be quite usual. This does not mean that social class has no influence. We can see from Table 32 that the majority of the middle classes have tended to vote Conservative whilst the bulk of Labour support has come from the manual workers and their families.

Table 32. *Class and voting 1964–74*

*Percentage of support for each party
at each general election*

	1964	1966	1970	1974 Feb	1974 Oct
Conservative voters					
Non-manual	57	59	54	63	58
Manual	43	41	46	37	42
	100	100	100	100	100
Labour voters					
Non-manual	17	19	22	25	27
Manual	83	81	78	75	73
	100	100	100	100	100

Source: adapted from Crewe, 1977

Table 32, however, also shows another important trend in the link between class and voting. Apart from the general election of February 1974, the proportion of manual and non-manual Conservative voters did not change greatly over the ten-year period. The pattern of Labour voting, however, shows an increase in the proportion of non-manual, or middle-class, voters. The problem in the sixties and early seventies was not one of 'deviant' working-class voters voting Tory but of 'deviant' middle-class voters who voted Labour. This change in the pattern of voting has been described as *class de-alignment*. This means that old patterns of partisanship based on social class are no longer important. Since 1974 there have been further changes in the pattern of voting and the extent of class de-alignment. Whilst the Labour Party continued to attract the vote of the traditional working-class groups, especially in the North of England, these became a smaller group within the electorate as a whole. In 1984 the so-called typical Labour voter – a manual worker, trade union member, living in a council house – made up no more than 5 per cent of the electorate and no more than 10 per cent of Labour supporters. Alongside this 'old working class' a 'new working class' has emerged. Many manual workers, who owned their own houses, did not belong to trade unions and probably lived in Conservative-held constituencies in the Midlands or the South, decided to vote Conservative.

Table 33. *The two working classes, 1983*

	Conservative	*Labour*	*Liberal/SDP*
The old working class			
Council tenants	19	57	24
Works in public sector	29	46	25
Lives in Scotland/North	32	42	26
The new working class			
Owner-occupiers	47	25	28
Works in private sector	36	37	27
Lives in South	46	26	32

Source: adapted from Crewe 1983

Analysis of voting in the elections of 1979 and 1983 has, therefore, shown a change in influence of social class on voting. In part these changes reflect changes within the social classes themselves. They also show a move to voting on issues rather than for parties. Although partisanship may still be important many voters are likely to be influenced by specific issues which they see as important. This has also led to an increase in voting across social class boundaries.

Political parties

We have already been introduced to some of the political parties which are active in Britain. These can be divided into four main types. Firstly there are the national parties which account for the great majority of votes cast in any election. These are the Conservative Party, the Labour Party and the Alliance of the Liberal and the Social Democratic Parties. In the 1983 general election these parties received 95 per cent of the votes. The second group is made up of the smaller parties which represent particular national interests within the United Kingdom. Scottish and Welsh concerns are each represented through their separate nationalist parties, Plaid Cymru for Wales and the Scottish National Party for Scotland. Northern Ireland, however, has a number of parties, including the Ulster Unionist Party, the Democratic Unionists, the Social Democratic and Labour Party and Sinn Fein. The final group of parties which puts up candidates at elections seldom wins any seats. Some of these are 'one-issue' parties, for example the Ecology Party, which has campaigned on environmental policies. Finally there are those 'fringe' parties which have their name on the ballot paper but which do not represent any broad range of interests. This group may include 'joke' parties, such as The Monster Raving Loony Party, and groups which have broken away from one of the major parties, as well as a number of 'independent' candidates.

A political party is more than the politicians elected to Parliament once every five years. All of the major parties depend upon large numbers of ordinary party members who attend local branch meetings, organise social events and raise funds for the party. At election time it is the party members who deliver leaflets and encourage people to vote. Between elections the party members meet to discuss party policy. Each party has some form of national organisation which acts as link between the party leaders and the 'grassroots' members in the constituencies.

This form of mass political party is a fairly recent development, having emerged at the end of the nineteenth century. Such parties are an important part of the political system. We have already considered how they may act as a focus for political affiliation, or partisanship. However very few of those who vote for a particular party are likely to be party members. Even among party members there are different levels of activity. Some people may simply pay their subscription and perhaps give a little help on election day but play little active part in the life of the party. Others will be more active, attending branch meetings, selecting candidates and giving up many hours of their own time to work for the party. There will also be party members who stand in local elections and who become councillors. These different levels of involvement and *activism* provide one basis for recruitment into political life.

The political leaders have often worked their way up through the party. This is not the only way in which individuals may enter politics. Active involvement in trade unions, community groups, business and the professions may also be a route into political activity. It is the party, however, which selects the candidates and therefore acts as an important *gatekeeper* on the way to Parliament. Political leaders are also elected by the parties. Though there are different methods for electing party leaders all of the political parties can claim to be led by people who have been chosen by the party members.

The parties also play an important role in *political socialisation* and *political communication*. They are one of the ways in which people learn about political ideas and policies, and acquire political attitudes. They also act as a bridge between the electorate, and in particular the party activists, and the political leaders, enabling policies to be communicated to the party members and the views of the membership to be passed back to the national leadership. This is done informally, through the contact which MPs have with their constituency parties and also formally through conference resolutions, elections to key party posts and formal 'policy groups'.

Political parties are most active during election campaigns. At the beginning of the campaign each party will publish its manifesto. This is a document laying down the policies the party would wish to implement if it were elected. These policies would have been developed in the period between elections and would cover a wide range of issues. If elected the party would need to make decisions on education, social services, industry, defence, agriculture and many other matters. The manifesto would describe what the party proposes to do in all of these areas.

Interest groups

Whereas a party will seek to take action in many different areas interest groups are concerned with a far narrower range of issues. Interest groups do not seek to gain power for themselves but instead to influence those who have power. They put pressure on those who both make and carry out policies and for this reason they are sometimes described as *pressure groups*.

In the Houses of Parliament the lobbies are places where MPs can be met and spoken to. The word 'lobby' is often used for any attempt to influence those in power while a 'lobbyist' is someone who tries to exert influence on ministers and MPs.

There are many different groups which attempt to influence the way governments run the country. Some are highly organised groups, often linked to particular commercial or industrial interests, which 'lobby' for support among MPs, ministers and senior civil servants. Other groups are less powerful and may only be concerned with local matters. The aims, methods and organisation of interest groups vary considerably.

TYPES OF INTEREST GROUP

Interest groups may have two main types of aim. At one extreme they are groups which seek to promote a particular issue. The successful campaign to introduce commercial television in the 1960s is an example of *promotional* activity. Groups at the other extreme

210

are more concerned to protect their interests. When, for example, a government department proposed a change in the regulations covering the design of electric light fittings the manufacturers, who would have needed to have spent large sums of money on changing over to the new design, mounted a *protectional* campaign to oppose the change. Very often the same organisation may act both promotionally and protectively. The Road Transport Federation, for example, may seek to promote changes which permit the use of larger lorries while also protecting its members' interests by opposing the introduction of lorry bans in city centres.

Whether a group's aims are promotion or protection may depend upon the basis of its support. Organisations such as the Confederation of British Industry and the Trade Unions Congress represent particular groups within the community. Their aims are to support the interests of their members. The League against Cruel Sports, however, seeks to promote a cause, the abolition of blood-sports. *Cause* groups, because they generally do not represent particular sections of the community, tend to have a more varied membership than *sectional* groups. They are also more likely to concentrate on one type of activity whereas sectional groups often do other things as well. The Automobile Association which seeks to protect the interests of motorists also provides breakdown services, publishes maps and route guides and arranges insurance for its members.

There are also important organisational differences between groups. In particular there are differences of life-span. Some groups may have a long history, having been established to represent particular interests on a permanent basis. Such groups usually have a professional organisation which works full-time on its members' interests. The Child Poverty Action Group, the RSPCA, the Pools Promoters Association are only a few of the many professionally organised *permanent* groups which put pressure on government. Other groups may be established for one particular aim and, having achieved it, will then disappear. These can be described as *ad hoc* groups. In 1969 the government established the Roskill Commission to select a site for London's third airport. Cublington, near to the Buckinghamshire village of Wing was one of the areas to be considered. Local residents formed the Wing Airport Resistance Association (WARA) to fight the proposals. Eventually the government accepted WARA's views and chose an alternative site. WARA then disbanded.

PRESSURE GROUPS METHODS

There are many different methods groups can use to influence the

211

government. The choice of methods depends upon the resources that the group can call upon as well as the power it has to make the government listen. At one extreme there are powerful, well established organisations which work so closely with the government that little real pressure is necessary. Such groups would be consulted on proposed changes and their views would be taken into account. Their leading members will be invited to serve upon important bodies and they may even be represented within the government. At the other extreme there are many groups who have little influence and no direct contact with those in power. Their views would not be asked for and they would be seen as a nuisance rather than a help. Such groups have to employ a wide variety of tactics to press their cause.

The mass media provides campaigners with an important way of making their views known. Established groups will use the media to ensure that their point-of-view is regularly presented. Less powerful groups will try to use the media to make people aware of their existence and to publicise their cause. Because the media depends upon a regular supply of news interest groups seeking to influence public opinion will aim to gain publicity by creating 'news'. In extreme cases this may involve violent protests or demonstrations. More often it is a matter of providing the media with a supply of 'interesting stories' which lend support to a particular cause or interest. Often the stories would need to be tailored to particular groups. Frank Field, former director of the Child Poverty Action Group, used the court pages of The Times

> to find out who was most often invited to Number 10 Downing Street and so was worth lobbying. One was also very careful about where to place publicity. If I wanted to influence ministers or civil servants I wrote to The Times. If I wanted to influence trade unionists on the way to a Labour Party liaison meeting I went for The Guardian. (*The Times*, 8 April 1980)

An important link between interest groups and the government is through Members of Parliament. Candidates for Parliament are often sponsored by particular organisations. Trade Union sponsored candidates will have part of their election expenses paid by the union as well as help with their constituency expenses once elected. In return the sponsored MP will advise the union on political matters and put its views across in Parliament. Many other MPs will be employed as consultants by interest groups or will represent groups in which they have a particular interest. An MP may be approached by an organisation, or by a professional lobbyist, and be asked to support a particular group or campaign. It is often possible for MPs to introduce Private Members' Bills which support the aims of interest groups. Organisations will have draft bills on key issues ready to be introduced. When the results of the ballot for Private Members' Bills is announced lobbyists will try to persuade the successful MPs to introduce bills on their behalf. They will then provide the MP with evidence to support the proposed bill, researchers and other staff to help with the campaign, publicity in the media, lobbyists to persuade other MPs to give their support and any other help the MP might need.

Members of Parliament in Britain do not have the kind of support from teams of researchers and advisors that is available to elected representatives in other countries. It would be impossible for them to keep up the work that is needed for a Private Members' Bill to be successful without help from outside groups. In 1979 the Society for the Protection of the Unborn Child (SPUC) persuaded John Corrie MP to present a bill on their behalf. Later, when the Bill had been through its Second Reading Mr. Corrie commented

> I am quite convinced that we would not have had the number of MPs turning up for the debate on my Bill if it had not been for the pressure group. They did the work of getting the members into the lobby. I had tremendous help from SPUC in terms of facts and figures and research. I simply could not have done the work myself. (*The Times*, 9 April 1980)

The practice of sponsoring MPs to act on behalf of pressure groups has caused some concern in Parliament. MPs are elected to represent their constituents and not to act on behalf of interest groups. The practice of paying MPs, either through consultancy fees or by contributions to election expenses could create a situation in which MPs were no longer impartial or even-handed in their actions. As a safeguard all MPs must make their financial interests public and they should declare when they have an interest in a particular issue.

Political movements

Pressure groups can usually be recognised fairly easily. They have specific aims, a membership, a structure of officials and committees and a name to call themselves by. Often, however, political pressure is applied in other ways and by less structured groups. We would call them political movements. Pressure groups may be part of a wider movement and may give directions to a movement but the movement itself is broader than any group which exists within it. J. R. Gusfield has defined social movement as 'socially shared activities and beliefs directed toward the demand for change in some aspect of the social order'. This definition has four parts. Firstly, they are 'socially shared'. They do involve groups of individuals though often without the formal membership we would normally see in pressure groups. Secondly, they involve activities and beliefs. A movement is more than a sense of discontent or a feeling that things are not right in the world. Movements take action to change things and they share certain beliefs. Those beliefs lead, thirdly, to demands. In more formally organised movements these may lead to a manifesto laying down certain demands. Often they are just expressed publicly by those who share the aims of the movement. Finally, these demands are for change in the social order. Social movements are always concerned with change in some form or another. It may be change towards a particular view of the future, an ideal society or Utopia, or it may be change back to the way society was in the past.

At the centre of the movement there is usually an organised group around which there may be a committed membership. Further out, however, the movement is less structured and people's involvement is less.

Typical movements are the movement for reform of the abortion laws, the environmentalist lobby, the women's movement, the 'clean-up Britain' campaign and the Campaign for Real Ale.

In the 1960s one of the best-known movements became known as 'Ban the Bomb'.

MASS MOVEMENT

For most of the 1960s there was considerable opposition to Nuclear Warfare and nuclear weapons testing. In Britain this opposition centred on the 'Ban-the-Bomb' movement at the centre of which was 'The Campaign for Nuclear Disarmament' (CND). The campaign worked through leaflets, public meetings and debates, demonstrations and an annual march from the Atomic Weapons Research Establishment at Aldermaston to London. It was through the 1965 Aldermaston March that sociologist Frank Parkin (1968) carried out a study of the movement. Sociologists who have attempted to explain the support for mass movements have often used the idea of alienation. It has been suggested that people who support movements such as CND share a particular view of their position in society, that they are in some way 'alienated'. They are 'in society' but not 'of society'.

214

One view sees individuals as isolated units with few links into society. These people turn to mass movements for social contact and a way of life. Thus the membership of CND might have been expected to have come from people who have few links with other groups in society. For most people these other groups provide a socialisation into democratic values, social relationships and personal contact, and a way of expressing particular views and interests. It has been suggested that democracy depends on such groups – political parties, trade unions, churches, voluntary associations etc. – if it is to generate effectively. Mass movements, it has been thought, depend on 'alienated individuals' who are outside of this network of groups. Parkin's evidence does not support this view.

Eighty-four per cent of the older sample belong to at least one other organisation. Only 16 per cent could be defined as 'alienated' on this definition. The majority of CND members in Parkin's sample were middle-class whereas in other studies of mass movements the 'alienated masses' come largely from the working class or from lower-middle-class groups who saw their status threatened. These groups do not seem to have been important areas of recruitment for CND.

Table 34. *Membership of voluntary organisations*

	%
Membership in 1 or 2 organisations	49
Membership in 3 or 4 organisations	24
Membership in 5 or more organisations	11
Membership in no organisation	16
	100

Source: Parkin 1968

POWERLESSNESS AND REJECTION

Another view of alienation sees it as powerlessness. In modern society individuals can feel weak, unable to influence the course of events. It could be suggested that CND support came from people who felt that they had little power to change things. Parkin asked his respondents to say whether they agreed or disagreed with two statements:

1. Ordinary people cannot hope to change government policies.
2. There will always be war; it's part of human nature.

The replies did not suggest that CND members felt powerless. Ninety-seven per cent disagreed with the first statement and 87 per cent with the second.

A third view of alienation sees the supporters of mass movements as those who reject the dominant values of the society. In a modern 'pluralist' society where people have freedom of speech and ideas there can be no single set of values which everyone holds. Parkin suggests that certain collections of values are more generally accepted and that other collections of values are likely to be seen as deviant. Support for the Royal Family, for example, is part of a collection of dominant values centred on the monarchy. Republicanism and opposition to the monarchy would then be seen as 'deviant values'.

When asked if they agreed or disagreed with the statement, 'The monarchy is an institution we should be justly proud of', Parkin's sample showed a clear rejection of the monarchy by all social classes. Their replies, supported by other evidence in the survey, suggested that CND members may well be alienated from dominant values in society. They are more likely to support 'deviant' values.

INSTRUMENTAL OR EXPRESSIVE

Political activity is usually regarded as activity aimed at achieving a particular result. We could say that people engaged in such activity have an 'instrumental' approach. They seek to achieve certain ends. The means by which those ends are achieved are not particularly important. For some groups, however, the 'means' are important and may outweigh the 'ends'. The activity itself becomes the focus of politics and the aimed-for-results slip into second place. This is an 'expressive' approach to politics. People who 'stand up for their rights' or 'defend principles' are engaged in 'expressive' political activity. Fighting for a change in the law which will benefit you directly (i.e. more money for school leavers) is instrumental. Most political activity combines instrumental and expressive aspects.

The CND sample were asked their views on the statement: 'Protests and demonstrations which fail to achieve their aims are a waste of effort'. If involvement in CND was largely instrumental you would expect most people to agree with the statement. Disagreement with the statement would indicate a more 'expressive view'. The survey showed that 86 per cent of the sample disagreed with the statement. For them participation in the movement's activities was enough in itself.

Parkin suggests that this more expressive emphasis points to the strong middle-class bias of the movement.

Civil servants

The role of Parliament is to legislate; to pass laws and decide on policy. Carrying out the laws and acting on the policy is the job of 'the Executive', which, as we have seen, is made up of ministers and civil servants. In all there are about three-quarters of a million civil servants, excluding those who work in government dockyards and industrial establishments. Most of these are engaged in routine clerical or administrative work, in employment exchanges, social security offices and for the Inland Revenue. One-fifth of civil servants work in London, mostly in 'Whitehall'. At one time all government departments were centred on a group of buildings in Parliament Square and along nearby Whitehall. The growth of government activities has forced many departments to move to new buildings further away from Parliament but it is still usual to refer to the central offices of the ministries as 'Whitehall'. As well as carrying out the routine work of government, administering the social services, collecting taxes, planning the environment and budgeting the nation's wealth, civil servants also advise ministers on their future policies. Senior civil servants investigate the likely result of a particular policy. They collect information, discuss the matter with interested groups and prepare a report for the Minister. Civil servants also undertake the drawing up of legislation to be put before Parliament.

In 1983 there were 648,900 civil servants employed by the British government. Most of these are employed in clerical, technical and executive grades. The main interest for sociologists, however, has been the small group of senior administrative civil servants who stand between government ministers and the specialist and technical civil servants lower down. The role of these senior administrators is to provide the information and advice which will help ministers to make decisions. Because the civil service do not change when the government changes they provide continuity. They are also considered to be politically neutral, favouring neither one party nor another. Critics of this view of the civil service claim that the top civil servants are secretive and resist any changes, particularly those which might weaken their own position. They are drawn from a very narrow social background with a high proportion of graduates from Oxford and Cambridge, very few of whom have degrees in scientific or technical subjects. In the period 1973–5 only 8 per cent of all graduates had been to Oxford or Cambridge. Of the men accepted as administrative trainees for the civil service between those years 27 per cent had Oxbridge degrees. Half of all university and poly-

Fig. 51. *Changes in the size of the civil service 1973–1983*

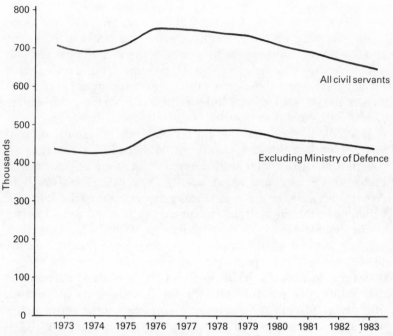

Source: Annual Abstact of Statistics 1983

technic graduates had science degrees compared to one-fifth of those who were accepted for the civil service. Despite many attempts to broaden the recruitment to the civil service the evidence still suggests that the senior administrators are appointing people who share their own particular background.

Theories of politics

A simple view of politics is that it is some kind of elaborate game. The contestants are organised in different groups with various roles to play. There are voters, MPs, ministers, civil servants, protesters and so on. The game is governed by certain rather vague rules and involves various kinds of activities. This is a view of politics which focuses on political institutions and on political processes. In real life politics does not seem to work out quite as neatly as such a simple view would suggest. Politicians always seem to be arguing. For much of the time their arguments are about the best course of action to take on particular issues. These are arguments about differences of

218

policy and they occur both between different parties as well as within a party. Often, however, political debates are about more than just policies. They are about the nature of politics itself. You could say that they are about the rules of the political game. To really understand politics it is important to understand these debates and the underlying theories which give rise to them.

Theories of politics can be divided into two opposite points of view, one based on ideas of consensus and the other on ideas of conflict. The consensus approach to politics is the view which is most often taken by leading politicians and by the mass media. It is often described as a *pluralist* or *liberal* theory of politics. Conflict viewpoints on the other hand are more likely to be based on a *Marxist* perspective.

PLURALIST PERSPECTIVES

The pluralist version of the political game sees it as a contest for power between a limited number of political parties each of which presents its policies to the electorate for them to choose. Once elected the winning party can claim a *mandate* for its policies. If it fails to govern in a way approved by the people then it will not be re-elected at the end of its term of office. When in power, however, the elected government has to make many decisions not covered by its mandate and it will have to respond to many unexpected events. It will find itself at the centre of many competing pressures and conflicting advice. The government will therefore have to decide on the best course of action consistent with its own policies and the advice available. Within the pluralist perspective the government is able to act in this way because the state itself is neutral, favouring no particular interests, and because political power within the state is clearly separate from economic power.

This 'classic' pluralist viewpoint sees the political will of the people as the main source of power within the state. Two important weaknesses of this approach have become obvious in recent years. Firstly, many aspects of government have become increasingly independent of political control. This can be seen in the growth of Quasi-Governmental Agencies and the importance of 'experts' within an increasingly complex society. Secondly, the power of certain elite groups within the political process has become generally recognised. Pluralist theories have therefore been adapted to allow for these developments.

This has led to two main variations of 'classic' pluralism. One can be described as 'reformed pluralism' and is the approach taken by politicians 'at the centre'. This includes the so-called 'Tory wets' on

Fig. 52. *The pluralist perspective*

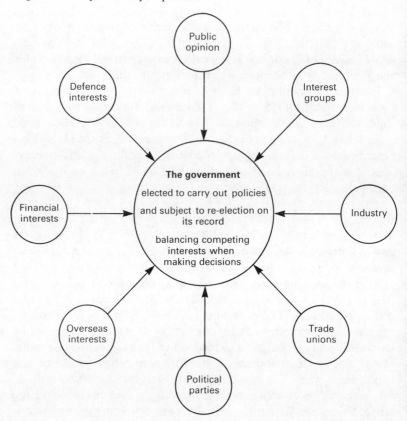

the left-wing of the Conservative Party and the right-wing of the Labour Party, as well as the Liberal/SDP Alliance. This viewpoint emphasises the power and authority of Parliament whilst demanding that all government agencies be made more accountable. The dangers of 'extremism' in politics are thought to be avoided by placing more emphasis on democratic principles such as 'one man, one vote'.

An alternative version of pluralism has developed on the political right, particularly within the right-wing of the Conservative Party. This *New Right* view of politics follows many of the basic principles of classic pluralism including the importance of a consensus and the expression of the popular will through elections. In other ways, however, it adopts a very different view of politics and of the work-ings of the state. Many of the ideas of the 'New Right' have been taken from economic theories which emphasise the role of the free market in giving individuals freedom of choice. New Right theories claim that government involvement in many areas of life has become too great and that less state intervention is needed. The greatest danger is seen as the natural tendency for the state to absorb more and more of the nation's wealth. The boundaries of state activity must therefore be rolled back and people given freedom to choose.

MARXIST PERSPECTIVES

Marxist views of the state are very different from pluralist approaches. Marxists begin by noting that all western democracies are also capitalist societies. It is therefore inevitable that they are organised in ways which support capitalism. Such societies, for example, are based upon the private ownership of property and the profit motive. Marxists reject the pluralist view that political and economic power are clearly separate. In their view the state represents a close alliance between the owners of capital and the political leaders. As evidence of this Marxists would point to the close links between those who control industry and commerce and those who administer government. The importance of the public schools and the old universities as sources of recruits to senior positions in business and government is one example of how this link is maintained.

Business interests wield considerable political power. Many are multi-national concerns whose budgets are greater than those of the state. They can use this economic power to ensure that the state does nothing to oppose their interests. They also maintain control over important sections of the mass media and use this power to

Fig. 53. *The Marxist view of the state*

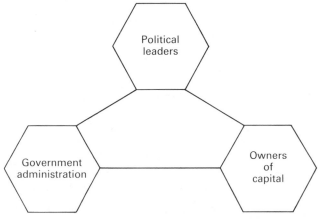

their advantage. Marxist writers also argue that state policies in areas of life such as social services and welfare are of direct benefit to the owners of capital. State education, for example, transfers much of the cost of training away from the employer to the state. The various different parts of the 'state apparatus' exist, they suggest, to support the needs of capital rather than those of the people. Running through Marxist arguments is the idea that democracy, as found in many western societies, is not true democracy. The so-called 'democratic institutions' act as a screen creating the illusion of democracy while allowing the owners of capital to exercise real power. This does not mean that the ruling elites always get their own way. At times of crisis they may be forced to accept changes in order to maintain order and prevent revolution.

These different political theories each attempt to explain the basic workings of the state. Each is closely linked to a particular political philosophy and influences how that philosophy is put into practice. As well as providing a basis of political action such theories also provide a way of understanding the actions of others.

11
Rich and Poor

He is of noble wealth and birth. So is she. Between them they own or have a stake in a sizeable chunk of Scotland and London. Now they have announced their engagement – and one day their fortunes will come together in a multi-million golden cascade. The 21-year-old Duke of Roxburgh and Lady Jane Grosvenor, 22, were pictured together at the Duke's home, 100-room Floors Castle in Roxburghshire, Scotland. As befits the occasion, the photographer too was an aristocrat, the Earl of Lichfield, who is Lady Jane's brother-in-law. (*Daily Express*, 24th August 1976, quoted in A. Giddens' 'The Rich', *New Society* 14.10.76.)

How unusual are the Duke of Roxburgh and Lady Jane Grosvenor? Are they all that is left of a dying aristocracy whose wealth has been reduced by taxes and inflation or are the rich, like the poor, always with us?

Income and wealth

Before we can answer these questions we must consider what 'being rich' means. We can judge how rich someone is on the basis of firstly what they earn, that is their income, and secondly, on the basis of what they have, which we would call their wealth.

In Fig. 54 we can see the official view of the distribution of income. The graph shows quite clearly that those people who are in the top 10 per cent of income-earners receive over 26 per cent of the total income before tax. The remaining 90 per cent of earners have to make do with the remaining 74 per cent of total incomes before tax. The bottom 10 per cent of earners only have 2·5 per cent of incomes to share among themselves before tax, though their proportion, while still low, does improve after taxation is taken into account. The inequalities are even clearer when we consider that the top 1 per cent shared 5·7 per cent of total incomes before tax (3·9 per cent after tax) and the top 5 per cent shared 16·7 per cent (13·6 per cent after tax).

The graph also shows that taxation does seem to have had some effect on the actual income people receive after tax is paid. Those with the smallest incomes pay little or no tax whereas those with the highest pay considerably more. However, this graph may not give us the whole picture. It is based on taxation returns and on people's *money* income. Taxation figures for the very rich are always likely to under-represent the true figure. 'Tax avoidance', or taxation planning, as it is more politely known, may often reduce an individual's apparent income. It is likely that the real incomes of the rich are more likely to be understated than those of the poor. In addition there is the problem of 'fringe benefits' or perks. Many employees receive additional benefits which do not count as income. They may have a car or a house which goes with the job, their children's school fees may be paid, they may even have interest-free loans for season tickets or house purchase. The benefits tend to be worth more the higher you are in the firm. Company directors generally receive

Fig. 54. *The distribution of personal income before and after tax*

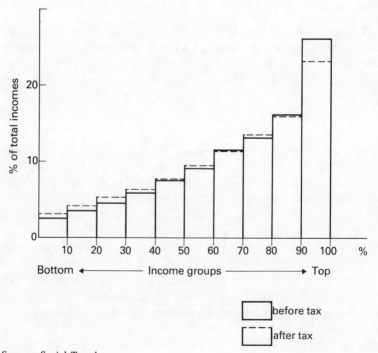

Source: Social Trends

more perks than managers and managers more than manual or clerical workers. These benefits are difficult to measure. It is however clear that they are more valuable to the higher income groups than to the lower groups. If anything they help to make the rich richer. Peter Townsend has calculated that when taxation and fringe benefits are taken into account the position of the richest 10 per cent has changed little in the last twenty years.

The second factor in 'being rich' is wealth. This can be made up from many different things. Your wealth includes any money you have under the mattress or safe in the bank, the value of your house if you own one, your household possessions, shares in building societies or with the Stock Exchange, Premium Bonds, Savings Certificates, mink coats, diamond bracelets and priceless Picassos. All of these things add up to your total wealth.

The ownership of wealth is even more concentrated than income.

Fig. 55. *The main types of private wealth*

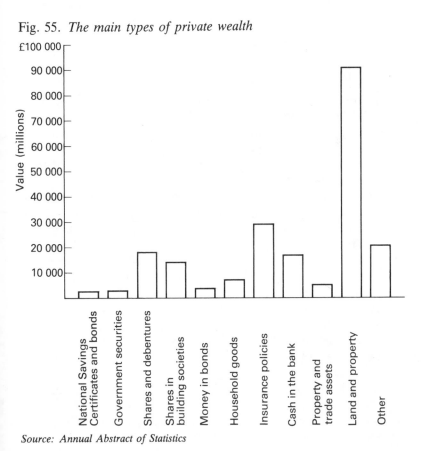

Source: Annual Abstract of Statistics

The top 1 per cent of wealth-holders own over a quarter of all personal wealth and the top 5 per cent own over one-half. This position has not changed greatly since the beginning of the century. In 1911 the top 10 per cent wealth-holders owned 92 per cent of all wealth, in 1960 they owned 83 per cent. Estate Duty returns do suggest that the small group of the most wealthy, the top 1 per cent, has shrunk in size since 1911. Whereas they then held 69 per cent of all wealth, by 1960 their share had fallen to 42 per cent. However, while the share of wealth held by the top 1 per cent declined, the share of the next 4 per cent down the ladder increased. This could mean that there are less very, very wealthy people and more not so very, very wealthy people; or that the wealth has been shared around the families of those very, very wealthy people in order to escape from taxes on inheritance. Early in this century estate duties brought in over 16 per cent of the government income. At the present time they bring in less than 4 per cent. Estate duty is another form of taxation which the rich have learned to avoid.

The rich

The world of the very rich is made up of three distinct groups of people. These groups are often closely interlocked with each other. The first group is small and on its own relatively unimportant. It is made up of those who could be counted as 'instant rich'. They are the pools winners and the pop-stars whose wealth is derived from activities which bring in very large incomes, often in a very short period of time. Though they may appear frequently in the press and on television they are not a particularly important section of 'the rich'. Most of the rich have either inherited their wealth (and along with it status and prestige), through established aristocratic families or through industry and commerce. Traditionally the British upper class was made up of the landed aristocracy whose members could often trace their ancestors back to William the Conqueror. Their wealth was in great country estates and their income came from farming. There are still many such families though not all of them are rich. Those that have kept their position have usually done so by merging with that other group of the rich – the commercial and business elite.

Whilst the base for the aristocracy was in the countryside, the base for the business elite is in the city, and more precisely in the City of London. It is here that the big banking and financial concerns operate. The Stock Exchange, the Commodity Markets, the

Merchant Banks and the Bank of England are all based in the City of London where fortunes can be made and lost very quickly. The 1960s were a period of property speculation and asset-stripping when some individuals made themselves into millionaires overnight. These people were the exceptions. The greater amount of city wealth is either in the hands of long-established banking and finance families such as the Rothschilds, or is owned by industrial or commercial magnates such as Jules Thorn or Isaac Wolfson. Often these families began with a self-made entrepreneur who built up the firm from almost nothing into a vast financial empire. The business, industrial and commercial rich may have had the money but often lacked status. The aristocracy had the status but for the last century, at least, have lacked the money. Today's rich are a combination of these two groups combining income, wealth and status, and often considerable power.

Poverty

You could say that the poor are all of those who are not rich. But what does it mean not to be rich? Compared to a property speculator with a fortune of £27 million most people seem poor. Yet if you ask them if they are poor they will deny it. The problem with poverty is one of defining it. Is poverty a fixed line below which people become poor? Is it a way of life, or a feeling that people have? This is a problem which has concerned sociologists and others for many years.

The earliest attempts to define poverty were based on the view that a family required certain basic commodities if they were to survive. If they were unable to provide these things then they were in *primary* poverty.

Seebohm Rowntree carried out a series of studies of poverty in York in the first half of this century. With the help of the British Medical Association he drew up a shopping list of necessary foods which should form part of a balanced, if meagre, diet for a man and his wife and three children under 14. To the cost of this basic diet Rowntree added an amount for clothing, fuel and light and sundries.

Other items bring the weekly bill to just over £5. This was Rowntree's poverty line. Families which existed below this line were said to be living in *secondary* poverty. At a still lower level were those families which were completely destitute and were in primary poverty.

The idea of a fixed poverty-line based on the necessities of life creates difficulties. There is no guarantee that people will spend

227

their money in the way laid down by the British Medical Association or any other official body. In normal life people do not agree about what their basic necessities are. Whilst a healthy diet may be important, some luxuries may be just as necessary – a night out at the pictures or a couple of bottles of brown ale for example. If you start asking people about poverty they will immediately draw comparisons. People see themselves as better off than some and worse off than others. Each individual relates his or her own position to the positions of other people. Poverty is relative. It is not a fixed line. Ideas of what poverty is change from time to time and in different places. A diet including half-a-pound of stoned dates

Fig. 56. *Rowntree's shopping list*

Table 1. **Dietary for man, wife, and three children (based on B.M.A. Report on nutritional needs, published 1950)**

Breast of mutton – 2½ lb. at 8d. per lb. (imported)	1. 8.
Minced beef – 2 lb. at 1s. 4d. per lb.	2. 8.
Shin of beef – 1½ lb. at 1s. 6d. per lb.	2. 3.
Liver – 1 lb. at 1s. 6d. per lb.	1. 6.
Beef sausages – 1 lb. at 1s. 3d. per lb.	1. 3.
Bacon 1¼ lb. at 1s. 11d. per lb. (cheapest cut)	2. 4¾.
Cheese – 10 oz. at 1s. 2d. per lb.	8¾.
Fresh full cream milk – 14 pints at 5d. per pint	5. 10.
Herrings – 1½ lb. at 8d. per lb.	1. 0.
Kippers – 1 lb. at 1s. per lb.	1. 0.
Sugar – 3 lb. 2 oz. at 5d. per lb.	1. 3½.
Potatoes – 14 lb. at 9 lb. for 1s.	1. 6½.
23½ lb. Bread – 13½ loaves at 5½d. each	6. 2¼.
Oatmeal – 2 lb. at 6d. per lb.	1. 0.
Margarine – 2½ lb. at 10d. per lb.	2. 1.
Cooking fat – 10 oz. at 1s. per lb.	7½.
Flour – 1¼ lb. at 9½d. per 3 lb. bag	4.
Jam – 1 lb. at 1s. 2d. per lb.	1. 2.
Treacle – 1 lb. at 10d. (in tins)	10.
Cocoa – ¼ lb. at 8½d. per ¼ lb.	8½.
Rice – 10 oz. at 9d. per lb.	5½.
Sago – ¼ lb. at 9d. per lb.	2¼.
Barley – 2 oz. at 9d. per lb.	1.
Peas – ½ lb. at 10½d. per lb.	5¼.
Lentils – ¾ lb. at 10½d. per lb.	8.
Stoned dates – ½ lb. at 10½d. per lb.	5¼.
Swedes – 6 lb. at 2½d. per lb.	1. 3.
Onions – 4½ lb. at 5d. per lb.	1. 10½.
Apples – 4 lb. at 5d. per lb.	1. 8.
Egg – 1 at 3½d.	3½.
Extra vegetables and fruit	1. 6.
Tea – ½ lb. at 3s. 4d. per lb.	1. 8.
Extras, including salt, seasoning, etc.	9.
	47. 4.

(1 shilling = 5p, 47s 4d = £2·37)

and six pounds of swedes may have been 'poverty' in York in 1950. It would be regarded as more than enough in some parts of the world where different standards of poverty are applied. A reasonable definition must relate poverty to the accepted standards within the wider society. If it is usual for families to own a refrigerator, a washing machine or a colour television then to be without one can be taken as a sign of poverty. We need to consider poverty in relation to the general standards within society.

It is therefore important to distinguish between poverty which is absolute – Rowntree's primary poverty – and relative poverty. A society may have few people living in absolute poverty but will still have a problem of relative poverty where large numbers of people are surviving at a level which most of their fellow countrymen would find unacceptable.

The idea of relative poverty is an important one but it does leave the sociologist with a problem. If the shopping list approach of Rowntree is abandoned, and we base our views of poverty on a person's position relative to the rest of society, how do you answer the question 'who is poor'? In this situation the sociologist must begin his answer 'well, it all depends . . .'. This is obviously not good enough if we want to get a clear idea of the number of people who might be in poverty or if poverty is disappearing or increasing. To get over this problem most social scientists use as a basis the level at which the government, through the Supplementary Benefits Commission, pays out Supplementary Benefit to people in need. It is not in any way a true measure of poverty. The S.B.C. scales may in fact be below the level at which we would say people are in poverty but it is a measure of poverty which is often used.

RELATIVE DEPRIVATION

Poverty is relative in another sense too. The poor are those people who are deprived of the things other people take for granted. But do people in fact see themselves as deprived? Do the poor, whoever they may be, see themselves as poor? Very few people look at advertisements for expensive watches and fast cars and say 'I can't afford that, therefore I'm poor'. Such things are outside of their frame of reference (Chapter 3). In normal life people relate their positions to those around them.

One of the areas in Banbury studied by Margaret Stacey was known as The Village. Wychtree Road runs through The Village with the council estates at one end in Upper Wychtree Road and the private houses in Mayfair Drive at the other.

Between the two is Wychtree Terrace where Mrs Kingpin lives.

229

She has strong links with many households in Wychtree Road as well as Wychtree Terrace and is the centre of an extensive gossip network. She distinguishes sharply between the Upper Wychtree Road people who 'live like pigs', 'drag up' their children and are a 'thieving lot' for whom she has no time, and the Mayfair Drive residents who are 'a cut above themselves' and a 'bit snobby'. (Stacey 1975)

Mrs Kingpin views her position in The Village relative to her neighbours. In that she is less well-off with not such a nice house as those who live in Mayfair Drive she is 'relatively deprived'. Compared to the residents of Upper Wychtree Road however she feels quite prosperous.

Poverty therefore is relative in so far as individuals lack things that others take for granted. Deprivation is relative because people see themselves within a fairly narrow frame of reference and not in the context of the wider society.

The idea of relative deprivation has been developed by Runciman who argues that people may fail to see themselves as deprived not only because they make comparisons within a fairly narrow frame of reference but also because they have come to see their situation as an inevitable part of the way society is organised. Poverty is seen to be natural and is justified as a normal part of life. This view suggests that inequality is inevitable and can never be changed. Poverty is even seen as a virtue, as in the old song 'she was poor but she was honest'. Such a view can be used as a justification for the continuance of poverty and as an explanation for the failure of any attempts to remove it. It is an ideological viewpoint (Chapter 7) which serves the interests of the wealthier classes.

Who are the poor?

In his early study of poverty in York, Seebohm Rowntree saw that 'the poor' were not a fixed group of people. During their lives people would go in and out of poverty as their circumstances changed.

'The life of the labourer', wrote Rowntree, 'is marked by five alternating periods of want and comparative plenty. During early childhood, unless his father is a skilled worker, he will probably be in poverty; this will last until he, or some of his brothers and sisters, begin to earn money and thus augment their father's wage sufficiently to raise the family above the poverty line. Then follows a period in which he is earning money and living under the parents' roof; for some portion of this period he will be earning more money than is required for lodging, food and clothes. This is his chance to save money . . . this period of prosperity may continue after marriage until he has two or three children, when poverty will again overtake him. This period of poverty will last perhaps for ten years, i.e., until the first child is fourteen and begins to earn wages; but if there are more than three children it may last longer. While the children are earning, and before they leave the home to marry, the man enjoys another period of prosperity – possibly however only to sink back into poverty when his children have married and left him, and he himself is too old to work. (Rowntree 1961, quoted in Coates and Silburn 1970)

Rowntree describes a 'cycle of poverty' through which people pass during their lives. The disadvantages experienced by each generation passing through this cycle of poverty are passed on to the next generation. Mothers from the poorest social groups have smaller babies and risk more infant deaths.

Table 35. *Birth and social class 1973*

Social class of mother	Stillbirths per 1 000 of all births	Average birthweight (grams)
I	7·4	3 359
II	8·5	3 346
III	11·2	3 273
IV	13·5	3 244
V	16·2	3 163
All classes	11·6	3 262

Source: Social Trends

Twice as many babies die in the first week of life in social class V as in social class I. Even though infant mortality has fallen steadily throughout this century social class V mothers have never been able to catch up their sisters in social class I. The inequalities which exist at birth continue throughout life.

Particular groups of people are more at risk than others. The families of the unemployed and the low paid, the sick or disabled, the elderly, single parents and their families and families with three

Fig. 57. *Health and social class*
Eyesight

% of 5 year olds with refractive error (1973)

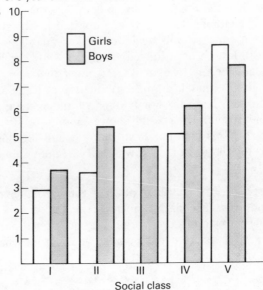

Social class

Fig. 58. *Health and social class*
Tooth decay

% of 5 year olds with tooth decay (1973)

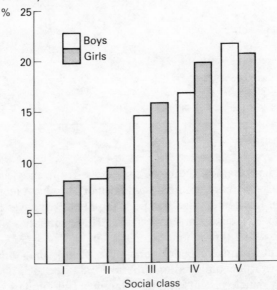

Social class

Fig. 59. *Health and social class*

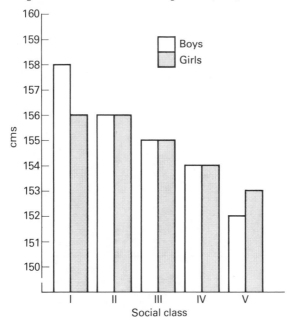

Height of school children at the age of 14 (1973)

Social class

or more children stand the greatest risk of getting into debt, of suffering the worst housing, inadequate diets and the poorest health.

Frank Field has written that
the cycle of inequality is complete. Even in death the significant differences between the rich and the poor stubbornly remain. We have seen that wives of professional groups have a far greater chance of giving birth successfully than the wives of semi-skilled and unskilled workers. The children of professional workers have a far greater chance of surviving the first year of life, and then of living longer.

These children are unequal when they start school and continue to draw away from their peers from poorer homes. The cycle of inequality is reflected in the income earned, the status at the work-place and in the housing rich and poor families occupy. These class differences appear again in the difference in health, and finally in death.

Despite growth in the national wealth the age-old inequalities remain. The position of the poor has improved. But so, too, has that of the rich. It is as if the poor have been placed on an esca-

Fig. 60. *Health and social class*

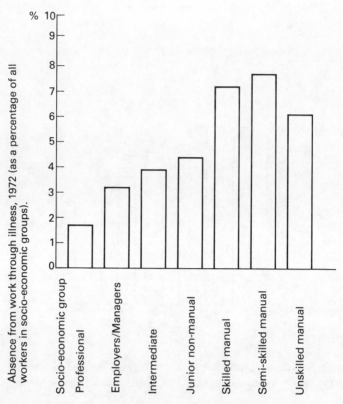

lator which gradually lifts their position. But the rich, too, are on board their own escalator which is moving just as fast, if not faster.
(Field 1974)

A culture of poverty

Poverty, as we have already seen, can be understood (a) as not having enough money for the basic essentials of life or (b) as being relatively deprived in comparison to other groups. Sociologists who have worked among people who live in, or near to, poverty have noticed that poverty has other important features. Poverty appears to produce its own attitudes and beliefs, its own behaviour and its own way of life. Coates and Silburn, in a study of a poor district of Nottingham, commented:

234

In nearly every interview we detected a basic sense of hopelessness or powerlessness. Although the degree of resignation or despair may vary from one man or woman to another there are still few people who express unqualified self-confidence or optimism. This is not to say that people in St Ann's are perpetually gloomy, far from it. One is constantly aware of a warmth, generosity, and humour – so often more characteristic of the poor than of those with more to lose. The difference we would emphasise is that cheerfulness and optimism find an exclusively private expression.

The overwhelming majority fail to have any broad social expectations, almost as though they have learned that such expectations are beyond their reach or control. When cheerful optimism is felt, it is not because things are getting any better, but because they are not getting much worse. (Coates and Silburn 1970)

Fig. 61. *Overcrowding, 1972 (percentage of households in each socio-economic group with no spare rooms)*

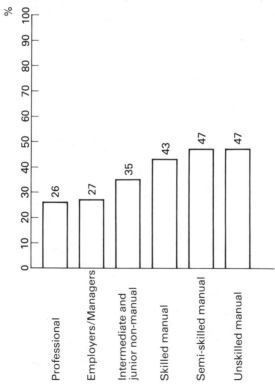

An American anthropologist, Oscar Lewis, has described this characteristic of poor neighbourhoods as a 'culture of poverty'. Poverty becomes a way of life which is handed down from generation to generation with its own customs, its own languages, its own values and view of the outside world.

Solving the problems of urban poverty

The 'culture of poverty' point of view led people to believe that to reduce poverty you had to change the culture. It was largely on this basis that both Labour and Conservative governments attempted to tackle the problem of poverty in the 1960s and early 1970s.

A string of official reports in the early 1960s drew attention to the problem of the inner cities. The Milner-Holland Report focused on housing in London, the Plowden Report looked at Primary Schools, Seebohm considered the social services and Ingleby, children and young persons. The problem came to be called 'urban deprivation'. It was believed that the problems of the inner cities were caused by the disorganisation of the people who lived there. If you could help the people to get themselves organised then they would break out of the 'culture of poverty' and the problems would be solved. First you had to find how to get people organised. A large number of separate projects were set up to do this. Urban aid was to 'provide for the care of our citizens who live in the poorest or most overcrowded parts of our cities and towns. It is intended to arrest, in so far as it is possible by financial means, and reverse the downward spiral which afflicts so many of these areas.' (Home Secretary, James Callaghan, addressing Parliament 2.12.68)

The E.P.A. or Education Priority Area projects sought to establish 'the kind of partnership between parents and teachers in relation to children that there should be in an ideal community'. The Neighbourhood Schemes put large sums of money into particular problem neighbourhoods. Inner Area Studies looked in detail at the problem of local authorities in six local areas. In 1969 the Home Office established 12 Community Development Projects which were based on three assumptions. 1. It was the deprived who were the cause of urban deprivation. 2. The problem could be solved by overcoming apathy and encouraging self-help. 3. Local research into the problem would bring about changes in local and central government policy.

In the 1970s came yet more projects but the approach began to change. It became recognised that 'the problem of urban deprivation cannot be tackled effectively by means of special compensatory programmes of the self-help or community development type'. The attack on 'the culture of poverty' had not worked.

The fault lay in the very idea of a 'culture of poverty'. The first criticism that was made was that if such a thing as a 'culture of poverty' did exist it was a result of deprivation and not a cause of it. To remove the poverty you had to remove the fundamental causes which very often lay outside of the deprived community. The Inner City Study Projects and the Community Development Projects both pointed out very clearly that 'social disorganisation' was not the root of the problem. The real problem lay in a shortage of jobs caused by closing factories and by insufficient investment in new ones. C.D.P. argued that instead of putting the blame on the poor the government should look more critically at the way industry was organised in a capitalist society. The second criticism of the 'culture of poverty' rejects the whole existence of a separate culture. This criticism is based on studies of poor communities which suggest that the attitudes and values of the poor are no different from those of 'rich' society.

Liebow, in a study of 'Tally's Corner' found that the unemployed men who hang around the corner placed little value on work. However the jobs the men were always offered were low-paid and had low status. 'The rest of the society', remarked Liebow, 'holds the job of dishwasher and janitor in low esteem if not outright contempt. So does the street-corner man.'

Coates and Silburn's study of St Ann's in Nottingham came to a similar conclusion. Rather than belonging to a separate culture they suggested that the people of St Ann's shared the same hopes and values as the rest of the people of Britain. Their poverty forces them to be realistic about what is possible and about what they can achieve.

The welfare state

Government action against poverty, ill health, unemployment and deprivation is not confined to the urban poverty programmes. The origin of the Welfare State goes back to the early years of this century when health and unemployment insurance were first introduced. Modern governments accept that they have a responsibility for the wealth and well-being of the nation. This has not always been so. The Acts of Parliament which form the basis of Britain's system of health, welfare and social security date from the end of the Second World War. Before that time governments were only prepared to accept responsibility for certain groups, or for the very poor. Most people had to make their own arrangements for insurance and medical care.

THE BEVERIDGE REPORT

The turning point came with the publication in 1942 of the Report of a committee of civil servants headed by Sir William Beveridge, on Social Insurance and Allied Services. In his Report, Beveridge described five freedoms which were the right of every man, woman and child in the country. These were freedom from want, disease, ignorance, squalor and idleness. The Report proposed a comprehensive system of social welfare for all. The idea of the state, or the community, providing for the needs of the least fortunate was not new. The Poor Law of 1601, the 1834 Poor Law and the 1911 People's Budget are earlier examples of state action. Men and women like Charles Booth, Edwin Chadwick, Octavia Hill, Eleanor Rathbone, Sidney and Beatrice Webb each made their own contribution. The Beveridge Report was unique in bringing so many ideas together to provide for people's needs, 'from the cradle to the grave'. The proposals of the Report were contained in a long series of Acts of Parliament passed between 1944 and 1948. The 1944 Education Act is discussed in Chapter 8. It was followed by the Family Allowances Act 1945, the National Insurance Act 1946, the National Insurance (Industrial Injuries) Act 1946, the National Health Service Act 1946, the Children's Act 1948, the National Assistance Act 1948, and others. Many of these Acts of Parliament have since been amended or replaced by new legislation but the pattern of the Beveridge Report remains.

FROM WOMB TO TOMB

The idea of a Welfare State is built around four basic concepts. First, there is the principle of social security. Richard Crossman has described this as a 'cushion of security against hardship due to unavoidable misfortune' which could lead to considerable hardship for the worker and his family. Workers could insure themselves privately against such catastrophes but many failed to do so. The Welfare State does it for them; providing compulsory National Insurance against accidents. Another misfortune might be ill health. In this case the state provides a National Health Service out of taxation. The second principle was that of 'equality of entitlement'. One of the lessons of the Second World War was that basically all men have the same needs. A rich man's house was as likely to be hit by a bomb as was that of a poor man. All men should be entitled to the same basic social welfare. A duke may collect the same pension, be treated in the same hospital, send his son to the same school, as a dustman. Above this basic minimum individuals could make their own arrangements, but the basic minimum was there as a right. The families of all lower paid workers have a right to the Family Income Supplement. All unemployed men have a right to industrial training and to the services of an employment exchange.

Central to all ideas of social welfare is the principle of concern for the individual. Because people have different needs and different circumstances they must be treated differently. A probation officer or child-care officer must treat each case on its individual merits, even though this may seem unjust. The final principle of the Welfare State is that of participation and community involvement. Ordinary local people serve on the Board of Managers of local primary schools as well as on the Regional Hospital Boards, and other bodies.

SOCIAL SECURITY

An important part of the Beveridge scheme was for a national system of social security. There had been limited schemes of health and unemployment insurance before but Beveridge progressed a scheme which would cover everyone. It was to be based on a government-run insurance scheme to which everyone contributed the same amount. The benefits of this scheme were to be available to all. At the outset therefore the scheme has three important features.

Firstly, it was a contributory scheme, secondly payment was on a flat-rate and thirdly benefits were universal.

In time, however, these features were changed. Whilst it remained contributory it was clear that Beveridge's hopes for a self-financing scheme were not justified. The government increasingly subsidised the scheme from taxation. The flat-rate paid by everyone was replaced by a two-tier system by which an additional 'earnings-related' payment gave many workers a higher level of benefit. Their contributions, and therefore, what they received at retirement, or if made redundant, was related to what they earned.

Many people had, and still have, a great dislike, or even fear, of the means-test – the declaration of income and resources before a social benefit can be received. For many it brings back memories of the 1930s when men had to prove that they were destitute before they could receive help. Social Security after the Second World War was not charity. It was an insurance paid for by all and therefore available to all as a right. Professor Richard Titmuss wrote 'There should be no sense of inferiority, pauperism, shame or stigma in the use of a publicly provided service'. This principle of universalism without means-test was not supported by everyone and strong arguments developed in favour of selective rather than universal benefits. Firstly, it was considered to be a wasteful use of limited resources to provide for everyone equally irrespective of their needs. Benefits, it was argued, should go to those in greatest need. The means-test enabled the providers of social services to know what people's needs were. Secondly, some politicians felt that it was morally wrong to give people something for nothing. People should stand on their own feet and should only be helped when in real need. Thirdly it was feared that universalism would mean that more and more of the nation's resources would be spent on social services and less would be available for investment and the needs of industry. The Conservative Party in particular had favoured a move towards selective benefits and away from universalisation. The Family Income Supplement is one example of a selective benefit. It is available only to those families whose income is below a certain level and provides a cash payment as well as free prescriptions, free school meals and other benefits. Means-tests are also used for rent rebates, payments towards home-helps, university grants and day nurseries.

The opponents of selectivity argue that it is in fact less effective in helping those in need. The stigma of claiming such benefits and the complexity of many forms prevents many from seeking help. It has been estimated that in 1975 non-take-up of benefits for those under retirement age was £175 000 000. Probably a quarter of those who should receive Family Income Supplement fail to claim. Often people do not know that they can claim these benefits, or they claim too late. It is likely that many of those who fail to claim are those in greatest need.

Another result of means-tested selective benefits is the creation of a 'poverty-trap'.

You would normally expect a person who gets a pay-rise or works more overtime to be better-off. The 'poverty trap' can mean that someone who receives means-tested benefits is in fact worse off if they work longer hours or get a pay-rise. This is because means-tested benefits fade away at the point where income tax begins. Whereas one week a wage-earner received a wage plus benefits a pay-rise the next week could mean that he not only loses the benefits but also starts to pay tax and is worse off. There have been attempts to reduce the effect of the poverty trap by introducing lower tax rates for low-paid workers and by taking some groups out of the tax system altogether but they have not removed the problem completely.

It can be seen that social security has moved a long way from its original principles. It is a very complicated system involving large numbers of civil servants to check claims, pay out benefits and investigate 'scroungers'. Despite this vast administration and sums of money spent the social security system does not seem to have succeeded in removing poverty.

The voluntary organisations

Long before the phrase 'Welfare State' was first used, voluntary organisations were involved in social welfare. The earliest schools, hospitals and poor relief came from private charities and though the state has taken over responsibility for these things the voluntary bodies still exist and perform useful functions.

While the Welfare State usually provides a basic minimum, voluntary groups are able to provide much-needed extras. The National Health Service provides all that is needed to make a hospital patient well. There are doctors and nurses, operating theatres and X-ray equipment. Because funds are limited, hospitals are seldom able to provide a library or a hospital shop, or a bedside radio service. These facilities are often provided by voluntary groups, by groups of 'hospital friends' or by a Rotary Club. These important extras involve fund raising and voluntary workers to run them. Raising money and organising voluntary workers are two important functions of voluntary organisations. They enable the welfare services' scarce resources of money and manpower to be used more effectively.

In some parts of the Welfare State the voluntary organisations have a far more important role to play. In the Children and Young Persons Act 1969 the officers of the National Society for the Prevention of Cruelty to Children are 'authorised persons' able to bring a young person before a juvenile court. Similarly Dr Barnardo's is a recognised agency for the care of children, working with local councils. This partnership between voluntary body and state or local authority should not be underestimated. Very often it is the voluntary organisation which introduces a new idea or a new solution to a problem. Later, when its value has been proved, the state may step in and give it finance or even adopt its ideas for its own purposes. Family Planning, Citizens Advice Bureaux, community care of the mentally ill are all schemes which began in a small way and were later supported by the state. Voluntary bodies are often able to provide a testing ground for new ideas.

Sometimes this 'testing ground' function of the voluntary organisation goes as far as sponsoring or even conducting research into a problem. Cancer research is an example of this. The money available for research through the government-backed Medical Research Council is limited. By raising funds from voluntary bodies, scientists are able to increase the amount of research being carried out. Voluntary bodies also have a certain independence from the government. This can be important if the organisation wishes to act as a pressure group, applying pressure on the government. Groups like the Child Poverty Action Group and Disablement Income Group are primarily concerned with this pressure-group function. They provide an independent check on the activities of the Welfare State. They also try to keep the public informed and to educate people. 'Shelter', the National Campaign for the Homeless, is an example of a voluntary body which devotes considerable effort to education.

Voluntary organisations have a very important part to play in the Welfare State. They perform useful functions in providing additional resources, initiating new ideas, involving voluntary workers and educating the public. The welfare society is a partnership between state, local authority and voluntary organisation.

12
Crime and Deviance

Crime is generally thought of as a problem in society. Frequently we are told that crime is getting worse, that the crime-rate is rising and that law and order are becoming more difficult to maintain. But what exactly is crime? How do we know that it is rising? and what has it to do with law, and with order? Can sociology help us to answer these questions?

Crime is universal

To begin with we must understand that there is nothing unusual about crime in society. There is no society in the world which exists without crime. There may be differences in the things people in different societies *count* as crime but no society is without crime in some form. This is not really very surprising. For there to be no crime, everyone would either have to think alike, which is obviously impossible, or they would have to be so tolerant that any actions would be permitted, even murder. In the end every society has a point where it says these actions are wrong and wrongdoers must be punished. Having said, however, that crime is found in all societies, what people count as crime, and what they do about it differs from society to society. They also differ at different times and even in different parts of one society.

Having begun with the idea that crime is usual in society, we must recognise certain basic features of what we call crime. For any action to be a crime it needs to be defined as 'crime' by people or individuals who have the power to do so. Parliament can make laws, so too can judges, but as we shall see later in this chapter there are other 'definers' – the police and the newspapers, for example. This means that what counts as 'crime' can change from time to time, and from place to place, laws change and actions which were once permitted become criminal.

Secondly, for an action to become a crime it needs to be decided by a legal process which will involve not just the police as 'law enforcers' but also magistrates, judges, juries, counsel and so on.

Before continuing to look at crime in more detail it is important to get a basic idea of how the law works and who is involved.

THE LAW

Law in England is made up of two strands. Parliament has the power to make laws. These laws are known as statutes. Sometimes Parliament gives power to make laws and regulations to other bodies. Government departments and local councils for example can make regulations which have the force of law as long as these regulations are not themselves against the law or in any way against the will of Parliament or the courts. As well as statute law there is the older tradition of common law. Statutes can never be designed to cover every possible event. Times change, new problems arise and statutes need to be interpreted. This is done by the courts of law. The decisions of the courts become 'precedents' which guide judges on how they are to proceed in the future. This is the basis for common law. It lays down the principles upon which judgements will be made. This does not mean that judges can do what they like. Parliament always has the power to decide what the correct interpretation is and can always pass a statute to close a 'loophole' should one appear. Just as Parliament has the power to change the law against 'precedents' laid down by the courts, so too can the courts give judgement against the Government when it breaks the rules.

As well as two kinds of law, statute law and common law, there are also two kinds of court. On the one hand there are courts which deal with offences against the law. These are criminal courts. Many court cases deal with disputes between individuals where no law has been broken and these are dealt with by civil courts. Robbery is a matter which would be dealt with by a criminal court whereas a civil court would deal with disputes over contracts, including business contracts, property and marriage.

Most criminal cases are 'non-indictable' which means that they are less serious than 'indictable' cases and will therefore be dealt with by the lower courts. The magistrate's court, which has a magistrate (or justice of the peace), instead of a judge and jury deals with over 90 per cent of all criminal cases including some of the less serious 'indictable' offences. More serious cases are dealt with by the crown courts. The Old Bailey in London is an example of a more famous 'crown court'. Civil cases are dealt with by county courts or by the various divisions of the high court.

When someone is allowed to 'appeal' against the verdict of a court, the case is taken to a higher court and possibly to the House of Lords which is the final Court of Appeal.

Offences by young people are dealt with separately. The law defines people under 14 as 'children' and those between 14 and 17 as 'young persons'. Many cases involving children and young persons will not get into court. They are likely to be dealt with by the Police Juvenile Bureaux or by social workers. Children under 14 are not held to be criminally responsible. Should a 'child' get into serious trouble with the law, the juvenile court would sit as a 'care proceeding' and seek to ensure that the child received whatever help or care was needed. Much of the work with children and young persons is carried out by social workers.

The enforcement of the law involves other groups of people as well as the courts. Most obvious amongst law enforcement agencies are the police. There are over 125 000 policemen and women in the United Kingdom assisted by a further 79 500 civilian employees, traffic wardens and part-time special constables. In addition there are the separate police forces for the railways, airports and military bases. On a number of matters, Parliament has also given powers of law enforcement to certain specialised groups of people. Factory

Fig. 62. *The courts of law*

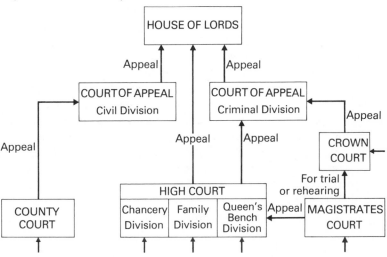

245

inspectors, weights and measures officers and public health officers all have powers of law enforcement.

Other groups are concerned with the treatment of offenders. Probation officers prepare reports on people who are being taken before the courts and supervise those who are put 'on probation' as an alternative to prison. Social workers have a similar role for those under 14. There are then the prisons and remand centres to which the courts may send convicted persons or those awaiting trial.

SOCIOLOGY AND CRIME

In their attempts to understand crime and other forms of deviant behaviour, sociologists have used different ways of looking at the problem. Some have thought of crime as a kind of illness which has particular causes and which can be prevented and cured. Others have viewed crime not as a disease but merely as a particular type of action which becomes 'criminal' because people with the power and authority to do so 'label' it as criminal. For this group of sociologists the way actions are labelled is more important often than the actions themselves. A third approach looks at crime in the context of a society in which most property is owned by a fairly small group of people who use their power to keep those with little property under control. In these debates about crime and deviance there is a basic problem of whose view of crime is correct. On the one hand there are those sociologists who accept the everyday definition of crime. They are often termed criminologists. They see crime as certain activities which the law says are criminal and which are therefore wrong. A wider view sees crime as activities which would be generally thought to be wrong but which may not come to the attention of the courts. Edwin Sutherland pointed to this kind of wrongdoing in his study of 'white-collar crime'. These are crimes usually committed by 'persons of respectability and high social status' in the course of their normal work. Business fraud, tax evasion and even free use of the firm's telephone all come in this category. A yet wider view sees crime as merely one form of deviant behaviour in a society which contains many forms of deviance. To understand crime you need therefore to understand deviance and how it arises. As well as problems of perspective and definition sociologists must also consider why they should study crime. Can the sociologists remain neutral? Is it possible to study something as important as crime or deviance for its own sake without having some interest in the uses to which that knowledge is put? Some sociologists accept that their role is to provide answers to questions posed by the law enforcers. They seek to provide the information which

Fig. 63. *Views of criminals and deviance*

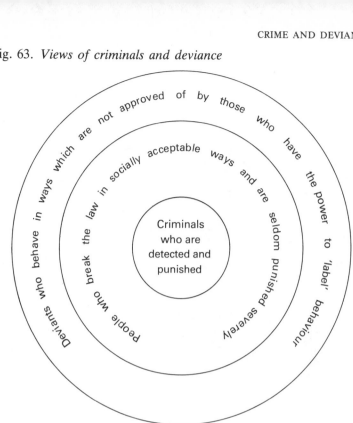

will guide the actions of judges and policemen, prison governors and probation officers. Other sociologists wish to remain independent, free from the influence and interference of those in authority. Indeed, they would argue it may be more important to study those in authority than to study the criminals themselves. These problems are basic to the study of crime and deviance and will appear again as we examine various approaches in more detail. You should consider your own viewpoint and discuss it with others.

Explaining crime

In looking for reasons for criminal behaviour, sociologists have worked from two types of explanation. Firstly there is a way of explaining crime which looks for causes in each individual. Crime is seen as a personal action caused by physical characteristics. This type of model could be called genetic as it is usually based on the study of genes and the chemistry of the body. An Italian scientist,

247

Fig. 64. *The criminal man from Lombroso's* L'uomo Deliquente, *1876*

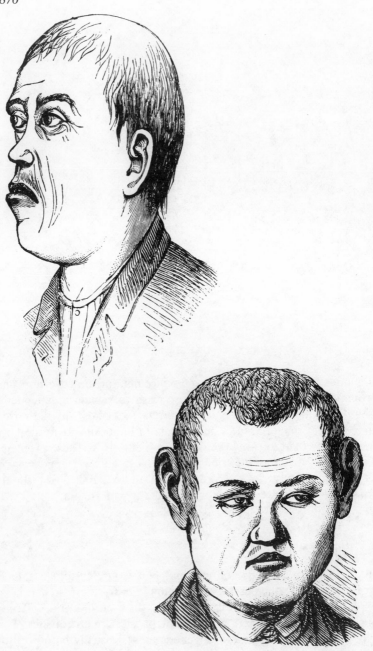

Lombroso, developed a theory on these lines in the nineteenth century. Criminals he claimed would easily be recognised by their physical characteristics, and he produced drawings that showed basic criminal types.

Lombroso's theories are not generally accepted today though some scientists still think of crime as having a basically biological cause.

The second type of explanation is concerned not with the make up of the individual but with the social environment within which the individual lives. Most sociological theories are based on some variation of this type of explanation which could be called 'environmental'. You will not have to think very hard to realise that crime is unlikely to have one single cause, whether you are concerned with one particular crime or with crime in society it is clear that there are many causes. Most theories of criminal behaviour are in fact 'multi-causal'.

In the 1920s Cyril Burt carried out a psychological and sociological study *The Young Delinquent*. He argued that there was no single explanation for criminal behaviour. Over 170 different causes were studied. Many of these were basically 'genetic' and in Burt's view were likely to be the major cause in roughly 35 per cent of the cases studied. The remaining 65 per cent were caused by mainly environmental factors. Burt's genetic, or physical causes, included low intelligence, temperament and physical infirmity.

Few sociologists today would be quite as confident as Burt in attempting to give percentages to particular genetic and environmental 'causes' of crime. Burt himself admitted that 'between what is instinctive (genetic) and what is acquired (environmental) there is no sharp clean-cut division', and also that no test could ever satisfactorily separate the two aspects. Most modern sociologists would say that Burt over-emphasised genetic influences and included as genetic many factors which were largely environmental.

ENVIRONMENTAL INFLUENCES

If genetic factors are not as important as Burt suggested more attention must be given to environmental influences.

One line of argument is based on the view that to become a law-abiding adult the child needs to be socialised into the important values of society. If that socialisation is not adequate or effective then the child will be likely to become a delinquent. This argument concentrates on the idea of family socialisation and on the effect of the family in a child's early life. Young children learn the difference between right and wrong at an early age. Naughty children are

Fig. 65. *The criminal area*

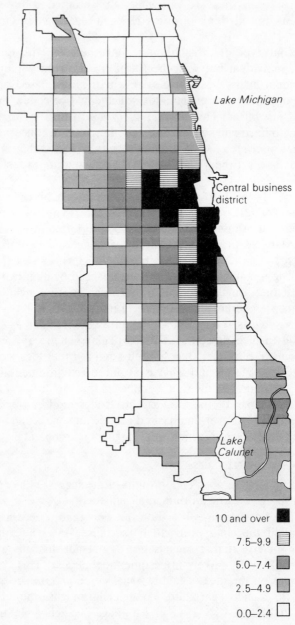

Rates of male juvenile delinquents, Chicago 1927–33

Rates per 100 male population in 10–16 age group

Lake Michigan

Central business district

Lake Calumet

10 and over

7.5–9.9

5.0–7.4

2.5–4.9

0.0–2.4

punished – with a smack or by being sent to bed. Punishment may also take the form of being denied affection. 'Mummy doesn't love naughty children' may be the kind of punishment used. Good behaviour on the other hand is usually rewarded, by a kiss and a hug or by actual rewards like a sweet or a biscuit. In so-called *normal* families rewards and punishments are given fairly and consistently. Naughtiness, if discovered, leads to punishment; being good gets a reward. What counts as 'being good' or 'being naughty' is usually clearly defined and reliably enforced. When this does not happen the socialisation is said to be faulty because criminals are therefore thought to be those that are not given the right kind of upbringing. The problem with this approach is that is tries to build its argument on the idea of a *normal* upbringing.

You have only got to look around you to see that family life differs very much from family to family. We must therefore treat any ideas of a 'normal' upbringing with some caution. What writers often refer to as 'normal' upbringing, or *correct socialisation*, is often the socialisation they are used to. Socialisation is also important when you consider the effects your friends have on you. 'Getting into bad company' or 'mixing with the wrong sort' are often given as explanations of criminal behaviour.

The American sociologist Edwin Sutherland recognised this in his theory of *differential association*. For Sutherland the way people learn to be criminals is much the same as the way other people learn not to be criminal. It just depends on the group from which you learn. The more closely you are involved with a group the more you learn from them. Other studies have taken a broader view and have tried to relate criminal behaviour to the environment in which people live.

Shaw and McKay studied the official statistics for crime in Chicago in the 1930s. They saw the city as a pattern of circles, like an archery target. At the centre was the business and entertainment area of downtown Chicago. Surrounding it was a ring of older housing (called the 'zone of transition') which though once prosperous had now fallen upon hard times and was the home of a shifting population of unskilled workers and immigrants. Beyond that lay the settled working-class communities surrounded in turn by the better-off residential areas and on the outer ring by the upper-class estates. On Shaw and McKay's evidence crime was centred on the 'zone of transition'. Even though the population of this zone was continuously changing, the delinquency rate remained the same. This zone of the city, it was suggested, lacked the established community sense to be found elsewhere. It was socially disorganised and this contributed to the crime rate. Shaw and McKay's 'ecological' theory has been criticised. In describing social disorganisation they neglected many aspects of the community which were not criminal. In addition their concentric zones do not fit the maps of other cities. They did, however, point to the fact that rates of delinquency are often higher in particular environments.

Who becomes delinquent?

Researchers who try to study the causes of criminal behaviour often have difficulty in studying a normal (non-criminal) group of people. Very often in the past criminologists have concentrated on studies of people who have already been convicted of criminal acts. Statements about the causes of crime are often made only on the basis of the evidence of those who have committed crime and seldom with comparable evidence on non-criminals in similar situations. This often means that researchers are looking back into the criminal's past in an attempt to explain his present behaviour. Frequently the evidence they require is lost or forgotten or wasn't recorded as no one thought it important enough.

The Cambridge study on delinquent development attempted to overcome these problems and to find the basic causes of crime among young people. Four hundred and eleven eight-year-old boys were selected from six primary schools in an area of North London. The boys all came from a fairly settled working-class area of North London. Information on the boys was collected in three ways:

1. The boys themselves were either interviewed or tested five times – at the ages of 8–9, 10–11, 14–15, 16–17 and 18–19.
2. Their parents were interviewed in the first year of the study and then once a year until the boys left school.
3. Criminal records of the courts and the police were used to keep a check on any offences committed by the boys.

The whole study lasted ten years and at the end was still in touch with over 94 per cent of the original sample of boys.

At the end of the study the researchers had evidence on over 150 different factors which might have had an influence on a boy's behaviour. These included the family background, housing, progress and behaviour at school, intelligence, height, health, friendship groups and criminal records for each of the 411 boys studied. On the basis of police and social services records the boys were grouped under four headings:

(a) Boys with more than one conviction.

(b) Boys with one conviction only.

(c) Boys with no convictions but who were known to the police through the juvenile bureaux or an unsuccessful prosecution.

(d) Boys with no convictions who were not known to the police.

In addition to the official records of delinquency the study also asked the boys themselves about their criminal acts. This evidence showed that the vast majority of boys had committed some kind of minor offence. Ninety-three per cent had let off fireworks in the street, over 90 per cent had seen an (X) certificate film when they were under age. A few boys had committed more serious offences such as house-breaking (7 per cent), shop-breaking (12:7 per cent), theft from cars (14 per cent). These self-reported crimes did not always match up to the official records. The official figures would seem to understate the true extent of criminal behaviour.

When the evidence on official and self-reported criminal acts is compared to the possible causes of crime, five factors stood out as important:

(a) low family income

(b) large family size

(c) at least one parent with a criminal record

(d) low intelligence

(e) parental conflict or lack of discipline.

The boys who suffered from at least three of these factors were statistically more likely to be in the group of persistent offenders.

The Cambridge study is useful in that it points to certain basic problems which would seem to affect criminal behaviour. Some questions did remain unanswered. The differences in self-reported crime and the official records may indicate some form of police bias. The boys in the delinquent groups may have fitted particular stereotypes of criminals more so than equally delinquent boys who were classified as non-offenders. It is not clear how far such a study of a fairly small group of boys in one area of London helps us to understand who becomes delinquent at other times and in other places.

Most importantly, however, the study emphasised the need to consider the effects of a number of inter-related causes of crime.

The Cambridge study on delinquent development suggests that delinquency arises from a complex interaction between the individual home atmosphere, the personal qualities of the boy and the circumstances in which the family live . . . a multi-causal theoretical approach seems necessary. (West and Farrington 1973)

253

Different amounts of crime and delinquency in different areas of cities or among different groups of people can therefore be explained in a number of ways. Poor housing conditions, large families, low wages may all be linked to crime but they need not be definite causes. Many people who live in poor housing, have large families or low wages do not always turn to crime. We may still be left with many of our questions about the causes of crime unanswered.

MERTON'S VIEW

Robert K. Merton has put forward a theory which may take us a little further forward in our search for explanations. Merton was concerned not only with crime but with other forms of deviant behaviour also. He recognised that instead of being a result of a breakdown in law and social control, deviance may in fact be a result of the very way society is organised. In their lives people want many things. They may want wealth, success, power, or just a comfortable home and a little peace and quiet. Merton calls these 'goals'. Some of the goals are encouraged by society. Others are not. Within society there are different ways of achieving these goals. Some of these ways of achieving the goals are approved of, and some are not. The ways the goals are achieved he called 'means'.

Most people have *goals* of which society generally approves. They want to earn a decent wage and to live in reasonable comfort. They use accepted *means* to achieve their goals. They work hard, spend their money carefully and try to make ends meet. Merton calls this approach 'conformity'. Other people have similar goals but may choose to use different means. They may use means which are not generally approved.

They will use other means to achieve their goals. They may turn to crime or ways of making a living which do not meet with general approval. Merton calls these 'innovators'.

A third group accepts the means but ignores the goals. These are termed 'ritualists' and while they work within the system they have no idea of where they are going or what they want from life. Merton includes two more groups – retreatists and rebels – who reject both the goals and the means. The 'retreatists' reject goals and means by dropping out of society. The rebels seek to change the society. You could probably recognise each of these types in your school or college. Schools and colleges have their own goals – being educated, passing exams, etc. They have means by which these goals are achieved: working hard, writing essays, turning up for classes, etc.

The *conformists* intend to pass their exams and do all that is expected of them. In extreme cases they are called 'swots'. The innovators want to succeed but they will use other methods. They may get higher marks by 'borrowing' other people's work. They may cheat in exams. Ritualists don't really know why they are at school. They don't have much ambition but they do all of the work just the same. Retreatists gave up long ago. They don't care about the exams and they don't bother with studying. Rebels think the whole system is rubbish and try to change it. They may want to abolish exams or make lessons voluntary. In particular they want to change what schools stand for.

Merton suggests that these different approaches are the result of the way society is organised. Certain goals – success, wealth, prestige, etc. – are encouraged within society. Many people however are not able to obtain these goals in ways of which society approves. They therefore adopt means which are seen as deviant.

Crime, therefore, arises when people are unable to achieve the *goals* which everyone regards as normal by the *means* which society accepts.

SUBCULTURE

A further approach to the problem of crime also recognises that criminal activity is concentrated in certain localities. Instead of blaming the physical environment – bad housing, unemployment and a lack of amenities – attention is directed towards the attitudes and values the people share. It focuses on the cultural factors.

The American sociologist Albert Cohen used the idea of subculture to describe the ideas and values of particular areas which were against the values of the whole society. In Cohen's view there was a kind of 'anti-culture' produced by problems of 'getting-ahead' in a world dominated by middle-class values. He suggested that young people in working-class areas become frustrated because they cannot gain the success which middle-class values suggest they should. This leads to a sense of rejection and turning to gangs and teenage groups where they can be accepted on equal terms. In Cohen's view delinquency and crime are the result of this status frustration imposed upon working-class youth by middle-class social values.

A slightly different view which also focused on the idea of subculture was developed by Walter Miller, another American Sociologist. Miller's view of sub-culture is broader than Cohen's. For Miller certain working-class communities are centred on a way of life which itself encourages certain kinds of behaviour. The desire for working-class youths to show that they are tough, quick-witted and daring combined with a belief in 'luck' are likely to bring them into conflict with the law. 'Getting into trouble' is seen as a normal aspect of slum life, as normal as being unable to pay the rent.

ASOLESCENT BOYS IN EAST LONDON

Peter Willmott considered these theories in his study *Adolescent Boys of East London* (1966). Many of the boys who were interviewed recognised the conflict between the values within their own community and the values demanded for success outside.

'There's a proper way of speaking everyone should have', said a 17-year-old clerk, 'and I'm trying to get it, I'm trying to change my accent to sound my aitches and say "good evening" instead of "watcher" and "goodbye" instead of "ta-ta".'

'You have to talk a bit different to what you do at home,' said a 15-year-old would-be bank messenger, 'that's if you want to get on well. Because you're in the City and talking to all posh people. You want to be able to mix with the right sort of people.'

Most of the boys interviewed rejected such changes.

'I don't want promotion. I just want to stay ordinary,' said an electrician's mate aged 19, 'a friend of mine went into a bank. He had to change his voice and now he says "Hallo"; you'd think he was a poof.'

'I couldn't change the way I spoke,' said a butcher's boy aged 18. 'I've been brought up like that. I know my way around here, anywhere else I feel out of place.'

Theories of 'status frustration' may have fitted some teenagers but it did not explain all of the delinquent behaviour. Delinquency in Bethnal Green was usually fairly trivial. Forty per cent of offences in the area involved stealing, often fairly minor theft though with some more serious 'breaking and entering'. Theft was more common among the younger teenagers. Older boys were more likely to be caught 'taking and driving away' cars or motorbikes, or riding a motorcycle without a licence. One in eight crimes involved some form of hooliganism or violence. Downes' research in a nearby part of East London showed that from the age of 20 the chance of being involved in crime falls rapidly.

Many of the boys interviewed by Willmott regarded stealing as 'normal behaviour'. An 18-year-old commented:

'We used to thieve now and again, same as anyone else, but I don't think we was bad, it was just the normal thing to do.'

And a 16-year-old was probably exaggerating only slightly when he said: 'There's not a boy I know who hasn't knocked something off at some time or another'. A friend who was present commented: 'They're not thieves or anything like that, they're just normal'.

On the surface there appeared to be a 'cult of toughness' among the boys of Bethnal Green. It was generally thought to be 'manly' to stand your ground when threatened or to fight someone if they abuse you. In Peter Willmott's view this toughness was more 'a matter of folklore than everyday behaviour'. Much of it was talk without action.

Any hostility the boys did feel was usually directed at adults, often those in authority – the police or council caretakers. It took the form often of shouted insults or vandalism, rarely of deliberate physical violence. Willmott concludes that rejection and frustration do cause some boys to turn to crime but that there are many other boys in similar positions who manage to 'go straight'. For most of the boys delinquency is fairly trivial, part of the basic tension between adolescents and the adult community and encouraged by the peer group, which begins to lose importance as the boys get older and as their attention turns to courtship and the prospect of marriage.

An alternative view

So far in this chapter we have concentrated on the approach we described as 'criminology', which attempts to find the causes of crime so that 'the problem' of crime can be solved. We have already seen how some sociologists have criticised this approach. They argue that sociologists ought to be looking at problems like crime from an independent viewpoint. Instead of accepting the popular view of crime and working from there the critics say that sociologists should be prepared to reject the popular view and seek to understand crime truly sociologically. To do this the sociologist must make his own questions and not take those questions which society – in the shape of judges and policemen and newspaper journalists – prepares for him.

Traditional criminology they argue has taken a one-sided view, only studying the criminal. More important perhaps is the study of those who decide what crime is and how certain actions become labelled as 'crimes'. This alternative approach is often called 'transactional' theory because it sees crime as the result of a 'transaction' between those who have the power to say what crime is and those

who are called 'criminal'. A further criticism is that traditional
criminology only looks at certain kinds of actions which have been
called 'crimes'. It fails to consider behaviour which, though not
criminal, is still thought by many people to be wrong, or at least not
normal. For this reason many sociologists prefer to focus not on
crime but on deviance. This is often known as *deviance theory* or
as *labelling theory* because of its concern for how certain acts
become 'labelled' deviant. We shall be using the term 'deviance
theory' to cover all of these alternative views including 'transactional' approaches and 'labelling'.

DEVIANCE

One of the best summaries of the deviance approach comes from
the book *Outsiders* by American sociologist Howard Becker.

> . . . deviance is created by society. I do not mean this in the way
> that it is ordinarily understood, in which the causes of deviance
> are located in the social situation of the deviant or in the 'social
> factors' which prompt his action. I mean, rather, that social
> groups create deviance by making the rules which when broken
> constitute deviance and by applying these rules to particular
> persons and labelling them as outsiders. (Becker 1966)

From this point of view deviance is not a quality of the act a person
commits but rather a consequence of the application of rules and
sanctions to an 'offender'. The deviant is one to whom the label has
successfully been applied; deviant behaviour is behaviour that
people so label. In the first part of the passage, Becker is taking a
different approach to that of Albert Cohen or Miller who see
'causes' of crime in society. Instead of focusing on the environment
which might cause people to break rules Becker looks at the way
rules are made and applied. To Becker deviance is not about the
way people behave but about the way others label that behaviour.
Deviance is seen then as 'a transaction' between someone who
behaves in certain ways and those who have the power to label that
behaviour and to apply rules to it.

This view of deviance therefore centres on three important
questions:
(a) Why is certain behaviour labelled 'deviant' in the first place?
(b) In what ways do people come to be labelled deviant and have
    certain rules applied to them?
(c) What are the effects of this labelling both for society and for the
    individual?

When sociologists try to answer these questions they are building their answers on certain assumptions. Firstly, deviance is relative. That means that actions which may be acceptable in one place or at one point of time may not be accepted elsewhere or at a different time. For example, killing people is legally acceptable in times of war if the person killed is an enemy. Killing people is not acceptable in the normal way of life whoever it is who is killed. However, Parliament could decide to re-introduce the death penalty for certain crimes in which case it is within the law for certain people – i.e. public executioners – to kill certain people – i.e. properly convicted criminals.

A second assumption is that people's ideas of what is acceptable or unacceptable can be influenced and that this affects how they react to particular situations. Deviancy theorists are, for example, interested in the way newspaper and television affect people's ideas of what is normal and what is deviant.

Thirdly, there is an assumption that certain people have the power to act on their beliefs about deviant behaviour. The police can arrest people whom they believe to be breaking the law. Often they have to use their discretion and this can mean that certain kinds of 'deviance' become singled out for action. Magistrates and judges also have the power to make statements which people generally listen to.

Fourthly, by labelling someone's actions as deviant, this can have an effect on the person who is labelled. If people say that you are 'idle' or 'nutty' or 'thick' or 'kinky' enough times you may well begin to believe them and even to act in the way 'idle', 'nutty', 'thick', or 'kinky' people are supposed to behave. A final feature of this approach is the idea of deviancy as a process, as something which happens with one event leading into another making it difficult to say which is a cause and which an effect.

We can see these ideas at work in Stanley Cohen's study of Mods and Rockers.

Mods and Rockers

Mods and Rockers were separate groups of teenagers. You could recognise a Mod by his rather snappy suits, or by the fur-lined parka he wore when riding on his scooter. Rockers on the other hand preferred motor-bikes and wore jeans and leather jackets. A study by Alan Little showed that both groups were basically made up of working-class young people with only slight differences in success at school, or earnings at work. In the early 1960s, however, Mods

259

and Rockers were a 'problem' – especially at seaside towns on Bank Holiday week-ends. After the Easter Monday 1964 the newspaper headlines were:

'Day of Terror by Scooter Groups' *(Daily Telegraph)*
'Youngsters beat up town – 97 Leather Jacket arrests' *(Daily Express)*
'Wild Ones invade seaside – 97 arrests' *(Daily Mirror)*

Magistrates spoke of 'sawdust Caesars' and great public concern was shown about what many people felt was a serious social menace. The Mods and the Rockers were society's most feared 'deviants'. How did it all come about? Who gave them this distinguished position?

Stanley Cohen, a British sociologist, studied the history of the Mods and Rockers and the way in which they became notorious. In addition to interviews with the young people themselves and with magistrates, local councillors and others involved, Cohen also studied the way in which the newspapers dealt with the problem.

It all started with 'an event'.

Clacton is an East Coast resort not particularly well known for the range of amusements it provides for its younger visitors. Easter 1963 was worse than usual – it was cold and wet. The shopkeepers and the stallholders were irritated by the lack of business and the young people milling around had their own irritation fanned by rumours of cafe owners and barmen refusing to serve some of them. A few groups started roughing it around and for the first time Mods and Rockers factions, a division at that time only vaguely in the air, started separating out. Those on bikes and scooters roared up and down, windows were broken, some beach huts were wrecked, one boy fired a starting pistol in the air. The vast number of young people crowding the streets, the noise, everyone's general irritation and the often panicky reactions of an unprepared and undermanned police force made the two days rather frightening. (Cohen 1967)

Cohen goes on to show that there were also some 'troublemakers' present who represented a hard-core of youths and most had criminal records.

From 'the event' there grows 'a myth'. Cohen argues that the deviant event makes people search for reasons and that the event itself becomes magnified. 'Violence and damage' were regular headlines, yet the damage was not really very great. At Whitsun 1964 it added up to £400 at Brighton, £250 at Margate and £100 at Bournemouth. Only one in ten of those arrested was charged with offences involving violence. Another aspect of the myth was that 'the riots' were bad for business, keeping people away from the seaside – deckchair hirings at Brighton were 8 000 down over the Whitsun week-end 1964 – but it was one of the coldest Whit Mondays for many years.

Myths about the affluence of the teenagers were also unfounded. The young people brought before the Clacton Magistrates after Easter Monday 1963 had an average of 15 shillings (75p) each for the whole week-end. The take-home for these young people was no more than the average for their age group. These beliefs about the Mods and Rockers were important. They were the basis on which 'society' justified its action against the deviants. Sociologists would describe them as 'stereotypes', that is when certain characteristics of a group are applied to all individuals in that group. Thus any young person wearing a fur-collared anorack was likely to be labelled 'a Mod' and if he arrived by train at a seaside resort on a Bank Holiday was likely to be put back on the train by the police. The myths justified the measures taken to control what was seen by many as a social problem. For example bail was often refused for very trivial offences and a number of magistrates' verdicts were later reversed on appeal.

Informal agents of social control also took up extreme positions. On the initiative of a group of Senior Aldermen and councillors the Brighton Council overwhelmingly passed a resolution calling for the setting up of compulsory labour camps for Mods and Rockers. A group of Yarmouth businessmen and hotelkeepers set up a Safeguard Committee which seriously debated setting up road-blocks outside the town to prevent any invasion. (Cohen 1967)

These were all part of the process of amplification which turns a series of delinquent acts into a major social problem.

Stanley Cohen argues that, at its simplest, this process involves six stages. In real life things are not always as simple but the stages provide a way of understanding 'Mods and Rockers'.

At the root of the phenomenon was the *initial problem*. The roots of this could be found in the position of young people in the early 1960s. They were better off than they had been ten years before. They were earning more and had more to spend. Against this they were still not accepted as adults. From this they developed distinctive ways of behaviour and styles of dress which gave the young people an appearance of separateness. The Who, one of the leading groups of the Mod era, sang:

> People try to put us down,
> Just because we get around,
> Things they do look awful cold,
> Hope I die before I get old.
> This is my generation baby.

This development of deviant action and style is the *initial solution*. This leads to a *reaction*. A myth develops which involves misunderstandings and stereotypes. The myth makes others sensitive to the problem. Forms of control are called for and the problem begins to grow. Cohen calls this *the generation of the control culture*. The enforcement of law and order against the deviants *separates* them off still further from the main body of society and increases the deviance. In the end the forces of law and order can say 'there, we told you so, there was a problem but we have contained it and brought the trouble-makers to justice'. The myth is *confirmed* (see Fig. 66).

POWER AND CONSENSUS

In the end, any study of crime and deviance of law and order must come down to the question of power. When the police or the courts enforce the law they are using their power to maintain order in society. Sociologists would say that they are agents of social control. But where does their power come from, and how is it used? One answer is that the law enforcers – the police, judges, prison governors, traffic wardens, park-keepers, teachers and others – gain their power, through a chain of responsibility, from the elected Parliament which in turn gains its power from the people who elect it. This means that the power and authority of the law enforcers depends upon the agreement of the ordinary people of the country. This is described as a consensus view and is based on the idea that each person gives up a little of their freedom to the state so that the state can use that freedom to keep everyone in order. This consensus also means that most people believe that it is in their interest for law and order to be maintained. The consensus view sees society as normally law-abiding and peaceful with the law there to prevent any occasional breakdown of order.

The alternative view is based not on consensus but on conflict. Society is not naturally law-abiding but is instead a mass of conflicting interests. The law seeks to keep the conflict under

Fig. 66. *Creating a myth*

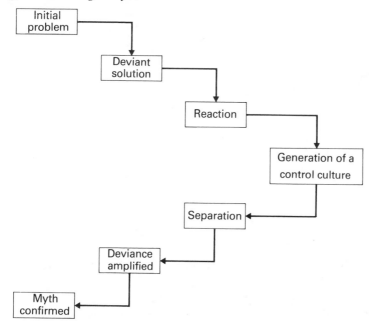

control. Those who take this view of society will point to the unequal distribution of property, wealth and power as the main causes of conflict. The law is as the way in which those who have power and influence control those who don't. This control is not only of course through the official 'law enforcers' like the police and the courts. Those who hold a 'conflict view' would say that control is also maintained by influencing what people think and their beliefs of right and wrong.

The mass media, education and the family play an important role in this aspect of social control. 'Order' is maintained in all sorts of social groups in many informal ways. If you want to test this kind of social control for yourself try pushing into a long queue at the front instead of going to the end. No one has the legal power to force you out but considerable 'informal' pressure will be used.

Crime and deviance is very much about the exercise of power; the power to define what is criminal or deviant, the power to control and punish those who misbehave, even the power to inflict pain or death. On the other hand crime and deviance may themselves be attempts to gain power. The thief attempts to gain power over property that is not his in a society where property is valued. The vandal may, using the only way he can, exercise power in a world which makes people increasingly powerless. The worker who puts a spanner in the assembly line may be using the only method possible to gain some control over his own work. Actions which are often said to be senseless may make great sense to those who do them even though such actions could not be condoned. Whether we call them criminal or deviant or not depends very much on our view of society and on the nature of law and order.

CRIMINAL STATISTICS

Sociologists have two main sources of evidence about criminal activity. Firstly, there are official sources which record the numbers of crimes reported, court appearances, sentences and other similar information. This information is provided by the police, the courts, prisons etc. and is collected together in *The Criminal Statistics for England and Wales* published by the Home Office each year. Secondly, there is the evidence collected by sociologists for their own purposes. This tends to be limited to particular areas or groups of people and usually focuses on the attitudes and behaviour of individuals and groups. Information on crime, especially official statistics, need to be used with care. Whilst the statistics are accurate in terms of crimes reported and cleared up, or sentences given, there are a number of reasons why they may not fully indicate the extent of real crime. If a crime is not reported to the police it is unlikely to become part of the statistics. There are cases where it is not realised that an offence has been committed. Often the victim of the offence does not wish to report the crime, either because they are a willing victim, as with illegal abortion or some sex offences, or because they have a close relationship with the offender and would not want them to be in trouble with the police. It is not unusual for the victim of sex offences to be too embarrassed to report the crime unless it is of a serious nature. Parents might not report acts of indecent exposure through a desire to protect their children from unpleasant questioning.

In other cases crime is unreported because the victim has little faith that anything can be done to improve matters or because they themselves are antagonistic to the police. Much poaching goes unreported because many people believe that country people have a right to the occasional pheasant or hare. Finally, there are those offences which are never detected and are known only to the criminal. Exceeding speed limits in built up areas is a common motoring crime which is only rarely detected.

More problems arise when we try to compare crime rates in different years. Changes in the law and in administration can produce apparent changes in the number of particular crimes. Cases of shopbreaking dealt with by higher courts fell from 8 848 in 1962 to 2 803 in 1963. This was almost entirely due to the Criminal Justice Administration Act which allowed such cases to be dealt with by magistrates' courts.

Finally, there may be occasions when juries are reluctant to convict for certain crimes or when offenders plead guilty to a lesser crime in return for evidence regarding other crimes with which they have been involved.

The problem of comparing crime rates is made more difficult by differences in police activity. Changes in police man-power or lack of resources can have a considerable effect on the detection rate and the number of crimes cleared-up. The police do not prosecute every crime they know about. They have considerable discretion. They may give 'a caution' or even ignore certain offences through lack of time to prosecute. The pattern of motoring offences in particular varies from place to place.

In some areas the police are tough on vehicle checks and unsafe tyres whereas elsewhere they concentrate on speeding offences. All of this has an effect on the level of reported crime.

CRIME TRENDS

Despite all of the problems of the criminal statistics it is still possible to get a general idea of the pattern of crime in Britain as a whole. It is quite clear that recent years have seen an increase in the amount of known crime. The two main areas of reported crime are theft and offences involving motor vehicles. This is a sign of the greater opportunities that exist for crime in our society. Modern supermarkets with their goods on open shelves make shoplifting much easier. More cars mean more motoring offences. There has also been an increase in large-scale organised crime.

Offences of violence against the person and criminal damage have shown the largest increases in the past twenty years though they still represent less than 3·7 per cent and 4·3 per cent of the crimes reported. Sexual offences have risen very little since the 1950s. The 'clear-up rate', that is those reported offences which lead to a conviction by a court, varies from year to year but is usually between 40–45 per cent of the known crimes.

The typical offender in our society is a boy, of school age, committing an offence with or without violence against property, or an older teenager involved in theft or vandalism. Men are generally more likely to commit than women though the crime rate among women is growing. The most likely punishment for any type of

Fig. 67. *Reported crime (U.K.)*

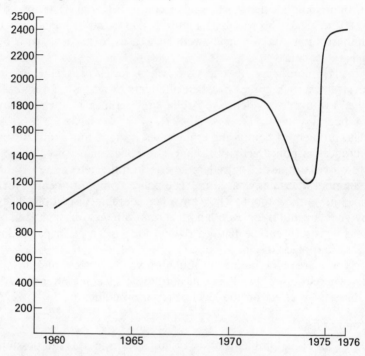

Fig. 68. *Types of offence 1976 (England and Wales)*

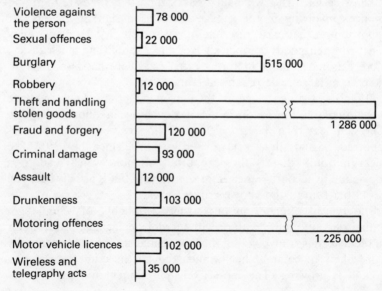

Violence against the person 78 000
Sexual offences 22 000
Burglary 515 000
Robbery 12 000
Theft and handling stolen goods 1 286 000
Fraud and forgery 120 000
Criminal damage 93 000
Assault 12 000
Drunkenness 103 000
Motoring offences 1 225 000
Motor vehicle licences 102 000
Wireless and telegraphy acts 35 000

offence is a fine. Alternative punishment such as attendance centres – at which offenders attend on Saturday afternoons – and community service orders – involving offenders in work for the community – are used for a small number of offenders.

Fig. 69. *Age and sex of offenders 1976 (persons found guilty per 1 000 of the population)*

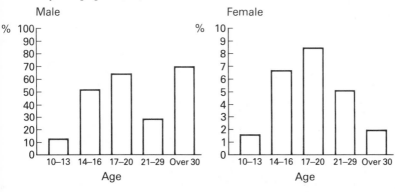

Fig. 70. *Sentences 1976 (England and Wales)*

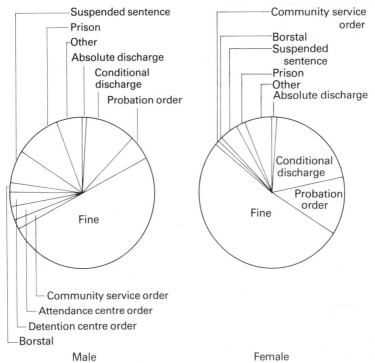

267

Police manpower has risen as the crime rate rises though nearly all police forces have less men than they could employ. In recent years there has been a rapid increase in the number of women police officers and in the number of civilians who assist the police in their duties, including traffic wardens.

Table 36. *Police forces (England and Wales) (thousands)*

	1961	1966	1971	1976
Policemen	72·7	82·5	91·8	101·0
Policewomen	2·3	3·2	3·8	7·0
Special constables	47·6	41·9	30·0	21·4
Cadets	3·3	4·1	4·5	3·7
Traffic wardens	0·3	2·7	5·8	5·9
Civilians	11·8	18·2	28·1	34·6

CONCLUSION

We can see therefore that in trying to understand crime in our society we need to take into account a number of factors. We must consider the social influences which are likely to lead to criminal or deviant behaviour; we need to look at the way deviance is defined and the way in which it is presented. Crime and deviance have been of particular interest to sociologists because they reflect society's view of what is normal and acceptable behaviour. By understanding crime and deviance we can also get a better understanding of what counts as normal.

13
Religion in Society

Sociologists have been interested in religion since the very earliest days of the subject. Some of the founders of sociology even thought that sociology would replace religion. Marx, Weber and Durkheim each considered the way religion affected the societies they knew. Their influence is still important.

Marx thought religion was like a drug. He called it 'the opium of the people'. He saw religion as one of the ways in which the ruling class prevented the oppressed workers from rising in revolt. Religion, with its promise of 'treasure in heaven' was often the only source of hope for those who had no chance of 'treasure on earth'. Durkheim also saw religion as central to the way society worked. For society to operate effectively it needed a set of beliefs and values which held everything together. For him, religion was the moral glue of society. Religion was at the basis of social life and part of the way men understood the world.

Weber's contribution is more far-reaching than that of either Marx or Durkheim. He looked at the way religious ideas related to other areas of life, particularly to the way the economy was organised and he considered how religious groups themselves operated. Many of the basic ideas we will use in considering religion in society come from the writings of Max Weber.

In this chapter we will consider three main aspects of the sociology of religion. Firstly, what is religion and how can it be studied by sociologists? Secondly, how do religion and religious ideas affect other areas of social, economic and political life? Thirdly, how do religious groups operate and how can they be better understood?

Before looking at these three questions, we must consider one question which should not concern sociologists. That is the question 'is religion true?' All sociologists have their own ideas about such a question, and as ordinary people would no doubt have an answer. As sociologists it is not a question they can even attempt to answer.

Questions of religious truth are a matter for theologians not for sociologists.

In October 1978 over 900 people living in a religious community in Guyana, called the People's Temple, apparently committed suicide by drinking fruit juice mixed with cyanide. They believed that others were about to take away all that they had worked for, that their only form of survival was death. One of the leaders of the movement wrote to a journalist shortly before he died, 'A man who hasn't found something to die for isn't fit to live, well we've found something to die for and it's called . . . social justice'.

Most people would say that the members of the Guyana People's Temple were wrong in their beliefs. Few people believe that suicide is the only way to prove your faith. But, people did believe such things, the suicide did take place and hundreds died. The People's Temple and its beliefs were a 'social fact'. To understand it fully the sociologist must put his own beliefs on one side and try to see such 'social facts' through the eyes of those who do believe. It is not the sociologist's job to prove or disprove the truth of such beliefs, merely to understand them.

What is religion?

Some would argue that the People's Temple was not really a religion. In many ways it seems more like a political or social movement. There is little mention of God in the Temple writings and even the faith healing depended upon belief in the powers of the Temple leader, Father Jim Jones.

This problem of actually saying what religion is, is an important one in sociology. We can see the problem more clearly if we consider someone who goes to church and ask ourselves the question – 'is that person religious?' We could answer that people who go to church are religious because they go to church, that evidence of churchgoing is reliable evidence of religion. You can probably already see the problems of this point of view. Firstly, it is a circular argument in which churchgoing is evidence of religion and religion is a cause of churchgoing. This is obviously not a sound argument. Secondly, and more important, it assumes that the *action* of going to church automatically indicates what the person *believes*. Belief in God may not be the only reason for going to church. There may be social reasons. Perhaps going to church on Sunday is an accepted thing to do, or a sign of social status. There may be very practical reasons for going to church. It may be that young people go so that

Fig. 71. *How religious do people think they are? 1968–69*

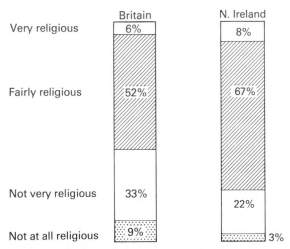

Source: *Religion in Britain and Northern Ireland* (I.T.A. 1970)

they qualify for membership of a church youth club or because it is a good place to meet people. Others may go because they enjoy the music or like singing hymns. There could be many reasons for going to church which have nothing at all to do with religion. It is also quite likely that many people who regard themselves as religious, who hold religious beliefs, may never go to church.

Social scientists must therefore be careful in separating the way people behave (their actions) from what they believe. Church-going means different things to different people. Understanding the meaning that religion has for people is an important part of the sociology of religion.

This still leaves us with the problem of defining religion. We have to decide which meanings or beliefs can be counted as religious. You could say that 'religion is a belief in spiritual beings'. Under this definition any belief in the supernatural or things beyond our earthly experience is religious.

Therefore, believing in luck, or horoscopes, or ghosts is religious. This sort of definition tends to include more than it excludes. Another 'inclusive' definition is that religion is that which is of 'ultimate concern'. If, therefore, your ultimate concern is that Leeds United win the F.A. Cup then you could say that 'football mania' is a kind of religion.

Inclusive definitions such as these are not very helpful to the sociologist. They include too many things to be useful for

271

comparison or analysis. Sociologists often find it easier to work with narrower, exclusive definitions based on particular evidence or events.

This does not solve the problem. You still need to decide what evidence you are going to use as a basis for your definitions. You could use evidence of what religion does. Durkheim wrote that 'religion is a system of beliefs which unite those that believe in them into a single moral community'. He defined religion in terms of what it does, or its function. We would say that it is a functional definition. Alternatively you could use a definition in terms of what religion is. This sort of definition normally selects a few important characteristics of any religion and uses them as a basis for defining it. Religion could be defined in terms of the belief in things which are beyond human activity and in terms of symbols which relate to those beliefs.

Defining religion is a problem, and one which cannot easily be solved. Sociologists use many different definitions, some are broad and inclusive, others are narrow and exclusive, some look at what religion does and others at what it is. It is important that when you read about religion you ask yourself why certain actions and beliefs are being labelled 'religious'. Ask yourself what kind of definition is being used.

CAN YOU HAVE A SOCIOLOGY OF RELIGION?

If religion is about beliefs, spiritual beings and the supernatural, how can it be studied by sociologists? It has been argued that because religion is individual to each person it can never be understood by science, even by social science. Sociologists would not in general agree with this view. Religious beliefs do not exist in a vacuum. Believers live in a social world. Their beliefs are acquired through social contact and are expressed in social behaviour.

The hermit in his cave lives by beliefs he learned from other people. Holy scriptures and religious writings communicate particular ideas and beliefs to human beings who live in social groups. The child goes to school or classes to learn about the Bible, Talmud or Koran, the adults belong to a church, synagogue or mosque, they are led and guided by a priest, rabbi or imam. Religion is a *social* phenomenon. It is, as we have already seen, a social phenomenon which is built on particular beliefs and meanings. These beliefs make up the cultural aspect of religion and make it possible for us to distinguish, for example, between religious groups and other groups such as political parties or social clubs. In studying religion we need to consider both its social and cultural aspects. To consider the social areas of religion, such as church attendance or religious obedience, without the cultural areas, such as what people believe, would give an inaccurate and one-sided view.

Religion and society

An important interest for the early sociologists of religion was the relationship between the beliefs people held and the social, economic and political organisation of society. For Durkheim the beliefs could not be separated from the way society was held together. The most elementary forms of religion began, he argued, when bands of primitive hunters came together. The feelings of friendship and togetherness which developed grew into rituals which, in the course of time, came to be regarded as sacred. In such a way religious beliefs grew from the very existence of society. They served to hold the society together and provided a basis for moral rules and social order. Durkheim went on to stress the evolutionary character of religion. Elementary forms of religion evolved into more advanced forms as primitive society itself evolved more advanced patterns of social organisation. At each stage religion provided the basis for social solidarity, and held the society together. Durkheim's approach has been the basis for a sociology which analyses religion in terms of the functions which religion performs. By using an open or 'inclusive' definition of religion Durkheim implies that any system of beliefs which functions to hold society together is religious. In this way nationalism and communism may be defined as religious. They are sometimes called 'functional alternatives' for religion because they carry out similar functions of social solidarity.

Durkheim's views have been criticised by other sociologists. His arguments were based upon what he took to be elementary forms of religion found among the Arunta Aborigines of the Australian desert. More recent studies have shown that even more elementary religions exist and their religious systems do not support Durkheim's view. Durkheim's functional definition has also been criticised because it is so broad that it includes many belief systems which should not really be termed religious. The idea of social evolution has also been rejected by many who question the idea that societies develop upon a straight path from 'primitive' to 'advanced' and Durkheim's approach has failed to show *how* religion changes. Whilst such criticisms are important they should not lead us to reject Durkheim's work which points to an important connection between patterns of belief and the organisation of society.

Another approach to the relationship between religion and society is found in the work of Max Weber. Whereas Durkheim was concerned with religious beliefs and social patterns, Weber's interest centred upon beliefs and the economic system. In the sixteenth and seventeenth centuries there grew up in parts of Europe a new class of capitalists whose wealth was based on the development of industry. Dominant among them were wealthy Protestants who followed the beliefs laid down by John Calvin. Weber noted that there was a great similarity between the religious beliefs of these new capitalists and the beliefs of Calvinism. Both sets of beliefs placed great stress upon the individual being responsible for his own success and salvation. Both emphasised the need for diligence and hard work which was for the glory of God. In his study of *The Protestant Ethic and the Spirit of Capitalism* Weber showed how these two sets of beliefs were linked, the one supporting the other. The theory has been questioned. It has been shown that there were capitalists who were not Calvinists and that much capitalist development came before Calvinism became important. However, Weber's thesis shows that religious ideas can form the basis for economic values. Weber emphasised that whereas the Catholic monk had a 'calling' to prayer and devotion the Calvinist saw his life as a 'calling' to work hard and to live simply. Industriousness and sober living were a duty to God. To the Calvinists salvation could not be earned. It was predestined by God. Your work and success in this life were signs that you stood among the chosen few who would inherit the kingdom of heaven.

Whilst Durkheim pointed to social solidarity and Weber emphasised the economic implications of belief other writers have looked to the political implications of religion. Marx viewed religion as part of man's alienation. Religion was something that man had produced but only served to maintain his oppression. 'Religion', he wrote, 'is the sigh of the oppressed creature, the heart of the heartless world, just as it is the spirit of the spiritless situation. It is the opium of the people.' (Karl Marx and Frederick Engels, *On Religion* 1844).

This kind of approach can be used to explain the impact of Methodism upon England in the eighteenth and nineteenth centuries.

During the 70 years before 1850 almost every country in Europe experienced a political revolution except for Britain. Why was Britain not affected? The rise of Methodism may provide part of the answer.

The origins of Methodism lay in the Church of England. When George Whitefield and John Wesley went out to preach to the people they did so because the Church of England had failed to keep the allegiance of the working people. The people who flocked to hear the Methodist preachers and who later formed the backbone of the new churches and chapels were mostly drawn from the ranks of the skilled artisans, the better-off members of the working class. Methodism gave them hope for the future and a way of using their talents. For many it provided an education and a bridge into the middle class. The values and beliefs of Methodism were, however, the values of the political and religious establishment. Methodism served to dampen down revolutionary feeling rather than encourage it. Methodism carried religion to the working people and with it there went a message which provided a justification for inequality. Each man's lot was appointed by God who will reward the sacrifice in the life to come. Methodism may have been one of the most effective means of social control to influence the English working classes.

The work of Durkheim, Weber and Marx provides us with valuable insights into the way religion is tied to the social, economic and political structure. They look at religion as it affects whole societies whereas other sociologists have focused upon smaller-scale issues and the operation of particular religious groups.

Church and sect

One of the first things that you notice when looking at religious groups is their diversity. Walk through any large town and you are likely to pass the places of worship of a great variety of religious groups. Some are local branches of large religious organisations, others are part of a looser federation of religious bodies and some may even be completely independent with no links to any other group. Churches like the Church of England or the Roman Catholic Church are very large indeed. In Britain alone these churches have nearly five million members between them without counting all of those people who may call themselves 'C of E' or 'Catholic' without ever going to church. The Salvation Army, The Society of Friends, Christian Science and other groups are also widely scattered across the country and have links with many other countries. The Church of England has over 17 000 church buildings in Britain. The Church of Christ, Scientist has less than 300.

Size is an important feature to consider, but it is not the only way in which religious bodies can be compared. An alternative would be to separate those groups known as 'churches' from those we might term 'sects'. In general churches are larger than sects but size is not

Fig. 72. *Changes in membership of religious groups (1970–75)*

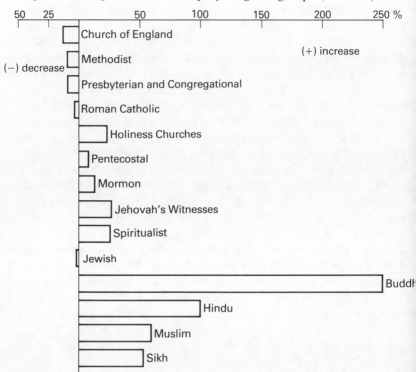

the most important difference. It is more important to compare their attitudes to the wider society and their society and their particular belief and practices.

This becomes clearer if we consider two main questions. Firstly, how does the religious group see itself and its beliefs? Does it believe, as many groups do, that there is only one path to heaven and that they alone hold the key, or does the group accept that there are many different views of religion and that it is only one of a large number of groups?

Secondly, we must ask how individuals join a particular religious organisation. Is membership open to all who wish to join or are there restrictions on membership which only allow certain people to enter? Those groups which accept that they are only one of many similar groups and which have fairly open membership would be termed denominations. Those which believe that their's is the only way and that all other groups are in error, and which have strict rules about joining, would be called 'sects'.

The Methodist Church is a good example of a denomination. It accepts that Methodism is only one branch of Christianity and can contemplate being united with other churches. To become a Methodist is largely a matter of attending a church regularly and being accepted as a member of that congregation. There are no tests of entry or formal rituals. The doctrines of the Methodist church are fairly open and while there are accepted views about moral behaviour and things like smoking or drinking they are not as rigidly held as with other groups. It is very unusual for someone to be expelled from the church for getting drunk, or going to a dance. Over the last two hundred years Methodism has changed and has increasingly tolerated behaviour which would once have been forbidden.

The 'Exclusive Brethren' is an example of a sect which believes itself to have the only path to salvation. To the Brethren all other churches and congregations have failed to follow the true (Brethren) way and are therefore 'in sin'. The Brethren keep themselves as much apart from society as is possible. They have not, as have some sects, taken themselves completely out of society, by setting up isolated communities in distant places. They do, however, maintain a high level of separation while still living and working within non-Brethren society. The focus of Brethren life is the family. Every meal is seen as a re-enactment of Christ's Last Supper and non-members may be excluded from it. This means that members of a family who remain outside the sect may have to eat alone. Failure to keep to the strict rules which forbid dancing, the cinema and other 'worldly' entertainment could lead to expulsion from the sect.

Between the extremes of the closed sect and the open denomination are a variety of other groups with different beliefs about themselves and the world. Some groups do change their ideas and beliefs and may become more sectarian or more like denominations. They may accept more worldly values or they may reject them.

TYPES OF SECT

The basic division into 'church-type' movements, or denominations and sects can be taken a little further by considering the various types of sectarian groups that exist.

Not all sects cut themselves off from the world as do the Exclusive Brethren. Many groups are very involved in the world's affairs, for many different reasons. Bryan Wilson has listed seven main types of sect in terms of the ways in which they see the world and their own beliefs.

The *conversionist* or evangelical sects are involved in the world because they want to change it. Their mission is to bring people to

277

salvation. Many Gospel Churches and Evangelical Assemblies come within this group. Their time is spent crusading for religious revival. Whereas such groups seek to evangelise in order to change the world other groups look forward to a time when the world will itself change. In particular, *revolutionary* sects look forward towards the Millenium, or the Second Coming of Christ. The Jehovah's Witnesses are a group which have always had a very clear idea of what will happen at Armageddon when only the saved will inherit the Kingdom. These two approaches – the conversionist and revolutionary are often closely linked and are very different from the approach of the third type, the *introversionist* sects, which, like the Exclusive Brethren, seek to withdraw from the world.

A fourth type of sect, the *manipulationist* sect, differs from those already described because its members accept the world instead of rejecting it. Sects of this type believe that they have special ways of gaining those things which all desire. Good health and a successful career are things which most people think are important. Manipulationist sects believe that men and women are only denied these things because they have not learned how to live the right sort of lives. Scientology, for example, teaches that people can be more successful if they clear their minds of unhealthy 'engrams' which prevent them from reaching their full potential.

Health and healing are important to many religious groups. They are central to the beliefs of *'thaumaturgical'* sects. Thaumaturge comes from a Greek word meaning wonder-worker. Such sects do often claim to 'work-wonders'. In particular they often believe that contact can be made with the dead whose help can be gained for the problems of the living. Spiritualist churches come into this group.

Wilson concludes his list of sect-types with the *reformist* sects, which seek to remain in the world while seeking to change it through social and political pressures (such sects are often very close to becoming denominations), and finally with *Utopian* sects which withdraw themselves completely from the world in order to live perfect lives in a new society.

These seven types give us an indication of the varieties of sect which exist in the world and some of their beliefs and practices. They are not seven completely watertight categories. Many real-life sects combine aspects from a number of different types. The Church of Jesus Christ of Latter Day Saints (Mormonism) is an example of a large sect which combines features of many of these different types. In the middle of the last century the Mormons cut themselves off from the rest of America by migrating West into the uncharted territory of Utah. The values they held were, however, the same values of success and achievement which were part of the 'Great American Dream'. The early Mormons believed that with the establishment of their church Christ's promises had been fulfilled and that America was the home of the new Millenium. Today the Mormons are very much an evangelical, conversionist group. A period of missionary service is an obligation for all young Mormons. Such a sect has every appearance of being a denomination, only keeping its sect-like character through its emphasis on its special knowledge and beliefs.

THE BEGINNINGS OF A SECT

Studies of religious groups have shown quite clearly that the organisation of sects, denominations and churches varies and that it is quite usual for groups to change. A sect may become established, its doctrines and pattern of membership may become more open, and it will become a denomination. A denomination may also change in the reverse direction. Where did it all start? How do religious groups come into being, and why?

One of the best known examples of the beginnings of a religious group is found in the New Testament. We can use it here as an example of the development of religious groups in general. In the four Gospels and in the Acts of the Apostles we find a detailed account of how the Christian Church began. Jesus was obviously a very impressive individual. He was a leader with considerable abilities who had the power to make others follow him. This is clear from any reading of the Gospels. He preached in a land which was occupied by a foreign army, ruled by a weak 'puppet' king where the established religious authorities were either powerless or collaborated with the enemy. There were revolutionary 'liberation' groups but they had little success. Because of his teaching and its effect on the people Jesus was executed. His followers escaped but later began to reorganise. They formed a tight little group which had considerable initial success preaching the words of Jesus. Their success was so great that some of their numbers had to give up preaching and attend to the day-to-day administration of what had by now become a Jewish sect. An official leadership developed and there grew up a need to communicate Jesus' sayings to those who had never heard him. Written records were essential. The teaching became particularly important when Christianity ceased to be an offshoot of the Jewish faith and began to take in Greeks, Romans and others. For its first few hundred years Christianity was a religion for slaves and the oppressed. It was not until the Roman Emperor

Constantine made it an official religion that it became an established religion.

If we analyse the rise of Christianity, we can see a number of features which are common to the origins of many religious movements.

Firstly, there was a leader with considerable influence and authority. His authority was not a traditional authority such as that exercised by the main religious leaders, the Pharisees, nor was it the legal authority exercised by the Romans. This authority was a part of the personality of the leader. Weber uses the word 'charisma' to describe this kind of authority and Jesus is a good example of a leader with charismatic authority.

There were, secondly, a group of followers with a very strong belief in their charismatic leader. Later some of these followers would become leaders. Their authority was derived from the authority of Jesus. Many of these men and women had particular skills of organisation and teaching.

Thirdly, there was a body of people who were in some way deprived. Many were very poor, others lacked power or sense of belonging as a result of Roman rule, many were physically handicapped.

Fourthly, the movement began as an offshoot of one religion and ended up as a religion of its own.

Finally, as the movement grew a greater proportion of its time was devoted to administration and less to the work of preaching, healing and so on and there developed a need to socialise the second generation into the group's beliefs.

If we bring the story up to date we can also see that what began as a sectarian religion ended up as an established church and that new sects began to arise out of it. The process started once more with new charismatic leaders, new followers, in answer to new needs out of which came new organisations.

The same pattern can be taken and applied to many other groups. Of particular importance are the role of the charismatic leader who leads the breakaway from the established groups, and the form of deprivation experienced by the followers. There is some evidence that particular kinds of deprivation lead to the establishment of particular kinds of church or sect.

Glock and Stark have identified five kinds of deprivation which may influence the evolution of a sect. *Economic* deprivation is another way of saying that people are poor. *Social* deprivation occurs when they lack power or status. *Organismic* deprivation occurs when individuals have a serious physical handicap. *Ethical* deprivation is caused by dissatisfaction with the values or ideals of the wider society and *psychic* deprivation is a state of despair and hopelessness. Liston Pope, in his study of churches in the mill towns of North Carolina, found that those churches which catered for the poorest and the most powerless members of society were those which practised 'ecstatic' religion. Other churches referred to them as 'Holy Rollers' because of their peoples' practice of dancing and rolling on the floor, often in a trance. This link between economic/social deprivation and 'ecstatic' religion has been noticed in studies of other groups. Similarly links can be made between other forms of deprivation and particular groups.

The origin of any religious movement can be related to particular social circumstances. To the sociologist religions don't just happen, they arise from social situations and involve leaders and followers, needs and aspirations.

Religion in Britain

Table 37 gives us a general picture of the pattern of religion in Britain. What does it mean and how reliable is it?

The table divides religious groups into three sections: Episcopal Churches, other Churches, and other religions. The Episcopal churches grouping is dominated by the Church of England which is the 'established' church. Otherwise known as the Anglican Church, the Church of England has never held a real monopoly of religion. Until the early nineteenth century it did have a very powerful position as the law prevented anyone who was not an Anglican from holding political office. At the present time it is only the ruling monarch who must still be a member of the established church. The 'Other Churches' section of the table lumps together a wide variety of groups from the Methodists, who separated from the Church of England in the eighteenth century, to the Roman Catholics from whom the Church of England itself separated two hundred years before.

Of the three columns: Members, Ministers and Church buildings, the last is probably the most reliable. At least most people are agreed about what a church building is even allowing for the fact that 'other religions' call them by different names. The problems of counting 'religious' buildings are, however, small when compared to the problems of counting members and ministers. It is a table in which it pays to read the small print first.

Church membership is an impossible thing to measure. What is

281

Table 37. *Church membership 1975*

	Members (Thousands)	Ministers (Numbers)	Church Buildings (Numbers)
Episcopal Churches			
Church of England	1 862(a)	14 379	17 212
Church of Wales	133(b)	896	1 720
Episcopal Church in Scotland	78(a)	235	335
Church of Ireland	176	375	495
Other	6	66	68
Other Churches			
Baptist Churches	256	2 394	3 560
Methodist Churches	596	3 098	9 138
Church of Scotland	1 042	2 261	1 964
United Reformed Church	175	1 795	2 068
Other Presbyterian and Congregational Churches	539	1 508	3 492
Roman Catholic Churches	2,413	8 032	4 100
Other Trinitarian Churches	574	9 239(d)	7 379
Mormon Churches	100	5 260	160
Jehovah's Witnesses	79	7 000(a)	600
Spiritualist Churches	57	233	594
Other Churches	70	164	1 001
Other religions			
Jews	111(c)	400(a)	315
Buddhists	21(a)	172(a)	30(a)
Hindus	100(a)	100	120(a)
Muslims	400(a)	1 000(a)	800(a)
Sikhs	115(a)	—	75

Notes

(a) – Estimate
(b) – Easter attendance
(c) – Heads of households (men and women)
(d) – Includes part-time ministers

a 'church member'? To be a member of the Church of England or the Roman Catholic Church you need to be baptised. For many people baptism, or christening as it is often wrongly called, is a ritual which takes place when they are still babes-in-arms. For full membership of these churches and the right to receive the Holy Communion you also need to be confirmed. You will notice that membership of the Church of Wales is based on 'Easter Attendance'. All active church members of Catholic and Episcopal churches are expected to attend the Easter Communion service. So Easter attendance may be a reasonable measure of membership. In other churches different 'membership rules' apply. Baptists regard adult baptism as a sign of church membership. Methodists are usually 'card carrying' members. When we get down to the 'other religions' section the problem of membership becomes immense. 'Jew' and 'Sikh' are not only religious terms, they also apply to a particular community of people. The fact that the Jewish figure includes 'heads of households' suggests that it is based on the Jewish community as an ethnic group rather than the active members of synagogues. It is not very surprising that not many of the figures for 'other religions' are given as estimates.

In the same way that definition of memberships vary so do definitions of minister. Some churches have elaborate hierarchies of deacons, priests and bishops. In some the 'ministry' could include 'priests' who have little 'ministerial' functions. They may be worker-priests in the week and clergymen on Sundays. Some may be full-time members of monasteries. Some religions do not even have professional priests. The Jewish rabbi is a teacher with a role very different from that of the Church of England vicar.

This table indicates some of the very real problems which arise when you attempt to put numbers to any area of religion. All religious statistics need to be approached with caution. Figures such as these can only give a very rough guide to the real pattern of religion in Britain.

The pattern of religion

When we look more closely at the evidence of religious activity and belief some sort of pattern emerges.

SEX DIFFERENCES

Women are more likely to be involved in religion than men. They are more likely to go to church, to pray regularly and to believe in God. Such differences are not, however, the same for all religious groups. American studies have shown that in Eastern Orthodox churches men are in the majority and we can see a similar pattern among Jewish congregations in Britain. The proportions of men and

Fig. 73. *Who is most religious? 1968*

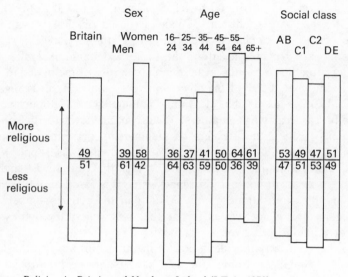

Source: Religion in Britain and Northern Ireland (I.T.A. 1970)

women in Roman Catholic churches are fairly similar whereas in Christian Science men are outnumbered by four to one. Argyle has suggested that such differences are caused by a combination of social and psychological factors. Women, he claims, are more likely than men to experience feelings of guilt and are therefore attracted to churches which promise salvation. Protestant denominations which have the higher proportion of women members emphasise God as a father figure whereas men are more attracted to churches, such as Roman Catholic, which place emphasis on the Virgin Mary as the Holy Mother. It may also be possible to explain the greater religious involvement of women in terms of 'relative deprivation'. Luckman points to difference in religious activity between working and non-working women and suggests that religious involvement may be linked to other economic and social roles. Women who go to work and have careers are less likely than other women to participate in religion.

AGE

Age is also linked to religious involvement. Older people tend to be more religious than younger people. Sociologists have put forward three possible models to describe the connection between age and religious behaviour. The *traditional* model sees a decline in religious activity from 15 years old until 30 followed by a gradual increase. The *stability* model sees no changes with age and the *disengagement* model sees continuous decline as people get older. Argyle has pointed out that it is not accurate to see religion as just one kind of behaviour. If 'church attendance' is separated from 'attitudes towards religion' and from 'belief in God' different changes occur at different times. Most people have established their religious ideas by the age of 18. A number of studies have shown that the peak period of religious conversion is between 15 and 20 years old. From 18–30 years old 'church attendance' declines, as you might expect from the *traditional* model. At this time, however, attitudes and beliefs are stable but positive 'attitudes toward religion' later increase, which is closer to a *traditional* model. From 60 years old, church attendance shows *disengagement*, probably because people are less active and prefer to watch religious programmes at home on the television to actually going to church. Attitudes and beliefs both show an increase at this time which supports the *traditional* pattern. The evidence shows clearly that religious ideas and behaviour do not stay the same throughout life. As we grow older our views and behaviour change.

SOCIAL CLASS

Religious behaviour and attitudes are linked to the social class of the individual. Writing in 1851 at the time of the Census of Religion Horace Mann commented, 'it is observable how absolutely insignificant a portion of the congregations is composed of artizans'.

The middle class are often thought to be more religious than the working class. This need not be true. Middle-class religion is often more obvious than working-class religion. It involves a religion of 'doing' rather than a religion of feeling. American research studies by Demerath showed that the lower classes were less likely to be church members but more likely to hold certain beliefs. Middle-class religion centred on a 'social gospel' and calls to help one's fellow men whereas more working-class groups emphasised salvation and hope for the life to come. This difference in emphasis also affects the denominations supported by different social classes. The larger denominations such as Church of England, Methodist and Presbyterian/Congregationalist, have a largely middle-class membership, whereas sects and 'independent' churches draw more upon the working class. There are, however, certain variations to this pattern. The Roman Catholic church has a large working-class following and some sects such as Christian Science have strong middle-class membership. Links between religion and social class also influence voting behaviour and may explain why Roman Catholics are more likely to vote Labour and why Anglicans tend to vote Conservative. The traditional link between the Methodist Chapels and the Labour Party may also explain the strength of the Methodist Labour vote.

THE GEOGRAPHICAL SPREAD OF RELIGION

As well as differences in age, sex and social class religious behaviour is also affected by geographical differences. Often different factors overlap. Social class affects where people live. Social class differences in church-going will, therefore, affect the location of particular churches. There are also historical factors which have influenced the location of religious groups. The most important of these has been migration.

When people move they take their religion with them. On arrival at their new home they seek out others of the same faith and seek to establish a religious community. When large numbers of people migrate their common beliefs and religious culture often form the basis of the community. We can see this clearly in the religious groups which surround the ports at which immigrants arrive.

At the end of the nineteenth century many thousands of Jewish refugees arrived at the London Docks. They came to escape persecution in Eastern Europe and were often destitute. On arrival they sought the help of their fellow Jews and eventually settled within a short distance of the docks. Synagogues were founded and Jewish industries were set up. As the people became established they began to move away into more desirable areas and new Jewish communities developed. Each stage of migration led to the establishment of new synagogues, food shops specialising in kosher foods, Jewish schools and social activities. Some members of the Jewish community drifted away and were absorbed into the wider community, often through intermarriage. For many their 'Jweishness' provided a basis for their identity in a strange land. Religion helped to hold the community together.

The same pattern is still being worked out in the districts surrounding London's docks today and around many other ports of entry. The new immigrants are from India, Pakistan and Bangladesh or from the West Indies. In East London the Jewish community has been replaced by a Muslim community. The synagogues have given way to mosques, kosher butchers to halal food shops and in the narrow streets Ahmed and Rasul now work in the rag trade once dominated by Cohens and Benjamins.

Whilst migration between countries can help us to understand the location of particular religious groups we must also consider migration within one country. For example, Methodism is much stronger in the Isle of Wight than in the surrounding areas of Hampshire and Dorset. The reasons for this are to be found in two historical events. Firstly, the success of the early Methodist preachers like George Whitefield and John Wesley in spreading their faith in Cornwall in the eighteenth century. Secondly, the migration of one group of Cornish Methodists from Cornwall to the Isle of Wight in the nineteenth century. On this basis Methodism became established on the Isle of Wight.

A similar pattern can be seen in Corby in Northamptonshire. Whereas most of the East Midlands has a fairly mixed pattern of Church of England, Methodist, Baptist and other churches, Corby is strongly Presbyterian. Once again the reason is migration. Earlier this century the Scottish steel firm of Stewarts and Lloyds opened a new factory on the iron-ore deposits which surrounded Corby. They brought with them a skilled force of Scottish workers who brought with them their church.

Migration does not always involve large groups who moved together. Migration can be the result of other factors. The Jewish community is well established at a number of seaside resorts. This is partly due to the desire of many Jewish families to stay at kosher hotels within reach of a synagogue when they go on holiday and to the wish of many older people to retire to the seaside while still keeping to their beliefs and practices.

RELIGION IN THE CITY

Patterns of migration, social class and age come together when we look at religion in the city. Most cities have more churches than they need. This is partly due to movements of population and a general decline in churchgoing but also is a result of the over-enthusiasm of our Victorian great-grandparents who built more churches than even they needed. It would be wrong, however, to base our ideas of city religion solely on the numbers of empty churches.

Most city churches were built and are still owned by the larger denominations. We have already noted that the membership of these denominations is largely middle-class, a group who tend not to live in the central parts of cities. The middle classes either build their own churches in the suburbs or on the housing estates or they travel to worship at certain prestige churches in the heart of the city. Religion in the poorer areas of the city is also likely to involve a number of smaller groups meeting in far less obvious buildings.

In the suburbs the church is often a social as well as a religious centre. The Sunday services share the church notice-board with details of dramatic societies, tennis clubs, scouts, cubs, guides and

Fig. 74. *Religion as leisure*

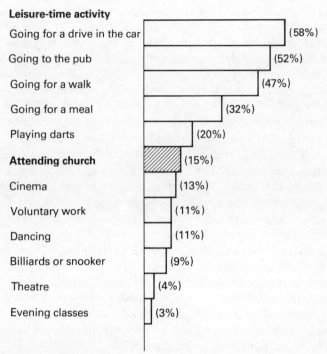

Leisure-time activity

Going for a drive in the car	(58%)
Going to the pub	(52%)
Going for a walk	(47%)
Going for a meal	(32%)
Playing darts	(20%)
Attending church	(15%)
Cinema	(13%)
Voluntary work	(11%)
Dancing	(11%)
Billiards or snooker	(9%)
Theatre	(4%)
Evening classes	(3%)

Source: Young and Willmott 1973

brownies. Going to church is merely part of a pattern of wider social contacts.

In attempting to make sense of the pattern of religion in Britain we need to consider the way these different factors work together. Population movements, age, sex, social class, all work together to produce a very complex pattern of religious activity.

Secularisation

The term 'secularisation' is often used to describe a process which is thought to be affecting religion in modern societies. 'Secular' is the opposite of 'religious' and *secularisation* means 'becoming less religious'. It is almost taken for granted that society today is in some way less religious than society in the past. For the sociologist of religion the idea of secularisation creates many problems. We have already considered the problems of defining and measuring religion. If it is difficult to define and to measure it is going to be very difficult to decide if it is diminishing. Different meanings people give to the word *secularisation* add to the problem.

The most obvious meaning of secularisation is that people are less religious. This means usually that less people go to church and Thomas Luckman has in fact called this 'a decline in church-oriented religion'. It is quite clear from the evidence on church-going, from the rate at which church buildings are being closed down and from the decline in recruitment to the ministry that there has been a considerable drift away from organised religion. A comparison of church attendance in Banbury on the last Sunday in March, 1851, with a similar Sunday in 1968 showed that there were more people in the Parish Church alone in 1851 than there were in all of the churches put together 117 years later. Whether or not this means that people are themselves less religious is another matter. We have no way of knowing that the people who filled Banbury Parish Church in 1851 were any more or less religious than those who go to church today.

We have already seen that church-going may be an accepted social custom, or part of the life of the community in which the person lives. Motives for going to church may have very little to do with religious belief. It is, therefore, not always accurate to draw a direct connection between beliefs and whether or not people go to church. An alternative view of secularisation focuses not only upon participation and church-going but on the connection between religious institutions and the state. In some ancient civilisations, and to some extent in Europe in the Middle Ages, it was not possible to separate religion from the state. The leaders of society were religious leaders, the laws were religious laws and the authority of the state rested upon the will of God. The presence of bishops in the House of Lords, the monarch's role as 'Defender of the Faith' and taking the oath on a Bible in a court of law are evidence of the connection between church and state in Britain. Whether these are examples of meaningful links between religion and the state or just hollow rituals is open to much debate.

A further problem arises when we try to discover when any religious decline began. Very often people speak about a 'golden age' when churches were strong and religion dominated the world. It is very difficult to decide when that 'golden age' might have been. It certainly was not during the Victorian period. The 1851 Census of Religion showed quite clearly that going to church was a middle-class activity. Nearly twenty years earlier Thomas Arnold, a leading churchman and headmaster of Rugby School, had commented 'it does not do to talk to the operatives (factory workers) about our pure and apostolic church. They have no respect for it. The church as it now stands no human power can save.' The most likely period for the title of 'golden age' is perhaps the twelfth century when the power of the church appeared strong and religion widespread. It can be argued, however, that the church in this period of history was so powerful and so closely aligned with the interests of the state that it was scarcely a religious organisation at all. Other candidates for the 'golden age' title might be Europe in the fourth century A.D., or Ancient Greece, or even the very dawn of civilisation. It is very difficult to agree on the most appropriate period.

Ultimately we must come to the view that secularisation has never been a consistent 'decline of religion'. Patterns of religious belief change and different ages have quite different features. The search for a golden age may be a wild-goose chase. David Martin has pointed out that 'when change becomes automatically secularisation then Europe has been secularised so often that it is difficult to see how any religion can be left.' (Martin 1969)

Although we may not get very far in a search for a 'golden age' it is clear that in recent history there has been some separation of social, political and religious institutions. The increased popularity of civil marriages gives us one example of this change.

Table 38. *Civil and religious marriages*

United Kingdom, 1971–76

	Religious marriages		Civil marriages	
	1971	1976	1971	1976
Total Marriages (thousands):	278	212	181	194
Percentage of all marriages:	61%	52%	39%	48%
Percentage change	−23%		+22%	

Source: Social Trends

Religious activities are playing a smaller part in people's lives and have less influence over political events. Whereas at one time church leaders were also political leaders, any modern bishop who comments upon politics is likely to be told to 'get back to his prayers'. This is all part of a general separation of church and state.

So far secularisation has been discussed only in terms of the relationship between religion and other areas of social life. We can also use the concept to consider changes which have taken place within religious groups. One of the main features of most religions is an interest in the 'other world'. Religious language includes words like 'heaven' and 'hell' and 'the life-hereafter' all of which indicate a concern for the 'life-beyond'. We often refer to individuals as being 'other-worldly' when we mean that they do not have a great interest in the problems of this life but are thinking about spiritual matters. However, religion is not only concerned about the life-hereafter. When people pray, or seek religious help, it is often to enable them to get on better in this life. When people were asked about the situations in which they were most likely to think about God, most gave examples of illness or bereavement or serious personal trouble. 'Death' was the one word most likely to make people think of God. While this does suggest an 'other worldly' attitude it is also clear that people do turn to religion to sort out the problems of this world. This is a form of secularisation. It shows a move away from religion which is concerned with spiritual matters towards a religion which is firmly based on worldly success. Studies of religious writings, for example, have shown that health, and wealth and success in this life have often been the aim of people who prayed or wrote testimonies thanking God.

This move from 'other-worldly' interests to 'this-worldly' interests can also be seen in the way many religious groups are organised. Peter Berger has suggested that many modern churches run on the same basis as big business in a market economy. They use the same techniques of management, they measure success in terms of the numbers of souls saved or donations pledged in any year and may even move into co-operation with other religious groups where it is thought likely to increase their share of the 'market'. Berger sees the religious scene as a market place of competing groups, 'the religious tradition, which previously could be imposed, now has to be marketed. It must be 'sold' to a clientele that is no longer forced to buy. The pluralistic situation is above all a market situation.' The development of religious advertising with hard-sell and soft-sell techniques, campaigns, doorstep witness and street-corner evangelism may be evidence for Berger's point of view.

Secularisation also involves the way people think about the world quite separately from any system of organised religion. All religions contain beliefs and mythologies which help them to explain why things are like they are. These beliefs explain not only spiritual matters but also human relationships, differences in opportunity and in success and the workings of the natural world. If you are poor, or persecuted, or handicapped, religion can provide a reason and a hope.

The Bible says, 'How blest are those who know they are poor;

291

the kingdom of Heaven is theirs . . . How blest are those who have suffered persecution for the cause of right; the kingdom of Heaven is theirs.' (Matthew, Chap. 6.) It is important to remember, however, that in the past religion has also attempted to explain the natural world, as well as the social and spiritual worlds. The movements of the sun and the planets, creation, the shape of the earth's surface and many other physical phenomena have been explained by religion. Often this has brought religion into conflict with science. As scientific discovery has developed it has shown that the natural world obeys physical laws which can be determined by experiment and by reason. This has led to a change in the way people think and in the ways they explain things. At one time it was believed that God created the earth in 4004 B.C. at 9.30 a.m. on October 23rd. Adam and Eve were created on October 30th. Today we know far more about the nature of evolution and would not attempt to explain the origins of mankind in purely mythical or religious terms. Our ways of thinking about cause and effect now depend far more on science than they do on religion. This 'rational' approach to understanding the world does not, however, confine itself to explaining the physical universe. Sciences like psychology and sociology also help us to explain the social world rationally. Secularisation of the way we think implies that men and women now look for reasons for all aspects of human life in science and reason and not in religion.

While there can be no doubt that the growth of science has led to a change in the way people understand the world we should not fall into the trap of pretending that we all are rational creatures all of the time. Superstition is still a feature of many people's lives. Abercrombie and others have described this as 'the God of the Gaps'. They found that superstition was far more commonplace than many people had previously thought and that it was important in people's lives.

> Over three-quarters of the sample touched wood in certain situations and almost half of them threw salt over their shoulders if some was spilled. There is then a big jump to belief in lucky numbers (22%) and charms (18%), the evasion of ladders, and the belief that black cats bring good luck (both 15%). Only one in ten people thought the number 13 was unlucky. (Abercrombie and others 1970)

Though people claimed to perform these actions, it is not certain that the actions have meaning for them. They could just be habits which could easily be broken.

We tried to discover more about the beliefs behind the practices by asking people whether or not they became uneasy if, for some reason, they did not perform the right action in the appropriate circumstances. Here it seems that the less common superstitious practices are more actively supported by those performing the actions. Nearly all of those who thought the number 13 unlucky said they would feel uneasy living in a house numbered 13. Just under half of those who tried to avoid ladders (for non-secular reasons) said they felt uneasy if they failed to do so, whereas only 8% of the wood touchers expressed a similar attitude. (Abercrombie and others 1970)

It is clear that though science and reason do form the basis for the way in which we understand and explain the world, for a significant number of people superstition and religion are still important.

Secularisation is, therefore, a topic which is difficult to pin down. In attempting to determine whether secularisation has taken place, and how it affects people's lives, we need to take into account a number of important factors. It is not enough to support the argument that secularisation has taken place solely on the basis of attendance at church on Sundays. We need to consider why people go to church, how the church sees its role in society, how people understand the world and the relationship between religious and other institutions.

14
The Mass Media

All communication involves *senders* and *receivers*, *messages* and a *medium*. When you write a letter to a friend you are the transmitter and your friend is the receiver. The message is contained in the words you have written. The words and the paper are 'medium of communication'. If there is more than one medium we use the word media. A letter therefore is a form of media for conveying messages between a transmitter and a receiver. The message is written in code using symbols we call words. Other forms of communication use numbers, morse code, musical notes or symbols.

Interpersonal communication

Talk is also a form of communication. It uses sound to carry the messages. When you have a conversation you use words to convey meanings to the person to whom you are talking. Communication between two people is *interpersonal communication* and it happens so frequently that we rarely give it much thought. It does, however, have its own rules and procedures. By understanding interpersonal communication better we can begin to learn more about mass communication.

If you listen to two people talking you will soon realise that they are both senders and receivers. Messages are sent first by one person and then by the other. If you listen carefully you will realise that each new message is influenced by the one before it and in turn influences the one that follows. You would find it a very odd conversation if each person spoke about something different without paying attention to what the other person had to say. Interpersonal communication depends upon feedback.

There is more to a good conversation than just listening to what the other person is saying. You also need to understand what is

Fig. 75. *Interpersonal communication*

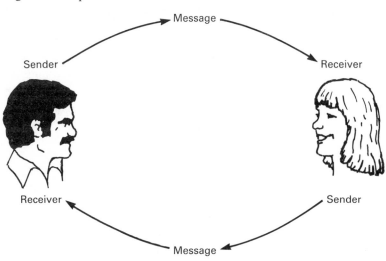

being said. You need to be able to decode the symbols. This means that you must first convert the sounds or symbols into something that you understand and then decide what it means. In everyday conversation we do this without thinking about it. It only becomes a problem when the symbols are strange to us, perhaps when we are learning a foreign language, or when we misunderstand what is meant. In a conversation the words do not stand on their own. We have a number of other forms of communication to help us. We use body movements, facial expression, gestures to help us to decode the meaning. Even in a telephone conversation where there are no visible clues we use the tone of voice to add meaning to the words. Another feature of interpersonal communication is the setting or context. Knowing where a conversation takes place helps us to make sense of it. A simple phrase like 'Can you help me?' means something different if it is said by a pupil to a teacher instead of by a drowning man. We could say that interpersonal communication is *context specific*. It takes place at a particular time, in a particular place and involves particular people.

Mass communication

Our brief introduction to interpersonal communication gives us a basis for understanding mass communication. In some ways the two forms of communication are very similar; they both use media to send messages, for example. In other ways they are very different. Mass communication also involves senders and receivers but whereas in interpersonal communication there are a small number of people who are both senders and receivers, in mass communication there is a small number of senders and a very large number of receivers. This large body of receivers, often numbering millions, rarely gets the opportunity to become senders. Mass communication is 'one way communication'. Opportunities for feedback are limited and the receivers become an audience for the messages that they are sent by others. To make mass communication possible it is necessary to use technology. Interpersonal communication also uses technology but it is an aid to communication. In mass communication technology is essential. As only a few people have access to the technology of mass communication the senders are likely to be full-time professional communicators working in mass media organisations.

The production of messages in mass communication is, therefore, very different from the process of creating a message in interpersonal communication. Mass media messages depend upon the existence of technology and media organisations such as newspaper publishers and television companies. These media organisations control and shape the messages that are produced. The production of media messages is similar to the production of any other product. Raw materials are shaped and processed to produce something that can be sold for a profit. In a newspaper the raw materials are items of news, photographs, paper and ink. The record industry processes songs, singers, vinyl discs and magnetic tape. The processes of media production bring about changes in the raw materials. Sheets of

Fig. 76. *Mass communication*

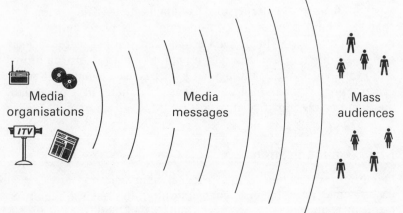

plastic are turned into records and news items are turned into stories. This process of change is called *mediation* and stands between the real world and the media audience.

CONCEPTS OF THE MEDIA

Various pictures are used to portray the way in which the media stands between the audience and reality. These different pictures tell us something about the way in which the process of mediation is seen. The media can be compared to a 'window' which allows images to pass through to those on the other side, or as a 'mirror' which reflects life as it really is. A more accurate picture of the media might be as a 'filter' only letting certain images pass through, or as a 'screen', blocking off the view of what lies beyond. These different concepts all point to the way in which the mass media, and particularly the news media, change, or mediate, the images that the audience sees. An alternative type of concept focuses on the role of the media in directing the audience's attention towards things. In this way the media can be seen as a 'signpost' or as a 'platform' which enables those who control the media to transmit particular viewpoints in the same way that a public speaker uses a platform to address a crowd. In a way the media is all of these things. It mirrors the real world, acting as a filter or screen to restrict the view. It can be both a signpost and a platform. The different pictures of the media are clues to the way the media can be seen. We must also consider how the media is used by the audience.

THE PASSIVE AUDIENCE

We have already seen how in interpersonal communication both senders and receivers are actively involved in the production and transmission of messages. In mass communication the audience appears to be passive rather than active. How true is this view of the passive audience? Do people just soak up media messages, such as television adverts, that are directed at them? Sociologists who have studied the ways in which members of the media audience use and respond to media communications tend to be critical of the idea of a passive media audience.

The audience can be active in many ways. A very simple action is to use the ability to choose. Television viewers may choose what to watch. You can choose not to buy a certain record or a morning newspaper. You make the decision to watch or to buy if you feel that it will bring you some satisfaction or benefit. Whether you choose to, or not too, is unlikely to influence the content of the media. Choice is a fairly limited form of action. There are other ways in which the audience can be active. When two people have a conversation they have to decode the messages and decide what they mean. The messages have to be interpreted. In a similar way the members of the media audience have to interpret the messages they receive. For the messages to make sense they have to be fitted in to what the individual already knows. People use their existing knowledge to make sense of the messages they get from the media. Consider what happens when you read the headline 'Football vandals strike again'. To make sense of those four words you need to draw upon your knowledge of events that might take place at football matches. You may need to use your knowledge of how the press has reported such events in the past, as well as your personal attitude to deviance and hooliganism. To interpret that short phrase involves you in some form of activity. Media sociologists have made the point that just to act as a receiver of media messages involves the individual in actively interpreting the messages received. This will influence how you are affected by the message.

Mass communication provides little opportunity for feedback. This does not mean that feedback is unimportant. Media producers need to know 'what the audience wants'. This does not mean that 'the audience' is a being with a mind of its own. 'What the audience wants' is made up of masses of individual likes and dislikes. These likes and dislikes are communicated to the television producers, the newspaper editors and the songwriters in many different ways. One important way is through the free market. If the public don't like it, it won't sell. Producers also rely on market research and letters from readers or viewers to give them some idea of audience views.

The development of mass communication

The earliest examples of mass communication date back to the twelfth and thirteenth centuries with the spread of hand-copied religious books throughout Europe. In the fifteenth century book production was revolutionised by the development of printing presses using movable metal type. By the seventeenth century the earliest newspapers were established. The development of power driven printing presses in the middle of the nineteenth century laid the basis for our modern newspaper industry.

The twentieth century has seen a rapid advance in all forms of mass communication. Radio (or 'Wireless' as it was then popularly known) became widespread in the 1920s and 1930s with television following in the 1950s. The film industry developed in the period

Table 39. *Cinemas and television*

	Cinema admissions (millions)	Television licences (millions)	Colour TV licences as % of total (%)
1971	176	15·9	3·8
1973	134	17·1	i9·4
1975	116	17·7	42·8
1977	103	17·9	55·4
1979	112	18·3	66·2
1981	84	18·6	74·0

Source: Annual Abstract of Statistics 1983

between the two world wars as did the record industry. Printed sheet music was the basis of the popular music industry until the 1950s when vinyl replaced shellac as the raw material for gramophone records. This made it possible to produce 45 rpm and 33 rpm discs which were cheaper and lighter than the old 78s.

Four main factors have had a influence on the development of the mass media. Firstly, each new form of mass communication has been based on a development in technology. Often the technology of mass communication is borrowed from other areas. Radio began as a means of communication on the battlegrounds of the First World War. Satellites, essential for modern radio and television transmission, developed out of the American space programme.

Technological change has not only made new forms of communication possible but has also increased the effectiveness of existing forms of communication. When the printing press was developed in the middle of the fifteenth century it was within a well-established multi-national book trade based on hand-copied manuscripts. The medieval scriptoria were able to supply an extensive market by employing large numbers of people to copy books. The introduction of the printing press increased productivity 100 times and enabled books to be produced much more cheaply. This led to a great reduction in the labour force and an increase in book production. A similar pattern can be seen in the modern newspaper industry. Twenty years ago newspapers depended on skilled compositors who converted the reporters' news stories into blocks of metal type from which the paper would be printed. Today the reporter can type his own stories straight into a computer which will then set the type photographically.

A second important factor in the history of the media has been the development of media organisations. When you walk into a record shop and buy this week's Number One disc you are at the end of long chains of production and distribution. This 'chain' includes the 'A and R' man who organised the recording session, the technician who shaped the sounds on the tape, the machine operators who pressed the discs, packers, publicity and promotions staff, the retailers and many others. Before you can listen to your new record you will need a record player, produced by another branch of the media industry.

Throughout the history of the mass media there has been a steady growth in the size and complexity of media organisations. This has been due to the combined effects of technological change, greater sales, and the need to increase revenue. It has also had an effect on the kind of messages transmitted. The experience of the newspaper industry is typical.

Increased production through improved technology could only be justified by creating larger markets and by eliminating competition. As newspaper technology developed the publishers had to sell more copies to cover the cost of the new machines. In order to keep their readers the papers needed a regular supply of entertaining stories and news items. These could only be assured if the newspaper had its own journalists and correspondents. The increased costs of producing newspapers which resulted could only be met by increasing income from advertisements. Advertisers, however, would only buy space if there was a large circulation. It became more expensive to run the newspaper and regular 'gimmicks' were needed to keep circulation high. As a result the proportion of space given to public affairs in popular daily newspapers in the last thirty years has declined by more than half. More people read cartoons and horoscopes than read political or economic news. In order to make profits the mass media industries have therefore needed large markets in which to sell their products.

The development of a mass 'public' or 'audience' is the third factor in the history of mass communications. Early newspapers were read aloud in taverns and coffee houses for the benefit of those who could not read for themselves, but the spread of newspaper reading in the nineteenth century depended upon an effective system of elementary education. It also required a fast and efficient transport system which could take the newspapers to the readers. This was provided by the railways and the developing road system.

In the early stages of each new technological development the development of a large audience has been restricted by the cost of the media. As long as the media, or the technology with which to communicate, was too expensive for the average person it was impossible to establish the mass public.

CONTROL OVER THE MEDIA

The final factor in the development of the media has been the issue of control. Mass communication involves the transmission of knowledge. Very often people feel that all knowledge should not be freely available. Information which might be of assistance to an enemy in time of war, for example, is kept secret. Pornographic books are not usually sold to young children. Throughout the history of mass communication those in power have attempted to control the knowledge that is communicated.

The early printing industry was very quickly controlled by laws and press censorship. In England the Tudor monarchs gave to the Stationers' Company extensive powers to control and licence printers. In the eighteenth and nineteenth centuries the Stamp Tax was used as a means of control by making newspapers too expensive for the average person. The Lord Chamberlain has always maintained control over the theatre while the cinema is under the British Board of Film Censors. Other forms of control include Obscene Publication Laws, Libel Laws and government 'D' notices which restrict publication 'in the national interest'.

The history of control over the media has, however, shown a steady move away from formal controls, such as laws and licences, and a move towards informal control through public pressure and the threat of political action. While it is in one sense true that there is a free press in Britain it is also clear that it is only free within certain limits. These limits become clear only when the media crosses the boundary which defines what is acceptable. In theory anyone is free to set up a newspaper and to publish their views. In fact few people can afford it and only the views of those who have wealth and power get into print.

How is the news produced?

It is late morning in a newspaper office in Fleet Street. The senior editors are meeting for the daily conference which determines the contents of the following day's paper. The News Editor reads out a list of the main stories of the day followed by the Features Editor,

301

Fig. 77. *IRA film stunt denied by BBC*

Source: Gibberd and *The Guardian*, 9 November 1979

Sports Editor and so on down the line. Overlaps between stories are sorted out, 'news angles' are explored and the order of importance of different stories is agreed before the meeting ends. By the middle of the afternoon news stories are beginning to pile up in the news room. Some are provided by the paper's own reporters sent out to chase up a story, others come through agencies or from the paper's correspondents around the world.

The flow of news from the various news gatherers is channelled through the newsdesk to the processors, the editors and sub-editors who occupy the 'back-bench'. Whereas the gatherers' job is to guarantee a supply of news the processor's job is to shape it into a form which fits the overall policy of the paper and to place it in a suitable position. Of the tens of thousands of words and the hundreds of pictures which flow into a newspaper office on an average day less than one-tenth will actually make it into print. The processors act as 'gatekeepers' controlling the flow of news from the gatherers to the final newspaper.

Galtung and Ruge, in a study of the ways in which four Norwegian newspapers handled major international crises, have suggested some of the factors which could cause an event to be newsworthy.

1. An event is more likely to become news if its *frequency* or time-span is close to the frequency of news publication. A murder takes little time and occurs between the publication of two issues of a newspaper. Building of a dam takes much longer and is less likely to be news, though the ceremonial opening may be.
2. News needs to be 'big'. Little events have less chance of being reported. This is the *'amplitude'* of the news. An ordinary birth is not news. The birth of quins is. In the same way the opening of a large dam will be more newsworthy than the opening of a small one.
3. There is also a need for *clarity* and precision in news items. If the meaning of an event is unclear it is less likely to be reported. The news depends on events that are not ambiguous.
4. News items are usually more meaningful if they have some *relevance* to the reader and if they are derived from a culture that is close to the reader. News of the American Baseball Leagues is not relevant to British readers and is culturally distant. It is seldom reported. On the other hand American tennis of golf, (games which are played in Britain) are reported regularly.
   It is often thought that news appears without warning; that it is totally unexpected. This is not true. Most news can be antici-pated. The more an event is expected the more likely it is to become news. Much news is predictable because it fits a time-

table. The monthly unemployment figures are published on the same day each month. Important people, who are usually news-worthy, have schedules of meetings and visits which are published in advance. State visits, football matches, economic conferences and similar events are all clearly predictable. This *predictability* is also important for the news media. It makes it easier for them to be in the right place at the right time, with the right technology. This is especially important for television news which needs a supply of pictures to accompany its stories.

It is possible for an event to be anticipated in such a way that it causes it to happen. Headlines which attempt to predict the calling of a general election or the resignation of an important figure may cause the very events predicted.

Once an event is established as news it will continue to be news even after its original *amplitude* has diminished. The news media has an interest in keeping a 'big story' going by finding 'new angles' on it. This justifies creating the story in the first place. Trouble at a football match can lead to news of the prosecution of so-called trouble-makers, reports of action to prevent further trouble, demands for tighter controls and so on.

Finally, news may be selected in order to maintain the *balance* of the newspaper or television bulletin. If all of the main stories of the day concern wars and revolutions in other parts of the world the news processors will be more likely to include a less important, but more cheerful, item of home news. Balance in the composition of the overall newspaper is an important factor in the selection of news.

BAD NEWS

The Galtung and Ruge study has been criticised because it focused only on foreign news and in particular on only three 'crises'. It only considered four newspapers and ignored television news. Research by the Media Group at Glasgow University, on the other hand, has focused on the way British television news handles economic and industrial disputes. It is often claimed that the news we see on television is neutral and balanced, presenting a fair and objective view of events. The Glasgow Media Group rejected this view.

> television news is a cultural artifact; it is a sequence of socially manufactured messages which carry many of the culturally dominant assumptions of our society. (Bad News 1976)

In other words news is a product which reflects the ideas, values and beliefs of those who produce it. Events are 'mediated' by passing them through the process of news production which shapes them in various ways. This mediation not only affects which events are selected as news but also how they are presented. The Glasgow Media Group has shown that television news works to a consistent and fairly uniform pattern. Not only do the different television news teams present similar items in their news programmes, they also presented the items in similar ways. The reporting of industrial disputes and economic crises consistently presented the official view and largely ignored the real issues at the heart of the events. The language used, the pictures shown and the personalities interviewed all tended to support the views of those in power and to conceal the views of the people involved in the dispute.

By video-recording all BBC and ITV news programmes over a period of a week or more the researchers were able to analyse both the content of the TV news reports and the way it was presented. One study analysed the television coverage of a strike by Glasgow dustcart drivers in 1975. In presenting the strike the TV news concentrated on the supposed health hazard and the expected arrival of the army. The cause of the strike was regularly described as 'demands for more pay'. The real basis of the dispute (a disagreement over equality of treatment for Heavy Goods Vehicle drivers employed by Glasgow Corporation), was never fully presented on the national television news. In part this was because the dustcart drivers themselves were never allowed to put their views until after the strike had ended. During the strike filmed interviews shown on television included a Professor of Community Medicine, a Fire Brigade officer, the Lord Provost of Glasgow, a City Councillor, the Secretary of State for Scotland, a Labour Member of Parliament, National Officials of the Transport and General Workers Union and a soldier. Only when the strike was over did the coverage include interviews with the striking drivers, balanced with a comment from a council refuse collector that the drivers should never have gone on strike in the first place. This lack of balance in TV interviews is not unusual. Of the 110 people interviewed on television in one week in May 1975 thirty-five were national politicians, eight were company chairmen, ten were industrial spokespersons or government officials and eight were trade unionists. There were also two professors, three doctors, one ship's Captain and one 'expert'. Of the remainder thirteen were wives and relatives of people in the news, nine were 'workers' and one was a blind demonstrator. Studies by the Glasgow Media Group have shown that similar biases can be detected in the length of time given to interviews with people of differing status, in the use of pictures and captions, and in the language of the news reports.

305

Grosvenor square

In presenting the news in newspapers and on television it is important that the news makes sense to the audience. It must be made to fit into our existing set of categories and definitions. A news story needs to have a 'news angle' which places it within a class of events with which we are familiar. The main news angle for the Glasgow Rubbish Strike was the feared health hazard. Frequently the news angle on a story changes as the events progress. A study of an anti-war demonstration in the 1960s showed that the 'news angle' on the expected protest developed in the fortnight before the march.

Three weeks before the march *The Times* carried a story about police preparations and reports of feared 'militant extremism'. This theme was developed later that week in a *Guardian* front-page story headlined 'Bombs and Arson on March'. On the following Monday a fire at the Imperial War Museum, deliberately started but causing little damage, reinforced fears of revolution and destruction of property. From this point the story developed with 'violence' and 'foreign extremists' emerging as the main news angles. The occupation of the London School of Economics by students objecting to the choice of a new director and a proposed ban on the entry into Britain of left-wing students as well as supposed disagreement between left-wing groups all contributed to the development of the main 'news angle'.

By the end of the week before the march the media coverage had developed three major themes. The dominant negative angle was the possibility of violence with little attention being paid to the reasons why the march was taking place. Against this the positive angle emphasised the preparedness of the police and their role in maintaining law and order as well as the peaceful way the vast majority of the marchers behaved. The third 'angle' focused on personalities, paying particular attention to the march organiser, Tariq Ali. These three angles – negative, positive and personality – emerged out of the pre-event coverage and determined how the march itself would be reported. On the day of the march, in the expectation of violence, the media concentrated its resources at those points where violence could be expected. Little coverage was given to the main part of the demonstration which marched peacefully to a rally in London's Hyde Park.

The construction of a set of news angles provided the newspaper readers with a framework within which the events could be fitted. By defining the 'event' as 'news' the media determined how it was to be reported.

Fig. 78. *The development of a new angle*

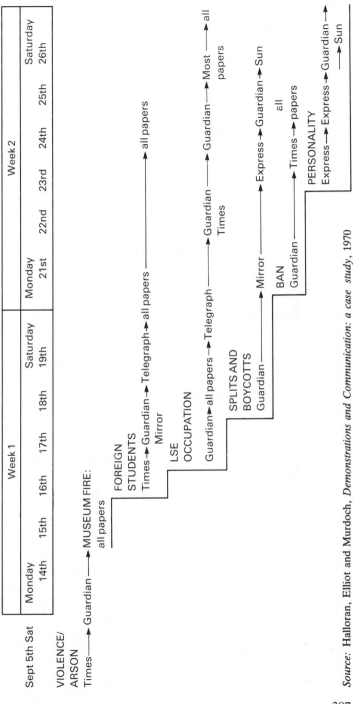

Source: Halloran, Elliot and Murdoch, *Demonstrations and Communication: a case study*, 1970

Crime in the news

For most people their closest regular contact with real crime is in the pages of their daily newspaper or on the television news. Crime is something you read about or see on the television. Our ideas about crime depend very much upon the way in which it is presented in the media. Not all media crime, however, comes under the heading of 'news'. Crime is also entertainment. On television, crime is portrayed in plays and films and the same heroes often appear in paperbacks and at the cinema. Usually we keep 'news-crime' and 'entertainment-crime' separate as though one is the real-life world while the other is make-believe. Such a division is not wholly accurate. The methods by which a news story and a piece of fiction are created are in some ways very similar. Firstly, crime fiction has a basis in reality. Some fictional stories are based on real-life events. This is not the only way reality provides a basis for fiction. Crime stories may not have happened in real life – but they could have done. They seldom stray far from what might have happened. The characters are modelled on roles and relationships which we recognise from real life. 'The police', 'the criminal', 'the innocent bystander', 'the victim', are all characters we can recognise. Crime fiction does not have to invent totally new characters.

Secondly, the way a crime novel is written depends very much upon the values held by the people who make up the audience. At the end of the story the 'good guys' usually win and law and order triumph. Entertainment-crime does, however, go a certain way beyond real life. The fiction writer or the television dramatist produces a story which entertains. It must be 'exciting' and 'gripping', holding people's attention and making them buy the next novel or watch the next programme. There is often a basic formula of suspense, violence, intrigue, romance, danger and suspicion. Put together in the right order they produce a readable book or an exciting film. Entertainment-crime is basically concerned with a product which needs to be sold to an audience and that audience must come back for more.

Newspapers are also a product. They need to be sold in very large numbers and people must be persuaded to carry on buying them day after day after day. This means that the basic rules for producing crime-news may not be very different from the rules which affect entertainment-crime.

News begins with events but not all events are news. Producing a newspaper means making a selection, or in fact a series of selections, from the available events. These selections are based on the idea of news value. A good journalist is trained to recognise 'news value' in a story. A good story has something about it which is unusual, unexpected or dramatic or which contains tension, romance or human interest. These are characteristics which do not differ greatly from those found in a good novel or a television play.

'There is this thing called a news story', commented a crime reporter on a national newspaper, 'I don't know how to recognise it, it's experience, I suppose. It's an odd quality. You can put six reporters in a court and they sit through six hours of cases and they'll all come out with the same story'. (Chibnall 1975)

In the course of an average day, a journalist comes across many events, reports, or leads which might produce a story. He or she selects on the basis of their potential news value. Often a story will need to be written-up in a way which adds to its news value. Words will be chosen which emphasise particular aspects of the event and interpretations will be given. Another crime reporter commented that news stories were: 'cliches set to music – you select the right cliche and write it up to suit the particular circumstances. Something like "tug-of-love" identifies a particular story and its theme'. (Chibnall 1975)

Reporters are not alone in selecting and shaping the news. Their stories are passed on to the sub-editors and those above them. Their role is to make further selections and to shape the news until it is ready to go into the paper. They have been described as 'gate-keepers' because of their role in restricting the amount of news that can pass through. A copy-editor studied by an American sociologist used 1297 column inches out of the 11 910 inches which were supplied to him. Their selections are, once again, based on the idea of news value though they also select on the basis of the newspaper's own policies.

The selecting and shaping of the news which takes place at these various levels has considerable influence on how crime is reported. A study by Roshier showed that the level of crime reporting in five British daily newspapers did not change much over a thirty-year period. There was no evidence to suggest that an increase in crime rates led to an increase in crime reporting. On one national daily the space given over to crime actually fell at a time when crime rates were rising fastest. Roshier also found that there was no connection between levels of particular crimes and their coverage in the press. Manslaughter, murder and drug offences involving the well-known were given far greater coverage than theft or motoring offences which affected a far greater number of people. In the words of a

crime reporter, 'company fraud is a difficult thing to write about
. . . there's no violence, no drama.' (Chibnall 1975)

THE CRIME REPORTER

In the newspapers studied by Roshier there was also a tendency to
place greater emphasis on the results of successful police action than
the actual 'crimes solved' rates would have justified. The picture
which emerged was one of more effective police activity than was
in fact the case. This may have been a result of the particular way
in which crime reporters work.

Crime reporters are an elite group in Fleet Street. Chibnall estimates that there can be no more than 70 journalists who regularly
report on crime and the police and that less than a third of these
are full-time crime reporters. As a group they are the main channel
of most of the news about crime. The news they handle is not strictly
'crime' news. It is police news, for the crime reporter's major source
of information is the police.

Much of his time is spent establishing relationships with police
officers who can give him the news he wants. Crime reporters need
to be trusted by their informants and to be able to provide favours
in return for the information given. The relationship between the
crime reporter and his police contacts is often very close. As one
reporter put it: 'over the years you get to know a copper . . . they're
not just business contacts, they're friends.' (Chibnall 1975)

This relationship can affect the news which is reported. The crime
reporter is unlikely to publish a story which might offend the police
as this could put a stop to further information. Similarly he might
include a story which is clearly favourable to the police or which
helps the police in their investigations.

Often the police will issue information which makes a good story
and say, 'well, if you print this it may help us catch this guy',
usually it's a case of leaking information that the police are getting
closer. Well, when he hears this the guy gets jumpy. (Chibnall
1975)

Particular problems arise when a crime reporter gets hold of a
story of police corruption. He could suppress, or write it up anony-
mously, or hand it over to a colleague. Seldom would the story be
given to another crime reporter. Journalism is a competitive activity.
The search for a scoop or an 'exclusive' story goes on all of the time.
The only way a crime reporter can be sure of his share of exclusives
is to keep as close as he can to his one main source of stories – the
police. This closeness inevitably affects the way the crime reporter

does his job and the view of crime which is presented in the news.

Steve Chibnall points out that 'Most crime reporters see their professional responsibilities toward the public as entailing the support of the police in the battle against crime. This means they are obliged to defend and promote the interests of the police.'

Advertising

Advertising seeks both to inform and persuade. The mass media could not exist without advertising which not only helps to sell media products but also provides a major part of the income of media publications.

In 1973 the Cadbury-Schweppes Group which produces chocolates and fizzy drinks as well as many other consumer products spent £104 million on advertising. In the same year the Group made a profit of £130 million. Every £1 of profit required £0.80 spent on advertising. A large proportion of this money went on buying space in newspapers, magazines, on television and radio. The majority of adverts are produced through advertising agencies. These are specialised firms which devise the advertising campaigns and co-ordinate production. Advertising is very much a team affair. A firm (client) with a product to sell presents the agency with a brief for an advertisement or for an advertising campaign. This will include ideas on how the product should be presented. These ideas will be developed by the 'account team' within the agency. Their experience of previous campaigns, the way competing products are advertised, the findings of market research and their own 'hunches' will be used to build up a particular approach to selling the product. This will then be used by the creative departments of the agency – copy-writers, artists, photographers and others – to develop the actual advertisement. Finally when the layouts are agreed, the words written, the artwork drawn and the photographs taken the pro-duction department will turn them into the advertisement on a bill-board, in a newspaper or on television.

The earliest advertisements appeared in newspapers in the seventeenth century. They were similar to modern classified adver-tisements. They advertised anything from 'powders for cleaning the teeth' to job vacancies for housekeepers and liverymen. An adver-tisement in 1658 stated – 'that excellent, and by all physicians approved, china drink, called by the Chinese Tcha, by other nations Tay, also Te, is sold at the Sultaness Coffee House, in Sweeting's Rents, by the Royal Exchange, London.' Such advertisements were

311

clearly informative and made no attempt to persuade the potential customer. Other advertisements did make ambitious claims for the products they sought to sell but their methods of persuasion were crude compared to modern advertisements.

Modern advertisements present a very particular picture of the world. It is not a picture of the real world but of a world which is one step above reality. The house you see in an advert is never your house but it may be the house in which you would like to live one day. Similarly the people in adverts are never like you though they may resemble the person you would like to be. Advertisements aim to fit people's aspirations, not their reality.

In everyday life there are many things that puzzle us. We may not understand why people sometimes behave in certain ways or what they mean when they tell us things. Life is full of ambiguities. Advertisements can never be ambiguous. Their meanings must always be clear for everyone to see. When we see an advert we must be able to attach meanings to the places, the objects and the people. We must be able to locate them in an established view of the world. For this reason adverts create a range of standard settings and characters. The harassed housewife, the career girl, the man-about-town, the trendy executive are all examples of recognisable characters. We could describe them as *typifications* which draw together a variety of features into a single character which can be recognised by all. These typifications are not 'real' either. They are images which are removed from the real world.

IMAGES OF WOMEN

Women are an important part of the mass media audience. Two-thirds of the listeners to day-time radio are women listening on average to 9.20 hours of radio each week compared to an average of 7.47 hours a week for men. Women spend £80 out of each £100 spent on consumer goods and control half of the savings deposited with Building Societies.

In many ways women are clearly a separate section of the media audience provided with its own magazines, radio programmes, feature articles and specialist advertising. The all-through readership of newspapers is evenly divided between men and woman. However women are more likely to read the letters pages, human interest stories and the horoscopes while men prefer to read about politics, sport, finance and the industrial news.

The ways in which the media portray women are also important. Gaye Tuchman, in a study of how American television presents women, agrees that women are trivialised and 'treated as child-like ornaments who need to be protected or kept within the safe confines of the home'. This process has been called *symbolic annihilation*. Tuchman is critical of soap operas which portray women as dependent upon men, either confined to the home and making themselves look pretty, or needing to be rescued by a man when they get into a problem elsewhere. In presenting women in this way the media are accused of reflecting the attitudes and values of a male dominated society. However, if the media reflects dominant social values it must also reflect changes in those values. The growing emphasis on equal opportunities is likely to lead to more women being shown in dominant positions in the media. Television drama serials which feature women in tough jobs in the police force may be part of this trend.

It would be wrong to assume that the position of women is similar within all parts of British society. Within the traditional working-class communities women hold a very powerful position at the centre of extended family groups or within local community networks. Television serials such as 'Coronation Street' reflect this dominant role of women. This is achieved by using roles which fit into specific 'strong woman' stereotypes – the hard-headed pub landlady, the widow who has become tough by surviving in a tough world, the hard-hitting, sexy barmaid.

The presentation of women in the mass media is not limited to television drama. Women feature extensively in advertising and in cartoons. The women of cartoons are either the extreme female stereotype of the seaside postcard – the sexy blonde, the fat lady, the harassed wife – or are pictured as ineffectively attempting to imitate male roles.

Making an advertisement

At first advertisements consisted solely of words. It was not possible to reproduce pictures in print until the nineteenth century, and the mass production of photographs in newspapers was not common until the early twentieth century. Today it is the pictures which form the major part of any advertisement. Words are much less important. In looking at advertisements we are, therefore, usually looking at pictures. It is very easy to imagine that such pictures do show us real things as they happened. This is not so. Advertising pictures, whether artwork or photographs, are carefully manufactured visual images produced within a commercial context. Every part of the picture is carefully planned, often at great expense. The characters within the illustrations are professional models and even the settings are carefully controlled. In an advertising campaign for a brand of vodka a girl holding a glass of vodka was pictured falling through the air without a parachute in a team of sky divers. The ground could be seen thousands of feet below, her hair blown back by the rush of the wind. The final photo was very different from the original, taken high on the side of a steep hill. Scaffolding pillars, which held the actors in mid-air, had been carefully painted out. The girl's hair had been re-drawn to make it appear more blown by wind from a wind machine, which also blew the smoke up from the sky-divers' flares.

The artificiality and 'unrealness' of advertising photographs can be used by sociologists to examine how advertisements convey certain images of the world. There are four basic ingredients in any advertising photograph. These are the product, props, a setting and the actors. It is the way these are used that creates the messages within the advertisement.

In putting these four things together the advertiser has four main devices at his disposal. These are often combined to produce a particular image. The majority of advertisements use the device of *product presentation*. The product being sold is clearly visible within the advert. It may be in its 'raw' state, for example, as a can of paint or a packet of soup mix, or it may be 'transformed' into a final end product – such as a painted room or a bowl of soup. The second device is *typification*. Typification is a device which involves actors who portray a type of character. The actors are clearly recognisable as a particular type of person. A third device, *association*, involves props and settings as well as actors. The product is linked to particular objects and gains some of the qualities of those objects. 'After Eight' mints pictured on a silver plate in a candle-lit dining room gain something of the sophistication of their surroundings and become more than chocolate coated mints. Some of the most effective advertising pictures go beyond product presentation, typification or association. They rely for their impact on the visual power of the image itself. Though often combined with other devices this supervisual aspect of advertising photographs enables the advertiser to convey a variety of subtle messages. Very often *symbolism* is used. An apple, especially one with a bite out of it, is a symbol of sexuality. The snake is a symbol of wickedness. Symbolism is also found in the way the people in advertisements relate to one another. Erving Goffman has pointed out that

> one way in which social weight – power, authority, rank, office, renown – is echoed in social situations is through *relative size*,

especially height . . . Indeed so thoroughly is it assumed that differences in size will correlate with differences in social weight that relative size can be used to ensure that a picture's story will be understandable at a glance.

In considering how gender relationships are portrayed in advertising photographs Goffman went on to identify five other categories of symbolism, as well as relative size. The *feminine touch* is used to suggest tenderness and affection. *Function ranking* tends to place men in the more responsible, commanding roles and to separate 'feminine settings' such as the kitchen from masculine settings like the sports field or the factory. *The family* is also used symbolically in adverts. Families in advertisements contain at least one girl and at least one boy. This ensures that a full set of family relationships can be portrayed. Girls tend to be placed in a relationship with the mother, boys with the father. Body position in advertisements often shows the *ritualisation of subordination*. Women are more likely than men to use the 'bashful kneebend' in advertisements. Similarly women are more inclined to be photographed with the head inclined to one side. The 'shoulder hold' symbolises one person possessing another. Goffman's final category is *licensed withdrawal* in which gestures or body positions enable actors to separate themselves from events. The hand in front of the face, 'finger-to-finger' position, finger in mouth, even twisting clothing symbolises withdrawal.

Goffman's study was particularly concerned with *gender advertisements*. The method he used, decoding photographs to uncover their symbols and rituals, can be used to analyse other types of advertisement. Images of children, social class, power and authority in society could all be studied by exploring the ways in which they are presented in advertisements.

Media effects

The study of the effects of the mass media has been of major interest to sociologists and social psychologists. The mass media has been blamed for changes in attitudes and values, increased crime, teenage violence, failure at school and for losing elections. It has almost become common sense to blame television, for example, for every sort of social ill. The media must have some effect on people. Advertisers would not invest millions if the advertisements were not going to sell the products. Even when we decide what to wear after reading the weather forecast, or go to see a film we read about in the newspaper, the media is having an effect on the way we behave.

315

Fig. 79. *Gender advertisements*

a. *Relative size*

b. *Feminine touch*

c. *Function ranking*

d. *The family*

e. *Ritualisation of subordination*

f. *Licensed withdrawal*

Source: Goffman, *Gender Advertisements*, 1979

It is wrong, however, to see the mass media as a *primary cause* of certain events. Remember that media messages originate within the social world and are transmitted back to that world.

The mass media can have effects at a number of levels. Individuals are affected when they buy goods because of the way they are advertised on television. Groups may be influenced as can organisations. Even wider social and cultural values within society may be influenced by views presented in the media. It may affect how we feel about things (*affective*), what we know (*cognitive*) or how we behave (*behavioural*). In his study of the effects of mass communication Klapper described three kinds of media effect. *Conversion* was a change brought about according to the intention of the communicator. *Reinforcement* occured when the receiver's existing beliefs were strengthened. The third category involved 'minor change' either in form or *intensity* of attitudes or beliefs. McQuail has extended these categories to include changes which may have been intended and media communication which prevents changes which might otherwise take place. There are also different time-scales of media influence. The person who switches off the television because the programme is too violent, too dull or too vulgar is making an immediate negative response to media messages. Changes in social values however take place over a much longer period. Using these two dimensions of time and whether effects are deliberate enables us to place them on a typology as in Figure 80.

SHORT-TERM EFFECTS

Advertising is one of our main sources of information about products that are available. The newspaper reader who sends for mail-order goods advertised in the paper, or the TV viewer who chooses one brand of catfood in preference to another on the basis of a televised commercial is making an *individual response* to a media message. It is a short-term response and is what the advertiser intended should happen.

A child who behaves violently following the display of violent acts on television is also showing an *individual reaction* to the media message. Again it is short-term but it is not an intended effect. Violence on television is intended to entertain not to cause violent behaviour. Groups of people may also be affected by the media in the short term. Whilst much advertising aims at influencing large numbers of people it approaches them as separate individuals, not as a group. Public relations campaigns, however, often try to win over whole groups. These are *media campaigns*.

Political campaigns may seek to win over trade unions or environ-

317

Fig. 80 *Media effects*

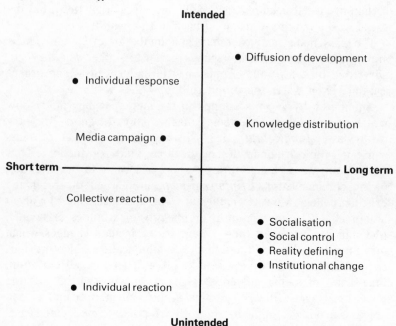

Source: McQuail, *Mass Communication Theory, an Introduction,* 1983

mental groups as a whole. They will use many different messages transmitted through different channels in an attempt to influence the group's shared viewpoints. An unintended group effect can arise when the media causes a *collective reaction* such as panic-buying of foodstuffs that are rumoured to be in short supply. When Orson Welles began his 1938 production of The War of the Worlds with a newsflash about alien invaders, people rushed out into the streets in a mass panic.

LONG TERM EFFECTS

In the longer term the media may be used for the diffusion of ideas (*diffusion in development*) needed in the development of society and for the distribution of knowledge (*knowledge distribution*). The radio serial 'The Archers', for example, has regularly been used to communicate new developments in farming techniques. A major purpose of the news media is the distribution of knowledge about the world. Yet in reality much of our knowledge comes not from the media but from personal contact. News gained from people we meet is more likely to be listened to and remembered than news in the papers. Although the progress of test matches or the Wimbledon final is communicated through the radio and television many people rely on other people for the latest score. In distributing knowledge the media also has the power to influence the importance we give to particular knowledge. Election campaigns, for example, have the ability to determine the issues which will be discussed. The media can influence the 'agenda' of issues. Whether or not the media actually determined the agenda is open to some debate. It has been argued that the agenda may arise from genuine public concern expressed through political elites and pressure groups. In this approach the media communicates agendas set by other groups within society.

Although a great deal of news and information is made available through the mass media we should not expect everyone to know everything. There is clear evidence of 'knowledge gaps' which are often linked to social class. The higher social classes are generally more likely to be better informed. In part this reflects the amount of news contained in different news sources. The 'quality' news-papers such as *The Times* and *The Guardian* contain far more column inches of news than popular dailies, such as *The Sun* or *The Daily Mirror*.

Finally the media may have certain effects in the very long term. In Figure 80 these are defined as *socialisation, social control, reality defining* and *institutional change*.

The mass media is so much part of our lives that it must have an effect on the socialisation of children and adults. Social values, attitudes and ways of behaving are picked up from the media. Many people would argue that the media's role is in fact 'desocialising' because the influence of television, books, magazines and comics goes against the socialisation which takes place normally within the family. It would be wrong, however, to see the television as a little black box in the corner of the living-room beaming out its influence to children who passively soak it up. Media messages are transmitted into social groups, particularly the family, and their influence is affected by how the group uses them. In this view the media is one of a number of socialising influences.

The ways in which advertisements, magazines and comics present male and female roles may for example have the effect of reinforcing other forms of socialisation. Situations in girls' comics are more clearly defined than they are in comics for boys. A typical story for girls takes place in or near to the home, family or school. Boys' stories take place anywhere. Whereas the heroes in the boys' stories are usually adult men taking action with a great deal of VROOSH,

319

SKREECH, BANG and AAARGH, the heroines of girls' comics are usually teenage girls trying to cope with problems of family or school or, in teen magazines, with romance. Stories in comics do not create male and female roles. They may, however, form part of a wider pattern of socialisation into gender roles.

Social control is important when the media socialise with attitudes and behaviour which support the existing social order. This may happen for a number of reasons. One view is that the media reflects the dominant values which exist within society. An alternative view is that the media is itself a very conservative force because it always needs to please everyone in order to survive. Workers in the media, it is suggested, have an interest in keeping things 'ticking over' smoothly and in 'not rocking the boat'. This may prevent them from taking up extreme positions on important issues. A third approach, argued by certain Marxist writers, is that the media's links with the ruling class turn it into a means for the spread of ideas and knowledge favourable to capitalism and the ruling elite.

The various theories of socialisation and social control are based on the view that the mass media is able to define reality. This means that the media, in some way, influences what people believe to be real. If situations are defined as real in this way they are likely to be real in their consequences. In times of war the media is used to convince the population of the reality of the enemy threat and to encourage people to fight. Politicians will use the media to portray them as they want people to believe they really are. They will try to convey an image of strength, resolution, confidence and wisdom. The media clearly has a role to play in forming opinions. Not only will the media present the dominant view of events but will also remain silent about alternative views. As the dominant views become generally accepted as the 'real' version of events there will be even less chance that alternatives will be presented. This has been described as a 'spiral of silence'.

A final long-term effect of the media is the change brought about in other institutions within society. The power of the media is considered to be so great that organisations which seek public support must change themselves to improve their media image. In election campaigns the media tend to focus on leaders. The issues and policies of the parties have tended to be pushed into second place behind the personality of the leader. The power of the leader within the party organisation has increased and the role of the 'grass roots' members has appeared to diminish. Similar changes can be seen in industrial concerns where 'public relations' and 'marketing' sections have gained increased importance because of their power to influence the media.

Children and media violence

Do violence and aggression on television cause children to be more violent and aggressive? Many people would say that they do but what is the evidence? When adults or children change their behaviour to fit the behaviour of others it is called 'modelling'. It is fairly normal for modelling to happen when adults and children are in many everyday situations. Does it happen through watching violence on television? For modelling to take place the individual must need to feel that a change in his or her behaviour is worthwhile. There must be some personal gain in following the model's behaviour. The model must also be recognised as someone who is worth copying. Watching television is a group activity and the attitudes of others in the group are also important. If the group is the child's family, as it often is, then family attitudes can have an important effect on possible modelling behaviour.

Studies of the content of television violence carried out in America in the early 1970s showed that most TV violence occurred in the past or in the future, less so in the present. It usually involved weapons rather than person-to-person contact and its consequences appeared to be slight. It involved little apparent suffering to the victims, the majority of whom were human. Seventy per cent of all leading characters were involved in some sort of violence. Attempts to measure the effect of such violence have usually involved experiments. The early studies by Bandura show the type of experimental methods likely to be used. A group of seventy-two children with equal numbers of boys and girls and ages ranging from three years to six years was divided into experimental groups and control groups. Each group was representative of different ages and of both sexes. The children in the experimental groups watched a film of someone making and then smashing a building toy and then hitting an inflatable doll. The control group saw the person building the toy only. At the end of the viewing session each child was placed in a playroom containing similar toys and was observed by the researchers. The child's behaviour was then noted. Smashing toys or hitting the doll were signs that modelling had taken place.

Experiments such as this have a number of important drawbacks. Firstly they take place in artificial situations and there is no reason to suppose that the same thing would happen in normal life.

Secondly, the samples of children were fairly small, even smaller in each age and sex group, and results might not be typical of all children. Thirdly it was often difficult to decide if certain acts were, in fact, aggressive. If a child hit the doll with a hammer aggression is being shown. What about tapping the doll with one finger, or gently patting it? Finally the model behaviour in the control and experimental scenes differed in other ways than just the level of violence. The experimental group scenes were more active whereas the control group watched very passive scenes. This may have had an effect. It is therefore difficult to draw very firm conclusions from such studies.

Those who carry out this research would, however, argue that modification to the design of the research, and the amount of research that has been done, do make it possible to draw some general conclusions. Children will imitate behaviour on television only if they see that behaviour as more rewarding than behaviour they would think of for themselves. This often means that children with many interests and a wider experience are less likely to be influenced by events in the media. The personality and the age of the child also has an influence. Young children who are inclined to be aggressive are more likely to imitate what they see. This appears to diminish as they get older but increases when they become teenagers. Children are also influenced by the position and competence of the characters who behave aggressively on television. Capable people who are shown to have a high status are more likely to be copied. When aggressive scenes show the horrific consequences of violence the non-aggressive child is likely to become anxious and this makes violent imitation less likely.

Selective bibliography

BALL, S., (1981) *Beachside Comprehensive*, Cambridge University Press.

BERG, L., (1972) *Look at Kids*, Penguin.

DOWNING, H., (1980) 'Word Processors and the Oppression of Women' in Forester, T., (ed.), *The Micro-electronics Revolution*, Blackwell.

GLASGOW MEDIA GROUP, (1977) *Bad News*, Routledge and Kegan Paul.

GOFFMAN, E., (1979) *Gender Advertisements*, Macmillan.

HEATH, A., (1981) *Social Mobility*, Fontana.

MARSH, P., (1978) 'Life and Careers on the Football Terraces' in Ingham (ed.) *Football Hooliganism*, Interaction.

McQUAIL, D., (1983) *Mass Communication Theory*, Sage.

MEAD, M., (1928) *Coming of Age in Samoa*, Penguin.

NEWSON, J., and NEWSON, E., (1976) *Seven Years Old in the Home Environment*, George Allen and Unwin.

RIMMER, L., (1981) *Families in Focus*, Study Commission on the Family.

SCHAFFER, R., (1977) *Mothering*, Fontana/Open Books.

SHARPE, R., and GREEN, A., (1976) *Education and Social Control*, Routledge and Kegan Paul.

SHARPE, S., (1976) *Just Like a Girl*, Penguin.

TUCHMAN, G. *et al.*, (1978) *Hearth and Home: images of women in the mass media*, Oxford University Press.

TURNBULL, C., (1973) *The Mountain People*, Cape.

WOODS, P., (1976) 'Having a Laugh: an Antidote to Schooling' in Woods, P., and Hammersley, M., (eds.), *The Process of Schooling*, Routledge and Kegan Paul.

Index